POLITICS IN
PAKISTAN

POLITICS IN PAKISTAN

The Nature and Direction of Change

Khalid B. Sayeed

PRAEGER

PRAEGER SPECIAL STUDIES • PRAEGER SCIENTIFIC

Library of Congress Cataloging in Publication Data

Sayeed, Khalid B
    Politics in Pakistan.

    Includes index.
    1. Pakistan--Politics and government. I. Title.
DS384.S29   954.9'1   80-13625
ISBN 0-03-041811-9

Published in 1980 by Praeger Publishers
CBS Educational and Professional Publishing
A Division of CBS, Inc.
521 Fifth Avenue, New York, New York 10017 U.S.A.

© 1980 by Praeger Publishers

123456789 145 98765432

Printed in the United States of America

for Janet

PREFACE

The nature and direction of political change in Pakistan has been largely explored and explained in terms of certain major variables emanating from both the external and internal environment. It may be seen that my earlier interpretation of the Pakistan movement presented in *Pakistan the Formative Phase* (1960 and 1968) and *The Political System of Pakistan* (1967) has been drastically modified in the sense that the earlier works emphasized Muslim nationalism and Jinnah's charismatic leadership as the two decisive forces, whereas the present work highlights the role of the British colonial regime in shaping and influencing political leadership and the socioeconomic situation that prevailed in Pakistan at the time of its establishment and during its early years. The Ayub regime described in Chapters 2, 3, and 4 was an attempt to strengthen the neocolonial foundations of Pakistan with this slight difference that it was the commander-in-chief supported by the United States who had emerged as the dominant force in the viceregal system and in shaping the nature and direction of socioeconomic change. We have characterized the Bhutto regime as a Bonapartist regime, using the term not in the sense of Napoleon Bonaparte but in the sense that Marx uses in *The Eighteenth Brumaire of Louis Bonaparte.* Pakistan's Bonaparte tried to rise above what he considered the narrow interests of both the landowning groups and other rural classes led by the small peasants, and certain urban forces drawn from the intelligentsia and industrial labor. His attempts were warped by both certain defects in his personality and the kind of political organization that he created. We have explained the role of the petty bourgeoisie supported by certain elements in the military in the overthrow of the Bhutto regime in Chapter 7. The last chapter deals with the social situation that is simmering but has not reached the boiling point. To the ferment of the socioeconomic forces must be added the external situation in which we have the Soviet-backed regime in Afghanistan and the U.S. and Saudi attempts to bolster the military regime in Pakistan. Our analysis suggests that certain fundamental changes are afoot. As to when exactly the floodgates manned by the military regime will be forced open by the tidal wave of change we cannot predict. Politics is not an exact science.

The book is dedicated to my wife without whose help and encouragement it could never have been written.

Khalid B. Sayeed

Queen's University
Kingston, Ontario

CONTENTS

PREFACE   vi

LIST OF TABLES   ix

Chapter

1   THE ORIGINS OF PAKISTAN AND ITS RULING ELITES —
    AN HISTORICAL EXPLANATION   1

    The Role of Islam in the Growing Support for Pakistan
    in Punjab   8

    Competing Roles of Pakhtun Ethnicity and Islam in Mobilizing
    Political Support in the North-West Frontier Province   16

    State Building versus Nation Building Under Jinnah   24

    Notes   28

2   SOCIAL AND ETHNIC CONFLICTS AND EMERGENCE OF CIVIL-
    MILITARY OLIGARCHY, 1947-58   32

    Disintegration of the Muslim League in the Provinces   35

    Disintegration of the Political Process   43

    Capitalist Development under Military Protection   46

    Notes   52

3   DEVELOPMENTAL STRATEGY UNDER AYUB KHAN   54

    Notes   63

4   CAUSES FOR THE SEPARATION OF EAST PAKISTAN   65

    Notes   82

5   BHUTTO'S POPULIST MOVEMENT AND THE
     BONAPARTIST STATE   84

     The Bonapartist State   89
     Agrarian Reforms   91
     Nationalization of Industries   95
     Labor Policy   99
     Autocracy and Coercion in the Name of National Interest   103
     Notes   110

6   PAKISTAN'S CENTRAL GOVERNMENT VERSUS BALUCHI
     AND PAKHTUN ASPIRATIONS   113

     Conflict between Growing Baluchi Aspirations and the
     Central Government   114
     Pakhtun Regionalism or Subnationalism   121
     Notes   137

7   MASS URBAN PROTESTS AS INDICATORS OF POLITICAL
     CHANGE IN PAKISTAN   139

     Urban Protests against the Ayub Regime   143
     Urban Unrest of the Early 1970s   152
     1977 Urban Conflict against Bhutto   157
     Notes   164

8   THE NATURE AND DIRECTION OF POLITICAL CHANGE
     IN PAKISTAN   166

     Probabilities of Urban and Rural Unrest   170
     Conservative Response of the Military Regime   178
     Notes   188

INDEX   190

ABOUT THE AUTHOR   195

LIST OF TABLES

2.1   Approximate Percentage of Industrial Assets, by Community, 1959   47

2.2   Increase in Investment for the Top 12 Major Industries, 1955-60   48

3.1   Estimates of Persons Below the Poverty Line in Rural Areas   60

3.2   Estimates of Persons Below the Poverty Line in Urban Areas   61

4.1   Background of Civil Service Officers in Influential Positions, 1965-70   72

4.2   Per Capita Gross Domestic Product in East and West Pakistan, 1959-60, Constant Prices   78

5.1   Comparison of State Government Under Ayub and Bhutto   90

5.2   Estimated Redistribution of Cultivable Land   93

5.3   Private and Public Sector Industrial Investment   95

5.4   Employees in Major Groups and Industries in Pakistan, 1970-71   99

5.5   Police and Security Expenditure   108

6.1   Gross Regional Product and Per Capita Gross Regional Product, by Province, 1968-69   123

6.2   Regional Distribution of Large-Scale Industry, 1969-70   124

6.3   Electoral Strength of Parties in the North-West Frontier Province, 1970-71   125

7.1   Population of Cities, 1961 and 1972   141

7.2   Urban Distribution, West Pakistan, 1961, and Pakistan, 1972   141

7.3   Labor Force by Major Occupation Groups, 1974-75   142

7.4   Number of Registered Trade Unions and Their Membership in Pakistan   142

7.5   Enrollment of Students, 1971-76   143

7.6   Percentage of Votes Won by Parties in Punjab and Sind in the 1970 Elections   152

7.7   PNA Processions, March-July 1977   158

8.1   Real Growth, by Sector, 1971-72 to 1976-77   171

8.2   Employment, FY 1967 and FY 1975   171

8.3   Labor Force Emigration from Pakistan   172

8.4   Income Distribution in Rural and Urban Areas, 1971-72   182

PAKISTAN

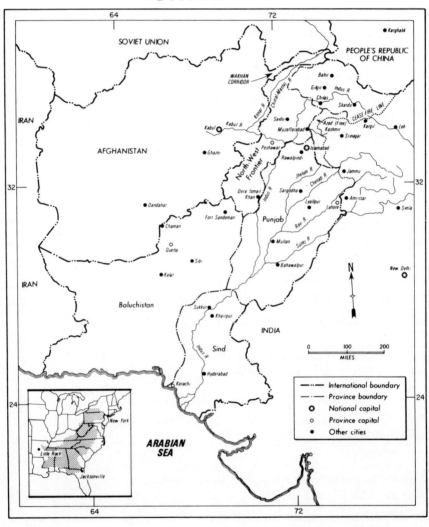

SOVIET UNION

PEOPLE'S REPUBLIC OF CHINA

● Karghalik

IRAN

AFGHANISTAN

WAKHAN CORRIDOR

Bahit ●
Gilgit ● Indus R
Chilas ●
Skardu ●

Kunar R
Chitral-Mastuj R

● Ghazni

Kabul ◎ Kabul R
Saidu ●
Muzaffarabad ●
Azad (Free) Kashmir
CEASE FIRE LINE
Kargil ●
Srinagar ●
Leh ●

Peshawar ○
Islamabad ◎
Rawalpindi ●
Jammu ●

North-West Frontier

● Qandahar

Fort Sandeman ●

Chaman ●

Dera Ismail Khan ●

Indus R
Jhelum R
Chenab R
Sargodha ●
Lyallpur ●
Lahore ○
Amritsar ●
Simla ●

Punjab

○ Quetta
Sibi ●
Kalat ●

Ravi R
Mullan ●
Sutlej R
Bahawalpur ●

New Delhi ◎

N

Baluchistan

Sukkur ●
Khairpur ●

INDIA

0   100   200
MILES

Indus R
Sind
Hyderabad ●
Karachi ●

New York ●
Little Rock ●
Jacksonville

ARABIAN SEA

—·—·— International boundary
—·—·— Province boundary
◎ National capital
○ Province capital
● Other cities

1
THE ORIGINS OF PAKISTAN
AND ITS RULING ELITES—
AN HISTORICAL EXPLANATION

In the eyes of most Westerners, Pakistan, whether regarded as an Islamic state or a Muslim state,[1] was an aberration from the norm. It was expected that the modern forces unleashed during the twentieth century, largely under the auspices of colonial powers like the British, the French, and others, were such that the newly independent states in Asia and Africa would tend to be secular and, if possible, even liberal and democratic. Thus many in Europe and North America were surprised that the Muslim-majority provinces and territories of India – West Punjab, Sind, the North-West Frontier, Baluchistan, and East Bengal – had broken away from India to constitute themselves into Pakistan with the primary purpose of protecting the rights and interests of its Muslim citizens and promoting an Islamic way of life.

This historical analysis of British colonial policies and the kinds of dominant groups that emerged during the colonial period is largely confined to areas like Punjab, Sind, the North-West Frontier, and Baluchistan because these areas constitute Pakistan as it exists today, that is, after the establishment of the separate state of Bangladesh in 1971. In another chapter explanations are given for the causes that led to the separation of East Pakistan and thus to the breakup of the former state of Pakistan in 1971. However, an historical analysis of British policies in northwestern India (which constitutes Pakistan today) and the kinds of ruling elites that emerged is useful because the ruling elites from West Pakistan tended to dominate the policymaking structures of the whole of Pakistan as it existed from 1947 to 1971.

1

Karl Marx in *The Communist Manifesto* referred to the all-engulfing economic power of the bourgeoisie that "compels all nations, on pain of extinction, to adopt the bourgeois mode of production; it compels them to introduce what it calls civilization into their midst, i.e., to become bourgeois themselves. In a word, it creates a world after its own image."[2] Marx knew that the British colonial power, even though it represented the British bourgeoisie, would encounter opposition in its onward march of expansion of trade and exploitation in the form of the Asiatic mode of production.

The Asiatic mode of production more or less depended upon self-sufficient villages with the role of the central power being confined to such matters as public works and irrigation facilities. This mode of production was different from feudalism because, lacking private property, it did not possess any internal mechanism of social change. "The whole Indian empire, not counting the few larger towns, was divided into villages, each of which possessed a completely separate organization and formed a little world in itself."[3] But when the so-called static and relatively unchanging Indian society came under British rule, Marx thought that economic and social changes would be introduced by the colonial power. In his article "The Future Results of British Rule in India," Marx predicted: "England has to fulfill a double mission in India: one destructive, the other regenerating — the annihilation of old Asiatic society, and the laying of the material foundations of Western society in Asia."[4]

But the process of history, as Marx himself knew, would not be determined purely by the kinds of policies that the British pursued. Marx himself had written earlier, "Men make their own history, but they do not make it just as they please; they do not make it under circumstances chosen by themselves, but under circumstances directly encountered, given and transmitted from the past."[5] It was true that the British government did draw the various parts of India closer by means of railroads and did improve the irrigation facilities, but it did not, as Marx expected, go all out to dissolve the Asiatic mode of production or village communities based on dominance of certain castes and tribal leaders.

The mutiny of 1857, which the British thought had been triggered by some of the reckless or enthusiastic policies of altering India's social conditions or ways of living, had cast a spell of caution over them. Moreover, why should they hasten the destruction of the empire itself through the dissolution of India's tribalism or the caste system? Above all, the empire had its own imperial interests and these could not be subordinated to the short-term or imprudent interests of industrial or merchant capital. A Marxist like Geoffrey Kay has pointed out that "capital created underdevelopment not because it exploited the underdeveloped world, but because it did not exploit it enough."[6] If the British had been ruthless and reckless in their policies of exploitation and had been motivated only by the interests of industrial or merchant capital, their empire would not have lasted as long.

Imperial interests demanded that tribal conflicts should be replaced by tribal quiescence and law and order. Therefore Thomas Thornton, who had been a foreign secretary to the government of India, in his biography of Sir Robert Sandeman, while paying tribute to the genius of the Sandeman system, pointed out that Sandeman resurrected the tribal organization of the Baluchis, which he found in a state of rapid decay. He reestablished the position and dignity of the *tumandar,* or chief. Some of these tribal chiefs had rendered yeoman services to the British government during the mutiny. Sandeman "organized these tribes under competent chiefs and headmen, composed their differences, enriched them by giving them work in canal excavation. . . ."[7]

The treaty of 1876 recorded the accord that Sandeman had brought about between the Khan of Kalat and his defiant tribal chiefs. The same treaty established the dominant position of the British in Baluchistan. In order to celebrate the signing of this treaty, Lord Lytton, the viceroy, invited the Khan of Kalat and his tribal chiefs to Delhi. The viceroy tried to create the impression among the Khan of Kalat and the assembled tribal chiefs that after signing the treaty they had joined a feudal system under which the viceroy and the khan were feudal lords with the tribal chiefs as their vassals. In order to mark the medieval solemnity of the occasion, the viceroy distributed heraldic banners among the assembled feudatories.[8] This policy of recognizing the Baluchi and Pakhtun tribal chiefs and the payment of allowances to them for the purposes of raising levies paid handsome dividends. Richard Bruce, who served under Sandeman, aptly observed that "we have bound Waziristan hand and foot, and are thereby pledged to mould our policy on such lines as will afford the Maliks efficient support and protection. . . ."[9]

The primary purpose of pacifying and controlling the Tribal Areas lying immediately outside the area of direct British administration in the Frontier was obviously the safeguarding and promotion of certain British imperial interests. It was through these areas that an external power like Russia was likely to launch an attack on India. An officer who served on the Afghan Boundary Commission discerned that the feared Russian invasion of India might be launched via Herat and Kandahar in Afghanistan and estimated that the Russians might require an army of 200,000 men for such an invasion.[10] Sandeman, in his memorandum "On British Relations with the Waziri and Other Frontier Tribes (1980)," observed:

All military experts, however, without exception, declare it to be necessary to secure Afghanistan from Russian aggression in British interests and for the defence of India. . . . The policy which I advocate has given us Baluchistan, the position at Quetta and on the Khojak, in Zhob and on the line of the Gumal. . . . If we knit the frontier tribes into our Imperial system in time of peace and make their interests ours, they will certainly not oppose us in time of war, and as long as we are able and ready to hold our own, we can certainly depend upon their being on our side.[11]

The relatively straightforward Sandeman system, or the "Forward Policy" of employing "the tribes as custodians of the highways and guardians of the peace in their own districts" in Baluchistan and the Tribal Areas of the Frontier, had to be bolstered by a relatively more complex form of political management in the Settled Districts of the Frontier and in western Punjab. As a result of the new legal system and proprietary rights in land created by the British, it was feared that the Muslim peasantry as well as the landlords in Punjab would soon lose the bulk of their lands because of their increasing indebtedness to non-agriculturalists like the Hindu moneylenders. Thus the Punjab Alienation of Land Act of 1900, while allowing free transfer of land within the agricultural tribes, prohibited permanent alienation of the land of agricultural tribes to nonagriculturalists. The imperial dimensions of this policy were clear to S. S. Thorburn, one of the architects of the act, who wrote:

> It is to be remembered that the Musalman peasantry of the Panjab, to the number of four millions, are chiefly congregated in the western districts between the Chenab and Afghanistan, are probably, except in some Trans-Indus tracts, more indebted and expropriated than any of the agricultural races in India, and have, in their own opinion at least, small reason to be satisfied with our rule — the unsettling effect upon their minds of the near approach of a "liberator" will be realised.[12]

It may also be pointed out that the areas of western Punjab and the North-West Frontier constituted not only the sentinel districts guarding the strategic routes but were also the homelands of the martial races who contributed the flower of the British Indian army.

The running of the British Empire in India depended not only on a sound strategic policy but also on an efficient and relatively inexpensive administration. Indian revenues had to pay for the maintenance of the army and the growing overheads of administration, including the construction of railways. It has been estimated that in the four decades preceding the First World War the expenditure on the Indian army constituted a third of the total expenditure of the Indian government.[13] Thus Anil Seal has pointed out:

> The British wanted to pull resources out of India, not to put their own into India. Therefore the administrative and military system had to pay for itself with Indian revenues. . . . The chief source of Indian revenue lay in land, and it had to be collected from millions of pay-ers. . . . It was in the administration of the localities that the vital economies in ruling had to be made. There, governance had to be pursued by simpler arrangements . . . by enlisting the cooperation of zemindars, mirasidars, talukdars, and urban rais.[14]

How inexpensive this administration was could be seen from the fact that Sir Michael O'Dwyer, referring to his early career in the Indian Civil Service as a settlement officer of a district in Punjab (where a settlement usually lasted for no more than four or five years), said that he "in the course of the Settlement summarily disposed of some sixty thousand cases of disputes as to inheritance, share, transfers, mortgages, redemptions of mortgage, sales, leases, boundaries, revenue-free grants, tenancies, village offices, generally on the spot in the presence of the parties and their friends and without the intervention of legal practitioners."[15]

In Punjab the British tried to set up homogeneous administrative units called zails comprising tribes and castes of similar origin or affinity, and over each zail the head of the tribe or the leading landlord was appointed as the zaildar. The deputy commissioner exercised his authority and collected government revenue largely with the assistance of functionaries in Punjab like the zaildar or the lambardar, village headmen appointed by the government from among the leading landlords. Whatever authority the village community had exercised was disintegrating under the British and gravitating toward the zaildars.

Referring to the unofficial wielders of power and influence in the districts of western Punjab, Malcolm Darling observed: "The peasantry, almost to a man, confess themselves the servants of the one true God and of Muhammad his Prophet, but in actual fact they are the servants of landlord, moneylender, and pir [spiritual guide]."[16] The Land Alienation Act of 1900, as noted earlier, had tried to eliminate, but with only partial success, the influence of the moneylender and also reduce peasant indebtedness. However, according to Darling, the Muslim peasant was still steeped in debt during the 1920s and 1930s. In some districts the big Muslim landlords had started acquiring the land of their neighbors. Thus, along with the pirs, the big landlords had emerged even more powerful in western Punjab. Though Punjab was supposed to be a province of small proprietors, what differentiated western Punjab from the rest of the province was the dominance of the landlord; "at a guess about 40 percent of the cultivated area is in the hands of men who own over fifty acres."[17]

The plight of the peasant, the tenant, and the landless laborer had to be seen to be believed. And Darling had seen it with his own eyes. Referring to their plight in one of the subdivisions of the district of Muzaffargarh, Darling observed:

> Every five miles or so is the house of a tribal or religious leader, who maintains a band of retainers to enforce his influence on his poorer neighbours, and to conduct his feuds with his equals. The poor man pays blackmail for his cattle to these local chieftains and for his soul to his pir, who may or may not live in the neighbourhood, but visits his followers yearly to receive his dues.[18]

The situation in Dera Ghazi Kahn was equally grim. Barring a few exceptions, "the landlord's maw was insatiable" and as a result of the Land Alienation Act he had doubled his acres. The small peasant, after satisfying the demands of the landlord, had to pay his dues and bribes to the moneylender, village mullah (preacher), and a whole host of revenue officials and village menials.[19] If this was the plight of the small peasant proprietor, in descending levels of degradation stood the tenant and the landless laborer.

Both in Muzaffargarh and in Dera Ghazi Khan, with the exception of about 5 percent who did not oppress their tenants, landlords were described as "all throat stranglers."[20] In Mianwali most of the landlords were "tyrants" (zalim).[21] The landlords in the district of Jhang and in some parts of Multan "were more powerful than 'officers,' that they inspired such fears in their tenants that they could take from them what service they pleased, and that they eat up the lands of the smaller folk, and rarely let their tenants stay long on a well for fear that they will assert their right of occupancy."[22]

The situation was different in the canal colonies. The canals fed by the Jhelum, the Chenab, and the Ravi had converted the four districts of Shahpur, Lyallpur, Jhang, and Montgomery into fertile tracts. Lyallpur was the largest district. The colonists were of three categories: the small peasant proprietor who was given a square of land (27.8 acres) was to be found mostly in Lyallpur district (in Shahpur he was given two squares); the yeoman farmer with his four or five squares; and the landlord, the representative of the landed gentry, who received between six to twenty squares (166.8 to 556 acres). The peasant proprietor was the most important, and in Lyallpur and Shahpur he owned about 80 percent of the land. The peasant proprietor in Shahpur had been recruited mainly from the northern districts but the peasant proprietors of Lyallpur had been almost entirely recruited from central Punjab. The Sikh Jats, who represented the flower of the Punjab peasantry in terms of their industry and thrift, fled to East Punjab at the time of partition. The Muslim Arains, who also came from central Punjab, were equal to the Sikh Jats in their thrift and industry.[23] The colonies had brought modern life into Lyallpur. The Lyallpur landlord controlled no more than 15 percent of the land. As for the influence of the pirs, it had already started declining in Lyallpur during the 1930s.

It may be noted that the kind of feudalism that had emerged in the neighboring province of Sind was probably a shade worse than what existed in western Punjab. Here the haris (tenants at will) numbered roughly 2 million in a population of 4.53 million in Sind in 1941. One cannot do better than to quote M. Masud, an Indian Civil Service officer who, as a member of the Government Hari Enquiry Committee in 1947-48, produced his Note of Dissent to the *Report of the Government Hari Enquiry Committee*. The conditions that the Note of Dissent described resembled those of serfs living in medieval times:

Fear reigns supreme in the life of the hari — fear of imprisonment, fear of losing his land, wife or life. The Zamindar might, at any time, get annoyed with him and oust him — he might have to leave his crops half ripe, his cattle might also be snatched and he might be beaten out of the village — he might suddenly find himself in the fetters of police under an enquiry for theft, robbery or murder or, more often, under Section 110 of the Criminal Procedure Code.

As was his counterpart in Punjab, the hari was under the spell of the pirs. He had imbibed the doctrine of taqdir (fate) from the constant preachings of the pirs. The message that came through was "He is low forever because God has made him so."[24]

The British must have been aware that the only justification for the kind of socially inequitable system that they had created in the rural areas was the furtherance of their own interests through a system of indirect rule resting on the semifeudal dominance of the landlords and the pirs. "This meant in practice that the British were winking at the existence of a legal underworld where the private justice of faction settled conflicts with the blows of lathis, or where, at the best, the strong could get their own way in the courts."[25] The cruelties and inequities of this system have been delineated graphically in the eyewitness accounts of Malcolm Darling referred to earlier. The Land Alienation Act of 1900, ostensibly designed to protect the interests of all agriculturalists, turned out to be, as already seen, a license for land grabbing on the part of the big landowners. Sir Michael O'Dwyer, a former Punjab officer who rose to be the governor of the province, wrote: "It is now regarded by hereditary landowners of all religions and castes as their 'Magna Carta.' "[26]

The big landowners who benefited from the act and who supported the British rule were keen that Punjab should continue to be the sword arm of India, that is, the central area from where the bulk of the Indian army would be recruited. The Punjab National Unionist party, established in 1923, emerged from the growing consciousness of their clear interests on the part of the big landowners belonging to the three communities — Muslim, Sikh, and Hindu. The Land Alienation Act of 1900 was aimed at undermining the control and influence of the urban-based Hindu moneylenders who were inclined to support the Congress. The purpose of protecting a vital area like Punjab from the incursions of anti-British national movements like the Congress was further reinforced by the formation of the Unionist party. Even a British officer like W. R. Wilson, district commissioner of Jhelum, pointed out that the government had created "a junker" class to defend British interests against the attacks of urban representatives in the legislature. "But as these 'Junkers' help to form the Government's bodyguard on the Council, this ever growing latifundia (which ruined Rome and the Provinces) is not likely to receive any check."[27]

THE ROLE OF ISLAM IN THE GROWING SUPPORT
FOR PAKISTAN IN PUNJAB

This analysis of British imperial policy in northwest India indicates how the British both in the pursuit of their military and strategic interests on the borderlands and in the matter of the day-to-day running of the empire through tax collection and the maintenance of law and order depended upon the support of certain tribal and landowning interests. It has also been pointed out that the British support of the big landlords in western Punjab meant that the British tolerated or connived at some of the worst forms of feudal exploitation of the Muslim peasants.

A British officer like Malcolm Darling had also reported that the peasants were becoming conscious of the kind of oppression and injustices that they had to bear under this kind of social system. Even though the Muslim peasants and tenants were inert and relatively helpless, there was the possibility of there being periodic eruptions among their ranks in the name of Islamic solidarity with Muslim states abroad or when certain disaffected tribes in the North-West Frontier rose against the British and tried to mobilize support through the Islamic appeal. One such uprising was the Khilafat movement launched by certain Muslim leaders in India to support Turkey in its struggle against the Western powers Britain and France during the First World War. "In the Punjab and in the neighbouring North-West Frontier Province . . . the Khilafat agitation has gone deeper than probably in any other part of India amongst large and very backward Mahomedan populations."[28] In the elections that took place in Punjab in 1921 for the provincial legislature, it was reported that in Lahore and other urban constituencies, because of the noncooperation organized under the Khilafat movement, no more than 5 percent of the voters went to the polls. On the other hand, in the Muslim rural constituencies, because of the influence of the landlords, the boycott was not effective.

Because of the religious appeal of Islam that could be used in support of social and political causes, the British had to pay considerable attention to the Islamic factor and use it skillfully for pursuing their imperial interests along the borderlands of the North-West Frontier Province and in the maintenance of the semifeudal status quo in western Punjab and in other areas. How the British manipulated the Islamic factor, particularly in the Tribal Areas, is discussed under the section relating to the North-West Frontier Province.

In Punjab, even before the advent of British rule, many of the sajjada nashins (hereditary custodians of the shrines or tombs where some of the well-known saints were buried) had become major landowners in some of the districts of west Punjab like Muzaffargarh, Multan, Montgomery, and Jhang. The British not only afforded protection to the families of these custodians by declaring them agricultural tribes whose lands could not be alienated under the Land Alienation Act of 1900 but also made the hereditary custodians zaildars, honorary magistrates, and district board members. As regards the Gardezi families associated with a shrine, the Multan *Gazetteer* said: "They are all thoroughly loyal."[29] About another leading custodian of a shrine, the *Gazetteer* declared: "The present Makhdum, Khan Bahadur Makhdum Murid Hussain, has precedence over all other unofficial Viceregal Darbaris in the district and is thus the premier peer of Multan. He possesses land in various parts of the district. . . . As guardian of the shrine of the saint Bahawal Haqq he is venerated by Muhammadans of the south-west of the Punjab and of Sind."[30]

Pakistan's national poet, Muhammad Iqbal, was contemptuous toward the claims of some of these custodians to be very religious and saintly because of their total loyalty to the British government:

> Closed is the long roll of the saints; this Land
> Of the Five Rivers stinks in good men's nostrils.
> Gods' people have no portion in that country
> Where lordly tassel sprouts from monkish cap;
> That cap bred passionate faith, this tassel breeds
> Passion for playing pander to Government.[31]

However, there were a few sajjada nashins who were concerned about the decline of Islam as a political and religious force under the British. They wanted to support a movement that would enforce the Shariat (Islamic law). They thus often found themselves in disagreement with the Unionist government, which even though it was led by Muslim premiers and enjoyed considerable support from Muslim landowners of the Punjab, was opposed to making the Shariat binding on Muslims in the place of customary law. The Unionist government knew that the enforcement of the Shariat with its provisions relating to the rights of inheritance of property enjoyed by female heirs would undermine the Land Alienation Act. Rights of inheritance if accorded to daughters according to the Shariat would mean that land would pass out of the control of the family or tribal unit when daughters got married.

In the urban areas of Punjab several other political groups and parties had emerged during the 1920s and 1930s that challenged the dominance of Punjab politics by the Muslim landlords and the sajjada nashins. Some of these groups were led by the ulama (learned authorities on Islam) and had developed pro-Congress sympathies, as in the case of the Ahrars.[32] These and other reformist groups, including those who were not pro-Congress, were not only opposed to British rule but were also committed to the view that superstitions like belief in magic and charms associated with the excessive veneration of saints were practices that were repugnant to the unitarian nature of the Islamic faith. In addition, there was a small group of Muslim Leaguers led by the poet Sir Muhammad Iqbal which, besides believing in Islamic renaissance, was also opposed to the dominance of Muslim politics by the pro-British Unionist landowners.

It was this kind of complex political mosaic that Jinnah faced during the late 1930s. He had to display extraordinary qualities of political craftsmanship first in steering a middle course between the urban and the rural interests and later in mobilizing political support both from the urban and the rural groups to batter down the Unionist fortresses in his onward march toward Pakistan. Before plunging into the Muslim League politics of the late 1930s, he was aware of the enormous hold that the British had over the Muslim landowners in the Punjab. He is reported to have remarked in 1932: "The Muslim camp is full of those spineless people, who whatever they may say to me, will consult the Deputy Commissioner about what they should do."[33]

One could see how influential the triumvirate (the deputy commissioner, the landlord, and the pir) turned out to be in the 1937 provincial elections in Punjab when the Muslim League won only 1 out of 86 Muslim seats, whereas the Unionists, supported by the triumvirate, won not only the majority of the seats in the provincial assembly (96 out of 175) but also the bulk of the Muslim seats. Soon after the elections, however, Jinnah, by appealing to Muslim solidarity, reached an accord with the Muslim Unionist premier of the Punjab, Sir Sikander Hyat. A pact with such pro-British conservative elements was distasteful to the Muslim League leader and poet Iqbal, for in his view it would undermine the prestige of the Muslim League among the Muslim masses. Jinnah was neither an ardent Islamic reformist nor a revolutionary but a hardheaded politician. Therefore he urged leaders like Iqbal to be patient and cooperate with him. He wrote to Iqbal, "I want to pull them [Muslims] up step by step and before making them run I want to be sure they are capable of standing on their own legs."[34] He was aware that the Muslim League, having displayed such a poor showing in the provincial elections, would be no match to the organized and entrenched power of the Unionist landlords.

In order to build a broad-based Muslim League movement in Punjab, Jinnah wanted to keep his options open by including the Muslim Unionists within the Muslim League without insisting on their ceasing to be members of the Unionist Party. Having gained only one seat in the Punjab provincial election, the willingness of the Muslim Unionist premier and his 80-odd Muslim Unionists to become associated with the Muslim League could only help Jinnah's prestige even though his urban supporters like Iqbal were unhappy.

But why did the Unionists agree to join a party that would benefit from such an association without the Unionists getting any advantages? The key to this puzzle lay in the simple fact that Jinnah had emerged, even after the 1937 provincial elections when he had gained no support in the North-West Frontier Province and Sind and won less than 40 percent of the Muslim seats in Bengal, as the most noteworthy all-India Muslim leader. His all-India stature was enhanced by the fact that the Muslim League had won a substantial number of seats in the Hindu-majority provinces. A more important factor was the concern of the Unionists to align themselves with a party that was by no means anti-British against the formidable and growing power of the Congress, which was successful in forming governments in seven out of the eleven Indian provinces in 1937.

Whether the passing of the Lahore resolution in March 1940 demanding the creation of a separate state for Muslims in the subcontinent was an act that had been methodically and deliberately designed or whether Jinnah and the Muslim League had accidentally stumbled on a gold mine has led to some speculation. According to some, Jinnah must have detected how the hitherto dormant Muslims could be aroused into action in the name of Islamic solidarity or Islam in danger during the Khilafat movement of the 1920s.[35] Commenting on the anti-Ahmadi demonstrations in Pakistan in 1953, the Court of Inquiry observed:

> If there is one thing which has been conclusively demonstrated in this inquiry, it is that provided you can persuade the masses to believe that something they are asked to do is religiously right or enjoined by religion, you can set them to any course of action. . . .[36]

The Qur'an promises earthly power to the faithful, and the Lahore resolution was also offering political power to the Muslims who had seen how Islam had decayed into impotence under British rule. But the Lahore resolution offered in addition the alluring prospect of jobs and opportunities to middle-class Muslims who first having lagged behind the Hindus were now in the process of catching up and felt that both the logic of numbers and the alleged Hindu discrimination stood in their way. This appeal of Pakistan in terms of jobs and opportunities for middle-class Muslims has been emphasized by both Marxist and non-Marxist writers. What is invariably missing from such analyses is that it also suddenly dawned on the minds of poorer Muslims in both the rural and urban areas that in Pakistan there lay the distinct possibility of improved material prospects even for the poorer people.

It is in this context that one can begin to understand the tremors that the Lahore resolution sent through the citadels of Unionist power in Punjab. British officials wondered why Sikander Hyat, the powerful Unionist premier of Punjab backed by all the British bureaucrats and supported by the Unionist landlords, had become so docile to Jinnah. In 1941 he was reported to have said "that unless he walked warily and kept on the right side of Jinnah he would be swept away by a wave of fanatacism and, wherever he went, would be greeted by the Muslims with black flags." The British official was not convinced at that time: "Subsequent events suggest that his reading of the situation was more correct than mine."[37]

A number of significant economic and social changes were sweeping both the rural and urban areas in Punjab during the late 1930s and the early 1940s. During Sikander Hyat's ministry (1937-42), the acts amending the Punjab Alienation of Land Act of 1900, namely the Restitution of Mortgaged Lands

Act of 1938, the Registration of Moneylenders Act of 1938, and the Relief of Indebtedness Act of 1940, were all clearly directed against the interests of Hindu moneylenders. Other legislative measures, such as a tax on urban immovable property, restriction of urban rents, and a general sales tax, were also interpreted by the Congress and other Hindu groups as having been specifically designed to hurt Hindu urban interests. The greater the Hindu-Muslim antagonism in the urban areas, the higher rose the political appeal of the Muslim League.

Because the Unionist ministry was supposed to be an alliance between Hindu and Muslim rural interests and tended to be hostile toward Hindu urban interests, one could see that the Unionists were likely to antagonize the Hindu urban interests and also lose their popularity among the Muslim urban interests. Between 1921 and 1941, the number of urban Muslims doubled, and in the central plains districts of Punjab, urban Muslims constituted almost 25 percent of the Muslim population. The Muslim League with its already established urban bases and the new demand for Pakistan could win over vast sections of this growing urban population in Punjab.

Even in the rural areas the Muslim League started making deep dents into the rural strongholds of the Unionist party. First of all, the Muslim League, being less conservative than the Unionists and led by the famous, Western-educated lawyer, Jinnah, would have greater appeal for those Muslim landlords who were acquiring Western educations and developing liberal outlooks. High prices for agricultural products during the war meant that even small and medium-sized landlords could assert their independence. In addition, when the Unionist party finally agreed to impose price controls, it was accused of being in league with Hindu businessmen and thus lost much of its appeal to the Muslim landlords.[38]

Jinnah must have sensed the political significance of the change that was sweeping both the rural and urban areas. After Sikander Hyat's death in December 1942, Khizr Hyat became the premier of Punjab. Jinnah must have been aware of the growing popularity of the Muslim League and the enormous political power that he himself had acquired when in 1944 he demanded from Khizr Hyat Khan that the Muslim League members of the Unionist party should owe allegiance only to the Muslim League and to no other party. Jinnah also wanted the name of the Unionist party to be changed to the Muslim League Coalition party.

Khizr Hyat refused to accept these proposals and reminded Jinnah of the Jinnah-Sikander pact, according to which the Muslim League was not to interfere in the internal politics of Punjab on the understanding that Sikander Hyat and his Muslim ministers would follow the policy of the Muslim League in all-India matters. Jinnah denied that his pact with Sikander Hyat had included such provisions. However, what was significant was that Jinnah felt that he could risk a break with the provincial ministry backed by fairly powerful interests and in a province where his party had won 1 seat out of 86 Muslim seats only seven years earlier.

Jinnah could claim that he was mainly motivated by considerations of national unity and party discipline. His stand was also vindicated by the fact that during the Simla talks in 1945 held by the viceroy to form a new executive council at the center, it was proposed by the viceroy that either Khizr Hyat would be included in such a government or he would be given the right to nominate a Muslim of his choice. Jinnah was adamant, and successful, in his opposition to a non-League Muslim being included in the proposed government because he felt that it would have dealt a deadly blow to his claim of being the sole spokesman of the Muslim nation and the Muslim League as the sole representative of Indian Muslims.[39] However, by treating this matter only in terms of power and representation, Jinnah probably set the tone for the future of Pakistan's politics. Jinnah did not attack Khizr Hyat on the grounds that he basically represented a constituency of feudal landlords who held their peasants, tenants, and landless laborers in political and economic servitude.

In the Punjab provincial elections of 1946, the Muslim League accused the British officials and the governor of trying to ensure the election of Unionist candidates. Lord Wavell admits having received such complaints from League circles, but does not mention the fact that he himself was accused that in his speech to the viceroy's durbar of notables in Rawalpindi he clearly hinted that votes in the forthcoming elections should be cast in favor of the "tried leaders."[40] In addition, Lord Wavell has lent credibility to these accusations and suspicions by showering high praise in his journal on Khizr Hyat for his pro-British attitude. Referring to his meeting with Khizr Hyat, the Punjab premier, Lord Wavell wrote:

> He did not talk much about all-India politics, said I knew his views; that the British ought not to leave, in fact he did not see how they could leave, that Pakistan was nonsense and any idea about exchange of populations madness, that he did not see how the Constituent Assembly would work, but that if I felt I should call it that was my business, that Jinnah's policy was all wrong; and that the Punjab would get on perfectly well by itself if only it was left alone.[41]

What sort of electioneering machinery could the Muslim League bring to bear against this entrenched power of the Unionists? The fact that by 1946 it had not developed an elaborate and efficient organization in Punjab was demonstrated when the Muslim League had to bring over more than 1,000 students from the Muslim Aligarh University to campaign for the League in Punjab and Sind. In one critical two-week period some 1,500 students addressed an estimated 700,000 Punjabis. The Unionists tried to counter this electioneering tactic by telling the voters that the Muslim League was insulting their intelligence by asking young students who had no knowledge or experience of life to preach to Punjab voters. In addition, on the surface, young left-leaning landlords like

Daultana had allowed certain intellectuals who were suspected of being communists to write the Punjab Muslim League Manifesto, which included planks like village uplift and the nationalization of key industries.

However, it must be borne in mind that the great bulk of the 86 Muslim constituencies lay in the rural areas of Punjab. The semifeudal landlords with their tenants and the sajjada nashins and pirs with their mureeds (followers) were concentrated in western Punjab in such districts as Dera Ghazi Khan, Muzaffargarh, Multan, Montgomery, Jhang, Shahpur, and Jhelum. Here the combined power of the bureaucracy and landowners could only be countered and finally overcome by the cry of Pakistan, which symbolized both Islamic solidarity and the political power of the promised state of Pakistan.

Thus, in order to appreciate how and why the Muslim League triumphed in the Punjab in 1946 (winning 79 of the 86 Muslim seats), one has to see the raw religious emotions and primordial passions that the Muslim League leaders and their supporters, the ulama and the sajjada nashin, aroused among the Muslim, masses. The central thrusts of their message were roughly as follows. Pakistan would have a government of the Qur'an. The supporters of the Muslim League constituted the only Islamic community and all the rest were kaffirs (unbelievers). Those who opposed Pakistan could not truly be called Muslims. Those who opposed the League might be excluded from burial in a Muslim cemetery and thus confined to hell after their death.

Does this mean that the unfurling of the banner of Islam in the election campaign had generated so much momentum and dynamism that the Muslim League leaders were being carried away by the enthusiasm of their followers? The flow and effusion of the religious rhetoric did suggest that. But the guiding influence was still that of Jinnah. His unswerving eye was on the results, and as a political leader his sole objective was to win such a crushing victory over his opponents in the heartland of Pakistan that his claim to be the undisputed leader of his nation and the Muslim League to be the only authoritative organization of the Indian Muslims would be vindicated. Once these objectives were attained, he probably thought the establishment of Pakistan would only be a matter of formal recognition by the British government and the Indian National Congress. Thus it was under his influence and guidance that the Jamiatul Ulama-i-Islam (the all-India organization of pro-Pakistan ulama) was called upon to set up its organization in Punjab.

Similarly, the Muslim League was successful in obtaining the support of the sajjada nashins of some of the prestigious shrines in western Punjab — Taunsa (Dera Ghazi Khan), Alipur (Muzaffargarh), Pakpattan (Montgomery), Sial (Sargodha), Jalalpur (Jhelum), and Golra (Rawalpindi). The pirs, the mullahs (preachers), and the maulvis (one who has had some formal schooling in Islamic theology and therefore qualified to lead prayers) had created such havoc for the Unionists that frantic telegrams from Unionist party organizers in the districts urged the party headquarters to send immediately not only supplies of gasoline but also as many maulvis as possible. They pointed out, as if they had discovered it for the first time, that 80 percent of their districts were pir-ridden and that fatwas (religious decrees) were the only antidote against League propaganda.[42]

The Muslim League victory, though impressive, was by no means decisive in all the districts. The constituencies where the Muslim League candidate won by a margin of 50 percent or more were Jhelum, Pind Dadar Khan, Chakwal, Gujar Khan, Rawalpindi East, Mianwali North, Montgomery, Okara, Dipalpur, Jhang East (acclaimed), Jhang Central, Jhang West, Lodhran, Mailsi, Khanewal, Kabirwalla, Muzaffargarh North, and Dera Ghazi Khan North. In constituencies like Shahpur, Sargodha, Attock South, Mianwali South, Multan, Alipur, and Dera Ghazi Khan Central, the Unionist party won. In Attock North, the Unionist party won by acclamation. There were other constituencies where the election results were either close or where the Muslim League won by a minority with the total vote of the opposition parties being high.[43]

One begins to wonder whether the Muslim League leaders in Punjab, most of whom were Westernized landowners, resorted to pure political opportunism in relying so heavily on the Islamic appeal. It was reported that some of them, like the Nawab of Mamdot, the president of the Punjab Muslim League, Shaukat Hyat Khan, son of Sir Sikander Hyat, Feroz Khan Noon, a former member of the viceroy's executive council — all city-dwelling and landowning elite members of the Lahore Gymkhana Club — were presented as pirs and sajjada nashins in the election campaign.[44] Perhaps the Muslim League, in its defense, could argue that it considered the goal of Pakistan so vital and noble that any means to defeat its opponents in pursuit of such a goal were justifiable. However, it was clear that Jinnah and the Muslim League could not have defeated the Unionists only with the help of the Quaid-i-Azam's charisma and the organization of the Muslim League. As noted, the Unionist party was a product of the British policy of supporting tribal and semifeudal leaders in western Punjab. In order to defeat this entrenched feudalism and landlordism, the Muslim League had to use skillfully the new political assets that were available — the promise of a new Muslim state, the unifying appeal of Islam, and the services of the ulama, the pirs, and the sajjada nashins.

As suggested earlier, the economic appeal of Pakistan should be seen in a broader framework than that of better prospects of jobs and opportunities for middle-class Muslims. The villagers and the poorer sections in the towns and cities also expected that in Pakistan they might be much better off materially because it was commonly believed that mostly the Hindus and Sikhs were in possession of bicycles and better homes and monopolized commercial outlets like shops and grain stores. Particularly those villagers and townspeople in the northwestern districts like Jhelum, Campbellpur, and Rawalpindi, who had been abroad as soldiers during the Second World War, appreciated the material appeal of Pakistan. Moreover, it must also be borne in mind that a canal colony area like Lyallpur had already started undergoing early forms of social and economic transformation. Here the peasant proprietor, particularly the Arain, besides being a Muslim was also thrifty and industrious. To him also Pakistan meant better economic prospects. Therefore, when one sets the Islamic factor and the role of the religious leaders in this broader perspective, one begins to see that the speedy success of Pakistan as a movement cannot be attributed solely to Islam, the pirs, and the sajjada nashins.[45]

How was it that the manipulators and mobilizers of the Islamic appeal were in command while the religious functionaries through whom this political asset of the Islamic appeal could be used were in a sort of dependency relationship? This was because the British had set in motion two parallel forces. The first was the particularisms and regionalisms that existed in the form of ethnic communities like the Pakhtuns, the Sindhis, and the Baluchis and then further a subdivision of these communities in the form of tribes, baradaris (kinship groups), and castes. On top of this political and administrative diversity the British created an overall imperial administrative system of India.

Alongside this imperial administrative system there emerged the two dominant all-India movements — the All-India National Congress and the All-India Muslim League. The expectation that the British would transfer power to such all-India movements gave a sense of unity to these movements. When the All-India Muslim League put forward the demand for Pakistan and the expectation grew that power might be transferred to such a movement, the religious leaders had no option except to cooperate with the Muslim League. The tradition of the faithful rallying around the banner of Islam was strong in the Muslim community and furthermore the hope offered by the Muslim League leaders that the future state of Pakistan would be based on the Shariat were compelling inducements for the religious leaders to follow a secular leader like Jinnah.

How this promise of an Islamic state was to be translated in the post-1947 period became one of the major and persistent areas of disagreement between the secular and religious leaders. The battles were fought not only in the chambers of the constituent assemblies of Pakistan but sometimes erupted into violent explosions as the one relating to the 1953 demand, particularly in Punjab, that the Ahmadi community be declared a non-Muslim minority.[46]

COMPETING ROLES OF PAKHTUN ETHNICITY AND ISLAM IN MOBILIZING POLITICAL SUPPORT IN THE NORTH-WEST FRONTIER PROVINCE

Going from Punjab to the North-West Frontier Province, one is in a different political world, a world of more developed political and ethnic consciousness. In Punjab the Muslim League found itself pitted against the government-backed Unionist party. In the North-West Frontier Province it seemed it was the Muslim

League that enjoyed government support. The Khudai Khidmatgars, who constituted the hard-core and dominant element in the Congress party in the North-West Frontier Province, were successful throughout the 1930s and 1940s in mobilizing political support of the Pakhtuns against government-backed interests and groups. The British government, through a system of tribal penetration and support of certain tribal leaders, had tried not only to keep the Pakhtuns divided but later, starting in the 1930s, had even used Islam and the mullahs to win Pakhtun support against both foreign powers and the influence of the Khudai Khidmatgars and the Congress.

Politically the North-West Frontier Province comprised the Tribal Areas of Malakand, Khyber, Kurram, North Waziristan, and South Waziristan[47] and the six Settled Districts of Hazara, Mardan, Peshawar, Kohat, Bannu, and Dera Ismail Khan. One could say that there was no ethnic group in Pakistan in 1947 that was more conscious of its separate linguistic and cultural identity than the Pakhtuns.[48] Particularly in the Tribal Areas, tribes like the Afridis, the Waziris, and the Mahsuds had been fierce in protecting their tribal customs and manners from the inroads of Western influence: "Therefore let us keep our independence and have none of your qanun [law] and your other institutions which have brought such havoc in British India, but stick to our own riwaj [tribal custom] and be men like our fathers before us."[49]

Even in the Settled Districts, where the Pakhtuns had been absorbed into the British administrative and educational framework, Pakhtun consciousness among both the educated and uneducated groups continued to be strong. They still adhered to Pakhtunwali (the Pakhtun code of honor), which imposed obligations of providing asylum to fugitives, hospitality to visitors, seeking revenge against enemies, and so on. This Pakhtun consciousness was not of recent origin. The famous Pakhtun poet, Khushhal Khan Khattak, had lyricized about the historic role of the Pakhtuns and how they had hurled defiance at the mighty Mughals.[50] One could see that this separate Pakhtun consciousness could not be submerged in the larger Islamic identity, for the Pakhtuns, though Muslims, had taken up arms against the Muslim Mughals.

Because the Tribal Areas lay at the strategic frontiers, the British had tried to gain a firm foothold in these areas by occupying and controlling certain commanding positions through a chain of posts and cantonments. This was supposed to be a policy "which combined strength with beneficence." "You cannot rule a Pathan by fear only. But neither can you rule him unless he respects you, and he will not respect you unless he also fears you."[51] It must have been clear to a number of British officers that the Pakhtuns could not be tamed into docility and quiescence, for there were periodic and frequent tribal eruptions against the British. In the Settled Districts as well the British had tried to keep the countryside under control by supporting the big khans (landlords) by giving them revenue grants and making them honorary magistrates, zaildars, and so on. Even the limited transfer of power to elected ministers available under the Government of India Act of 1919 was not introduced in the North-West Frontier Province until 1932.

However, one could discern the major directions and goals of British policy. As in Punjab, so in the Frontier they were trying to help progovernment groups and factions to gain political ascendancy. When limited self-government was introduced in the Frontier in 1932, Sir Abdul Qaiyum, a retired civil servant, became the first minister of the province with elected ministers exercising control over limited areas like health, sanitation, and public works. Even though the Frontier was poorer than Punjab and lagged behind in the number of qualified personnel to run the administration and the economy, yet the more egalitarian and ethnocentric Pakhtuns were capable of displaying greater political independence.

The Pakhtuns found in Khan Abdul Ghaffar Khan probably their first and most outstanding leader to give expression to their native independence and defiance of British rule. Here was a member of a landowning family, whose brother, Dr. Khan Sahib, had joined the Indian Medical Service, deciding to resist temptations of higher education and government office in favor of a long and more risky political service to his community. One could detect a certain pattern in the kind of political service that he wanted to render to his people. Even though he was attracted by the anti-British agitation that was going on in the country and had also taken part in the Khilafat agitation, it seemed that his main concern was for the well-being of the Pakhtuns. He had started social work under the influence of the Haji Saheb of Turangzai, a well-known leader of the Mohmands in the Tribal Area to whom he was related by marriage. King Amanullah of Afghanistan, who had been deposed under the influence of the British, became his hero. In one of his early speeches to the Khudai Khidmatgars (servants of God), an organization that he established in 1929, he said: "I have been told that Amanullah Khan used to call himself the revolutionary King of the Pakhtuns. And indeed it was he who inspired us with the idea of the revolution."[52] He also extolled Amanullah Khan's efforts to make government employees learn the Pushtu language. When a Khudai Khidmatgar was sworn into the organization, he promised not only to refrain from taking part in feuds (a common Pakhtun weakness) and lead a simple life, but also to "treat every Pathan as my brother and friend."[53]

The Khudai Khidmatgars had not only become popular in the Settled Districts but also in the Tribal Areas. In April 1930, when Abdul Ghaffar Khan was arrested by the British for stirring unrest, his arrest first led to massive protests resulting in rioting in Peshawar. Abdul Ghaffar Khan's former leader and relative, the Haji of Turangzai, leading a force of 2,000 Mohmands and other tribes, appeared on the outskirts of Peshawar district. There was widespread rioting in areas like Mardan with thousands of Afridis and Mahsuds launching attacks on Peshawar cantonment and other areas in support of the Haji of Turangzai. Martial law was imposed all over the Frontier on August 15 and the British had to break up the Mohmand and Afridi forces by air bombardment.

One could see the first beginnings of an all-Pakhtun massive and even armed movement emerging from the modest stirrings of the Khudai Khidmatgar. Twenty or 30 years ago the British had ruled out such "combined synchronous action" on the part of the Pakhtun tribes.[54] One could also see how Khan Abdul Ghaffar Khan as early as the 1930s was trying to combine factors of history, geography, culture, and language to transform the relatively backward, divided, and disorganized Pakhtuns into a national community. The common language, culture, and history of the Pakhtuns enabled him to reach out to both the Tribal Areas and as far as Afghanistan with the hope of uniting the divided tribes into an organized community against the British. Referring to his long-held goals and dreams, he said: "I want to knit the divided tribes of the Pakhtuns, spread out from Baluchistan to Chitral, into one community, one brotherhood, so that they can share their sorrows and sufferings and can play a vital role in serving humanity."[55]

It was clear to Abdul Ghaffar Khan that in order to carry on his struggle against the British and pursue his political goals, he could not depend only on the Pakhtun cooperation available in the province. He had been in touch with both Muslim and Hindu leaders belonging to parties and movements like the Khilafat, the Congress, the Muslim League, and so on. It was obvious that he did not wish to cooperate with the Muslim Leaguers, who were avowedly pro-British in his eyes. But it seems that he could not get along with other Muslim leaders, including the Khilafat leader, Muhammad Ali. He also had developed quite an aversion to Punjabi Muslims, even during the 1920s, probably because, like other Pakhtuns, he resented their growing presence in the administrative and commercial spheres in the Frontier.[56] On the other hand, he seemed to be much more at ease with Congress leaders partly because he admired their determined anti-British stand and partly because he was confident that the dominant Hindu leadership in the Congress party would not be able to establish any direct foothold in the Pakhtun areas and would have to depend upon him for enlisting Pakhtun support to their movement. Thus, though the Khudai Khidmatgars remained intact as a social service movement, they aligned themselves with the Congress for political purposes in August 1931.

The Congress, with its hard-core support from the Khudai Khidmatgars, was able to win the 1937 provincial elections having captured 19 out of 50 seats. Even though the Congress won only 15 out of 36 Muslim seats, the Muslim League had not been able to win even one Muslim seat. However, with some of the non-Congress Muslim members joining the Muslim League, the Muslim League emerged as the principal opposition in the assembly. Khan Sahib, the brother of Abdul Ghaffar Khan, became the Congress chief minister of the province.

One of the first measures that the Congress ministry passed was aimed at the power and privileges of the big khans. They were stripped of offices and

D G Tendulkar

positions like those of honorary magistrates, zaildars, and so on that the British had conferred upon them. Even a more serious blow was the abolition of revenue in inams (gifts). Sir George Cunningham, the governor, noted in his diary that by early 1938 the khans were complaining to him that the Congress influence in the rural areas had even disabled them from recovering their rents. The Muslim League, with its growing support in the non-Pakhtun districts of the province like Hazara and also among some of the urban areas, made a concerted effort to enlist the support of the big khans.

The Congress through the antikhan measures had been fairly successful in winning the support of the lower classes. But the Muslim League countered this move by branding the Congress as a Hindu organization and thus tried to become popular among the lower classes as well. Some of the crucial variables had started slowly working against the Congress. Cunningham's diary records: "I also noticed about the middle of 1938 that Muslim officials as a body were beginning to lean towards the Muslim League."[57] In November 1939, the Congress ministry of Khan Sahib resigned following the lead given by Congress ministries in other provinces and the province remained under the direct rule of the governor for three and a half years. There must have been a significant waning in the political support of the Congress. Again, to quote Cunningham:

> He [Abdul Ghaffar Khan] seemed to have realized the unpopularity he had earned by stirring up the lower classes against the Khans, and when, at the end of April, he announced the suspension of satyagarh . . . , as he was now frightened of India being dragged into the war, he was obviously thinking of defence in terms of an all-Pathan organisation and not of Congress or other party body.[58]

Probably more by design than by accident the British propaganda dovetailed with that of the Muslim League. Congress policies during the war period tended to be directed against a successful prosecution of the British war effort in India. Particularly in the Frontier, the situation was even more sensitive because of the threats the Khudai Khidmatgar often posed in trying to extend their propaganda activities into the Tribal Areas. Cunningham's policy note dated September 23, 1942 reads: "Continuously preach the danger to Muslims of connivance with the revolutionary Hindu body. Most tribesmen seem to respond to this."

It looked as if British officers like Cunningham and others through their years in the Frontier and their mastery of the Pushtu language and culture knew the Pakhtuns so well that they (non-Muslims themselves) were confident of skillfully using the Islamic appeal through the mullahs. Thus the Cunningham papers, referring to the period 1939-43, stated: "Our propaganda since the beginning of the war had been most successful. It had played throughout on the Islamic theme." The mullahs could be pressured into issuing fatwas against every enemy of the British government. Such fatwas were issued not only against the Germans, Italians, and the Russians but also against the "idolatrous" Japanese. The underlying tone of all this propaganda was also anti-Congress. Sir George Cunningham in a personal note to the author wrote that in 1942 the Afridis passed a solemn resolution at a big jirga (council of tribal leaders) in Tirah that any Afridis joining any political party from India would be put to death.

Even though the basic social service cadres of the Khudai Khidmatgar consisted mainly of peasants and artisans, yet from the program and pronounce- ments of Abdul Ghaffar Khan it was clear that he did not advocate any radical agrarian program apart from making modest demands for lower land taxes. He himself belonged to the landowning class, and second, in order to maximize the ethnic appeal of his movement, he did not want to create any class conflicts among the Pakhtuns. In fact, as noted earlier, Abdul Ghaffar Khan had become concerned that the Congress ministry through some of its policies had antag- onized the big khans.

When the crucial provincial elections took place during the early part of 1946, the Muslim League thought that by appealing to Islamic unity and particu- larly to the fact that the Frontier support to the Muslim League would ensure the establishment of Pakistan, it would be able to win an easy victory. The Congress, on the other hand, stressed heavily the ethnic appeal, the record of its short-lived administration, and above all its anti-British struggle. According to Khan Abdul Ghaffar Khan, the League used the services of Muslim religious leaders from Punjab and the Frontier and during the election campaign the British openly supported the Muslim League.[59] In contrast to the situation in Punjab, where the Muslim League had used Islam and the religious leaders to defeat the Unionists backed by the government forces, in the Frontier the Muslim League was also using Islam and the religious leaders but presumably had government support against its Congress opponents.

In Punjab the Muslim League won, but in the Frontier the Muslim League, in spite of its stress on Islam, lost. The total vote polled by the League was 147,880, whereas the League's opponents polled 208,896 in the Muslim constit- uencies. Of the 36 Muslim seats, the Muslim League won 17 with the Congress winning 19. In addition, the Congress won 11 non-Muslim seats for a total of 30 seats in a house of 50 members. It may be noted that in the Pakhtun areas the Congress won 16 of the 22 seats. The League was mostly successful in the non- Pakhtun Hazara district and in the urban constituencies and won only 4 seats in the predominantly Pakhtun areas.

Again, one of the most perceptive evaluations of the election results was given by Cunningham, who felt that the main reason for the League's failure was lack of organization and internal feuding. The Congress succeeded because of its appeal to the lower classes. The Muslim League at that stage could hardly mobilize any support on the issue of Pakistan because the suggestion of Hindu domination was "laughable" to the average Pakhtun villager.[60]

The attractiveness of Pakistan and the possibility of Hindu domination might not have impressed an average Pakhtun in January 1946 when the provincial elections were held, but 18 months later, when the referendum was held in July 1947, the Pakhtuns in sufficient numbers voted in favor of joining Pakistan and against acceding to India. How had this come about? The Congress leaders in the Frontier, particularly the Khan brothers, had not thought things through. According to Wavell, when Khan Sahib met the cabinet mission in April 1946, he created the impression of being "woolly in his ideas." He would not consider Pakistan as a possibility. "Nor had he considered what Hindu domination at the Centre might entail. He talked in fact entirely from the Provincial angle, as if the Pakhtuns were a separate nation living in Pathanistan."[61] The Khan brothers continued to support the idea of the Frontier remaining a part of India and the Frontier representatives taking part in the Indian constituent assembly.

The Mountbatten June 3, 1947 plan, announcing in effect the partition of India, and later his decision to hold a referendum in the Frontier, took the wind out of their sails. The British officers had worked steadfastly to undermine the influence of the Congress in the Frontier and it was obvious that they were not going to leave India with the strategic areas of the Frontier sandwiched as an island between Pakistan and Afghanistan. It looked as if Jinnah and the Muslim League had methodically outmaneuvered the Congress and the Khan brothers. When the June 3 plan was announced, it was apparent that the choice that lay before the Frontier with its over 92 percent Muslim population was to join the Congress-dominated assembly in Delhi and thus agree to become a part of Hindu-dominated India or send their representatives to an assembly consisting of representatives from the Muslim-majority areas, that is, Pakistan.

Even though such a plan ran totally counter to its dream of a united India, the Congress had to face the emerging reality. It could not possibly support the Khan brothers in their desire for the creation of the separate state of Pakhtunistan, for this, they feared, could lead to the further balkanization of the subcontinent with ominous implications for the future of India itself. Azad, reporting about the discussions in the Congress Working Committee relating to partition, has pointed out that Abdul Ghaffar Khan was completely stunned by the Congress giving up its opposition to partition "without even consulting the Frontier and its leaders" in its eagerness to come to terms with the Muslim League. "Khan Abdul Gaffar Khan repeatedly said that the Frontier would regard it as an act of treachery if the Congress now threw the Khudai Khidmatgars to the wolves."[62]

Another factor that helped the cause of Pakistan and induced the Pakhtuns to change their attitude toward the Muslim League was the increasing ferocity of the Hindu-Muslim conflict in India resulting in, from the Muslim point of view, mounting Muslim casualties. Direct Action Day was launched by the Muslim League on August 16, 1946 to demonstrate Muslim opposition to

Congress domination of the interim government and also to show the British that the Muslim League was as powerful as the Congress.[63] This unfortunately resulted in Hindu-Muslim riots in Calcutta followed by similar communal killings in Noakhali and Bihar.

All this must have created the impression among the Pakhtuns that the Muslims were a beleaguered minority community in Hindu-dominated India and that therefore if Pakistan were not formed, the fate of Muslims even in the Muslim-majority provinces might be jeopardized. When Nehru visited the Frontier and the Tribal Areas in November 1946, he was greeted with black flags and anti-Congress slogans and there were fears for his life. "Dr. Khan Saheb and other Ministers who had come to receive Jawaharlal were themselves under police protection and proved completely ineffective."[64] Nehru also realized that the situation had probably gone beyond their control.[65]

The Muslim League knew that the political tide in the Frontier had to be taken at the flood so that it might lead it on to good fortune. Jinnah was known for his great sense of political timing. On February 20, 1947, Abdul Qaiyum Khan, a former Congress leader in the Frontier who had become a Muslim League leader in the Frontier legislative assembly, was arrested in Mardan where the League had just won a by-election. The League seized this opportunity and launched a massive civil disobedience movement against the Congress government. As many as 2,500 Muslim Leaguers were arrested. To make matters worse, Hindu-Muslim communal rioting had erupted in Peshawar and the Pakhtun tribesmen from the Tribal Areas started pouring into Punjab to sack Hindu villages and shops. The Muslim League wanted to create the impression that it had a mass following and was capable of launching a mass movement. Qaiyum Khan, writing to Jinnah from prison, claimed that the League had been transformed and that never again would it be said that it was incapable of making sacrifices.

There was no doubt that religious leaders like the Pir of Manki Sharif with his following of more than 200,000 could take credit for having injected into the Muslim League a new religious and political fervor.[66] But it would not be accurate to suggest that the astanadars (pirs and custodians of shrines in the Frontier),[67] the ulama, and other religious leaders had played a predominant role without which the Muslim League would not have been able to win the referendum in July 1947.[68] First of all, the religious leaders could not claim credit for the turn of events. Their intervention came after the situation was ripe. Second, the pirs and custodians of shrines did not always exercise a completely dominant influence over the Pakhtuns. It was true, as Fredrik Barth has observed, that the Pakhtuns relied considerably on the saints in the matter of mediation of disputes.[69] However, he has also pointed out: "Politically powerful Pakhtuns can denigrate the sacred status of Saints and claim rank equality with them; Saints on the other hand are adamant in their claim that all Saints *ipso facto* rank higher than all Pakhtuns."[70] Third, it must be borne in mind that Islam had won a contest in which the ethnic forces as personified by Khan

Abdul Ghaffar Khan and his Khudai Khidmatgars had boycotted the referendum. Their plea was that they wanted the Frontier referendum to provide a choice in which Pakhtunistan should have been the alternative to Pakistan and not India or Hindustan.

This boycott was reflected in the returns, for only 50.99 percent of the eligible electorate of the North-West Frontier Province took part with 289,244 expressing their support for Pakistan and 2,874 for India. In the referendum only 292,118 people had participated out of a total electorate of 572,799. Even in the provincial elections of 1946, the number of voters polling in Muslim constituencies alone was 356,776. It must be borne in mind that the elections and the referendum were held on the basis of restricted franchise in the sense that out of a population of about 3.5 million in the Settled Districts of the Frontier, only 572,799 were eligible to vote.[71] People living in the Tribal Areas and the Frontier states were not eligible to vote either in provincial elections or in the referendum. Thus one could say that the Pakhtun ethnicity had probably suffered a partial eclipse but not extinction. The Pakhtuns on the whole were very shrewd pragmatists. From their vantage point on the northwest borderlands of India they had watched the ebb and flow of many historic currents, but their Pakhtun identity had remained intact. Without discarding this identity, they had chosen in 1947 to become a part of Islamic Pakistan.

STATE BUILDING VERSUS NATION BUILDING UNDER JINNAH

The role of Quaid-i-Azam Muhammad Ali Jinnah as the founder of Pakistan should be considered as both a nation builder and a state builder. These two roles of Jinnah can best be understood in terms of his personality and the different phases of his political leadership. It is not suggested that the key to an understanding of the historical development of Pakistan is the personality of its founder. What is being suggested is that the strengths and weaknesses of some of the dominant ruling classes like lawyers, bureaucrats, and merchant capitalists in the formative phase of Pakistan were encapsulated in the personality of Jinnah.

At first, that is, before the mass politics of Gandhi and the Congress emerged during the 1920s, Jinnah's primary role was that of a mediator. He was the architect of the Lucknow pact of 1916 when he was described as the ambassador of Hindu-Muslim unity. Though he personally believed in joint electorates, as an advocate of his clients and as a skillful composer of constitutional differences, he was successful in extracting from the Congress separate Muslim electorates and their introduction in provinces like Punjab and the Central Provinces as a concession to Muslim demands. In 1928, when the famous Nehru report was produced, the Congress leaders both on political and intellectual grounds rejected separate electorates and special safeguards for Muslims.

Jinnah offered his Fourteen Points as amendments to the Nehru report. His compromise solution in the Fourteen Points was to combine a strong federal form of government, which would please the Congress, with separate electorates and special safeguards for Muslims. However, this compromise formula was rejected by the Congress. Jinnah soon realized that without political power he could neither persuade the Congress nor could he speak with much authority as a spokesman of the Muslim community.

It is said that after the rejection of his compromise proposals by the Congress in 1928, Jinnah had considered seriously leaving India for good and in fact settled down in England for a few years to practice as a lawyer. However, with the passage of the Government of India Act in 1935 he probably felt that he could still play an important role in Indian politics both as a member of the Indian central legislature and as the president of the All-India Muslim League. The provincial elections that were held in the early part of 1937 not only brought him in contact with the Muslim masses but also made him aware that perhaps Muslims could consolidate their power in certain provinces where they were in majority. If the Muslim League were to succeed under his leadership in bringing this about, Muslims would be in a position to come to terms with the Hindus not as a relatively weak religious minority but as a strong community backed by their entrenched political power in Muslim-majority provinces like Bengal in the east and Sind, Punjab, and the Frontier in the west.

Thus, by 1940, one could see the transformation of a lawyer fighting for the constitutional and political safeguards of a community into an advocate of the two-nation theory and a proponent of the separate state of Pakistan. Some of the crucial and strategic mistakes made by his main adversary, the Indian National Congress, the favorable disposition of the British toward the Muslims, and above all the Islamic appeal and the hopes and aspirations the idea of Pakistan aroused among the Muslim masses brought to Jinnah a speedy and spectacular success. Comments have already been made on his political strategy and his impeccable sense of political timing in the discussion on Punjab and the North-West Frontier Province.

A middle-class lawyer, having originated from the Khoja trading community, and with his professional and business contacts with families or commercial houses like the Adamjees, the Ispahanis,[72] and the Habibs, Jinnah thought that the diversities and particularisms of regions, castes, communities, and sects would all be swept away in the future state of Pakistan if certain forms of state apparatus were built speedily and methodically. To Jinnah, "economic development and economic power was the most important of all the departments of life" and therefore during 1944-45 he was constantly urging his followers and commercial magnates to establish an all-India Muslim chamber of commerce with branches in different provinces. Again, at his urging, four big companies in such vital sectors as banking, shipping, insurance, and airlines were established prior to partition. Jinnah was also reported to have advised some of the leading commercial magnates in early 1947 to "pack up from Bombay and proceed to Karachi."[73]

When one merely lists the kinds of activities that Jinnah, through his leadership and initiative, had set in motion, one begins to wonder how one individual could have concerned himself with plans and programs relating to the establishment of chambers of commerce, a national press, four fairly big commercial and industrial enterprises, and a number of committees commissioned to produce reports on problems that the future state of Pakistan would face in such areas as education, industrial development, and so on.[74]

As regards the political and administrative framework of the new state, he tended to follow the traditions and legacies that the British Raj had left behind. He imposed a highly centralized constitutional system like that of the adapted Government of India Act of 1935 on a country that was both culturally and physically heterogeneous. Under Jinnah, three of the four provincial governors in provinces like West Punjab, the Frontier, and East Bengal were British. The Muslim League cabinets and the political machinery were handed over to the control of governors and bureaucrats. It was a Mudie or a Cunningham who sent detailed reports about cabinet and party factions. The kind of advice that Jinnah was receiving can be seen in the letters of these British governors. The main tenor of these letters was that the politicians were not allowing the government machinery to function with its preindependence bureaucratic efficiency. Jinnah could have drawn two conclusions from this: one, to place the politicians under bureaucratic tutelage; and two, to improve the party machinery to eliminate some of the factions and accommodate others. He was, after all, a dying man and could think of only immediate short-term remedies. In settling for the first alternative, he not only took care of the immediate problems but laid the foundations for future actions and policies of his successor governments that outdid him in establishing bureaucratic control over politicians. It may also be noted that the Civil Service of Pakistan became even a more centralized bureaucracy than its predecessor, the Indian Civil Service, because it discarded the provincial cadres that had been set up under the latter.

An exclusive emphasis on this kind of state building made the task of nation building exceedingly difficult if not impossible. A centralized bureaucracy dominated by members drawn from one province, Punjab, was bound to create misgivings among the less developed regions like Bengal, the Frontier, or Sind. Because in areas like policymaking and allocation of federal resources among regions the centralized bureaucracy was bound to exercise dominant influence, and because the central bureaucracy like the Civil Service of Pakistan tended to dominate policymaking departments in the provinces as well, people in the less developed provinces were bound to feel that their provinces remained underdeveloped because of their lack of access to decision making at the national and provincial levels.

The Quaid-i-Azam, even before the establishment of Pakistan, had influenced the development of certain economic and commercial institutions and had clearly indicated that the central philosophy behind economic policy would be based on principles of capitalism and private enterprise. Again, this kind of economic development with the entrepreneurial class drawn from certain commercial communities that had come from India and with their investment decisions guided almost solely by the profit motive was bound to result in both class and regional conflicts. This is a theme that will recur frequently in later chapters.

In his last independence day message, Jinnah declared, "The foundations of your state have been laid, and it is now for you to build, and build as quickly and as well as you can." Unfortunately, in the laying of these foundations an impression had been created that the interests of certain dominant classes or groups like the bureaucrats, the lawyers, the upper-middle-class intelligentsia, and the landlords had been uppermost in the minds of the decision makers. In their defense the ruling elites could argue that the policies that had been pursued were probably the only practical and prudent measures necessary for the speedy development of the country. But one may ask, where did the interests of the great majority of the people who lived in the rural areas of West Punjab, Sind, the Frontier, and East Bengal, namely, the small peasants, the tenants, and the landless laborers, fit into such policies? Most of these refugees were poor peasants and could have been rehabilitated if the large estates in West Punjab had been broken up through land reforms. Jinnah as the founder of the state and as the governor-general of Pakistan could have used his political influence and constitutional power to introduce land reforms as an emergency measure. Unfortunately, this was not done even though Mian Iftikharuddin, minister for rehabilitation of refugees in the West Punjab government, pressed for such reforms and resigned when his plea was rejected.

The Quaid, who had advocated the two-nation theory as the raison d'etre for the creation of Pakistan, probably felt after the establishment of the state that he could calm the religious passions so that communal carnage and killing might be brought under control. He preached tolerance to the constituent assembly and it seemed that the embers of liberal secularism of the early Jinnah were still flickering. An acute observer of the Indian scene had referred to Jinnah as "a sword of Islam resting in a secular scabbard."[75] This was further confirmed in his first address to the constituent assembly when Jinnah declared, "You will find that in course of time Hindus would cease to be Hindus and Muslims would cease to be Muslims, not in the religious sense, because that is the personal faith of each individual, but in the political sense as citizens of the state."[76] However, later in his speeches in Bengal and the North-West Frontier, when faced with the problem of emerging regional conflicts between Punjabis and Bengalis or between Punjabis and Pakhtuns, his exhortation would be that these regional groups should think of themselves as Muslims and Pakistanis first rather than as Bengalis or Punjabis or Pakhtuns.

This kind of thinking suggests a number of things. First, the leadership had not gone much beyond political rhetoric or invocation of the Islamic appeal for purposes of nation building. Second, as it became apparent later, the ulama and other religious leaders could also use this fissionable material for their own purposes. Third, in essence this was leadership by remote control. Leadership by remote control in the unusual political climate that existed in the subcontinent had produced Pakistan. The leadership, without becoming fully aware of the kind of Islam that existed at the grass-roots level and without responding to the concrete economic and social issues like semifeudal exploitation of the rural classes, had been able to achieve Pakistan. Jinnah perhaps was the best example of this anglicized, middle-class leadership. It has been reported to the author that when the governor-general addressed a jirga of the Pakhtuns in the Frontier, his English speech was translated into Pushtu by the British governor, Sir George Cunningham.

The power elites that emerged soon after the formation of Pakistan were the middle-class professional groups like lawyers and civil servants, merchant capitalists, and the big landowners drawn mostly from Punjab and Sind. This loose coalition had been brought to power by Muslim nationalism, but its chief instrument, the Muslim League, was not a well-organized party and had not been able to develop any firm grass-roots support in the countryside. The result was that every time there was a popular uprising, the ruling classes had to rely almost exclusively on the coercive apparatus of the civil service.

The next chapter shows how the increasing inability of the ruling coalition to cope with some of the major political and economic problems resulted in the civil-military oligarchy capturing all effective power in Pakistan.

NOTES

1. Muslim League leaders almost invariably presented the concept of Pakistan as an Islamic state to the Muslim masses, whereas the dominant group among these leaders planned and expected that it would be a Muslim state, the policies of which would be liberal and modern though influenced broadly by certain Islamic principles. The Muslim League leaders did not discuss the issue as to what would happen if there were a conflict between the principles or dictates of the Shariat (Islamic law) and the requirements of a modern state.

2. Karl Marx and Friedrich Engels, *The Communist Manifesto,* ed. Samuel H. Beer (New York: Appleton-Century-Crofts, 1955), p. 14.

3. Cited in Shlomo Avineri, ed., *Karl Marx on Colonialism and Modernization* (Garden City, N.Y.: Doubleday, 1969), p. 8.

4. Ibid., pp. 132-33.

5. Karl Marx, *The Eighteenth Brumaire of Louis Bonaparte* (Moscow: Progress, 1972), p. 10.

6. Geoffrey Kay, *Development and Underdevelopment: A Marxist Analysis* (London: Macmillan, 1975), p. x and Chap. 5.

7. Thomas Henry Thornton, *Sir Robert Sandeman: His Life and Work* (London: John Murray, 1895), p. 30.

8. Ibid., p. 94.

9. Richard Issaq Bruce, *The Forward Policy* (London: Longmans, 1900), p. 298.

10. A. C. Yate, *Travels with the Afghan Boundary Commission* (Edinburgh and London: Blackwood, 1887), pp. 433, 440.

11. Thornton, op. cit., pp. 358-59.

12. S. S. Thorburn, *Asiatic Neighbours* (Edinburgh and London: Blackwood, 1894), p. 51.

13. John Gallagher, Gordon Johnson, and Anil Seal, *Locality, Province and Nation: Essays on Indian Politics 1879-1940* (Cambridge: Cambridge University Press, 1973), p. 9.

14. Ibid., pp. 7-8.

15. Michael O'Dwyer, *India as I Knew It 1885-1925* (London: Constable, 1925), p. 53.

16. Malcolm Lyall Darling, *Rusticus Loquitur* (London: Oxford University Press, 1930), p. 214.

17. Malcolm Lyall Darling, *Punjab Peasant in Prosperity and Debt* (London: Oxford University Press, 1932), pp. 102-03.

18. Ibid., p. 103.

19. Ibid., p. 104.

20. Darling, *Rusticus Loquitur,* p. 286.

21. Ibid., p. 291.

22. Ibid., p. 264.

23. Darling, *Punjab Peasant,* pp. 122-23.

24. M. Masud, *Hari Report: Note of Dissent* (Karachi: Hari Publications, 1948), pp. 2, 6.

25. Gallagher, Johnson, and Seal, op. cit., p. 8.

26. O'Dwyer, op. cit., p. 39.

27. Cited in Norman G. Barrier, *The Punjab Alienation of Land Bill of 1900,* Monograph no. 2, Duke University Commonwealth Studies Center, p. 94.

28. Valentine Chirol, *India Old and New* (London: Macmillan, 1921), p. 208.

29. *Punjab Gazetteer, VII, Multan District 1923-24,* Part A (Lahore, Government Printing, Punjab, 1927), p. 108.

30. Ibid., p. 109.

31. V. G. Kiernan, trans., *Poems from Iqbal* (London: John Murray, 1955), p. 58.

32. The Ahrar were a party of nationalist Muslims. Although they seceded from the Congress, they continued to be anti-British and anti-Muslim League and organized protest movements in support of Kashmiri Muslims against their Hindu rulers.

33. A. H. Albiruni, *Makers of Pakistan and Modern Muslim India* (Lahore: Ashraf, 1950), p. 209.

34. *Dawn* (Karachi), December 25, 1955.

35. R. Russell, "Strands of Muslim Identity in South Asia," *South Asian Review* 6, no. 1 (October 1972): 23.

36. *Report of the Court of Inquiry Constituted under Punjab Act II of 1954 to Enquire into the Punjab Disturbances of 1953* (Lahore: Government Printing, Punjab, 1954), p. 231.

37. Penderel Moon, *Divide and Quit* (Berkeley: University of California Press, 1962), p. 38.

38. David Gilmartin, "The Rise of the Muslim League in the Punjab and the Destruction of the Unionist System," term paper presented to the History Department, University of California, Berkeley, June 15, 1973.

39. For details regarding the Simla conference and how it failed because of Jinnah's firm stand, see Khalid B. Sayeed, *Pakistan, the Formative Phase 1857-1947* (London: Oxford University Press, 1968), pp. 126-33.

40. For Muslim League accusations, see Penderel Moon, ed., *Wavell, the Viceroy's Journal* (Delhi: Oxford, 1977), p. 178. For accusations against Wavell, see Firoz Khan Noon, *From Memory* (Lahore: Ferozsons, 1966), p. 192. According to Noon, the viceroy, Lord Wavell, by the term "tried leaders" meant Khizr Hyat and the Unionists who had been in power and therefore tried as compared to the Muslim League candidates whose party had not been in power.

41. Moon, op. cit., p. 379.

42. The source for this information is David Gilmartin, who told the author that he had personally examined the Unionist party papers.

43. This analysis is based on a summary of the Punjab elections that is to be found in the India Office Library, London, in the series *Transfer of Power*, vol. L/P & J/8/472, folios 8-16.

44. *Report of the Court of Inquiry*, 255.

45. The author is indebted to David Gilmartin for the invaluable insights he has provided about the crucial role that the sajjada nashins played in enabling the Muslim League to defeat the Unionists in the 1946 elections. David Gilmartin, "Muslim Religious Organization in the Punjab and the Movement for Pakistan" (draft). This is a part of his forthcoming Ph.D. thesis for the University of California, Berkeley.

46. This resulted in violent clashes between the government and the religious groups resulting in considerable loss of life in Punjab in 1953. The same question arose in 1974 when the Bhutto government finally had to concede and the National Assembly declared the Ahmadis to be a non-Muslim minority.

47. Tribal Areas were divided into agencies, with each agency being placed under a political agent.

48. Use of the Indian word Pathan, which is also used by a number of English writers, has been avoided and the term Pakhtun is used instead because it is used both by the inhabitants of the area and by well-known leaders like Abdul Ghaffar Khan and even by his opponent, Abdul Qaiyum Khan.

49. See Preface, Evelyn Howell, *Mizh: A Monograph on Government's Relations with the Mahsud Tribe* (Simla: Government of India Press, 1931).

50. Quoted in James W. Spain, *The Pathan Borderland* (The Hague: Mouton, 1963), p. 91.

51. C. E. Bruce, *Waziristan 1936-1937* (Aldershot: Gole and Polden, 1938), p. 78.

52. Badshah Khan, *My Life and Struggle* (Delhi: Orient, 1969), p. 95.

53. Ibid., p. 97.

54. P. W. Thorburn, *The Punjab in Peace and War*, quoted in Hugh Kennedy Trevaskis, *The Punjab of To-day* (Lahore: Civil & Military Gazette, 1931), p. 18.

55. D. G. Tendulkar, *Abdul Ghaffar Khan* (Bombay: Popular Prakashan, 1967), p. 529.

56. For his attitudes toward non-Pakhtun Muslims, see Badshah Khan, op. cit., pp. 98-100.

57. The citations refer to Cunningham's Diary "B," September 1937-November 1939. It may be noted that these citations from Cunningham's papers are from the same papers found in the India Office Library. The references, however, are different because the citations are from the papers that are in the author's possession. In these citations the titles as given by Cunningham are followed.

58. Cunningham's Diary "C," November 1939-May 1943, p. 15.

59. Tendulkar, op. cit., p. 367.

60. Cunningham's Diary "D," May 25, 1943-March 16, 1945, p. 36.

61. Moon, op. cit., pp. 232-33.

62. Maulana Abul Kalam Azad, *India Wins Freedom* (Calcutta: Orient Longmans, 1959), p. 193.

63. For details, see Sayeed, *Pakistan the Formative Phase*, pp. 151-54.

64. Azad, op. cit., p. 171.

65. According to Wavell, Nehru's letter to the governor of the North-West Frontier Province suggested that he "seems to have realised that the Frontier and the Tribes had better be left alone for the present." Moon, op. cit., p. 378.

66. Spain, op. cit., p. 195.

67. *Astanadar* literally means "place possessor – one whose ancestors in remote or recent time acquired the title of 'Zhurg' of 'Buzurg' or 'Saint.' " *N.-W.F. Province Gazetteers. Peshawar District,* vol. A, 1931 (Lahore: Civil & Military Gazette, 1934), p. 155.

68. For an alternative point of view, which emphasizes the crucial role of the religious leaders, see Stephen Rittenberg, *The Independence Movement in India's North-West Frontier Province 1901-1947* (Ph.D. diss., Columbia University, 1977).

69. Fredrik Barth, *Political Leadership Among Swat Pathans,* London School of Economics Monograph on Social Anthropology, no. 19, 1959, p. 96.

70. Fredrik Barth, "The System of Social Stratification in Swat, North Pakistan," in *Aspects of Caste in South India, Ceylon and North-West Pakistan,* ed. E. R. Leach, Cambridge Papers in Social Anthropology, no. 2, 1960, p. 140.

71. These figures have been taken from *In the Supreme Court of Pakistan: Written Statement of Khan Abdul Wali Khan* (Peshawar, 1975), p. 81.

72. M. A. H. Ispahani, besides being his political follower, was also his adviser in personal matters like investments in stocks and shares. Z. H. Zaidi, ed., *M. A. Jinnah-Ispahani Correspondence 1936-1948* (Karachi: Forward Publications Trust, 1976), pp. 392, 402.

73. Hanna Papanek, "Pakistan's Big Businessmen: Muslim Separatism, Entrepreneurship, and Partial Modernization," *Economic Development and Cultural Change* 21 (October 1972): 13-14.

74. A number of pamphlets under the title Pakistan Literature Series were published under the authority of the Committee of Writers of the All-India Muslim League. Some of them were *Muslim Educational Problems* (Lahore: Ashraf, 1945), *The Future Development of Islamic Polity* (Lahore: Ashraf, 1946), and *The Industrial Pakistan* (Lahore: Ashraf, 1947).

75. Reginald Sorensen, *My Impression of India* (London: Meridian, 1946), p. 109.

76. *Constituent Assembly (Legislature) of Pakistan Debates,* vol. 1, no. 2 (August 11, 1947), pp. 18-20.

2
SOCIAL AND ETHNIC CONFLICTS AND EMERGENCE OF CIVIL-MILITARY OLIGARCHY, 1947–58

During 1950-58, Pakistan had seven prime ministers and one commander-in-chief, whereas India had one prime minister and several commanders-in-chief. Those who compare the political development of India and Pakistan very often tend to explain the divergent paths that the two countries have followed since independence in terms of certain disadvantages that Pakistan was plagued with during its early years. That Pakistan lost its founder in 1948 and its able prime minister was assassinated in 1951 are often cited as the origin of Pakistan's political misfortunes. The fact that a geographically and ethnically split country was to be run by a political party like the Muslim League, which had neither the organization nor the experience of its counterpart, the Indian National Congress, is used to explain political instability and the erosion of democracy in Pakistan. These explanations do not explain in depth the real problems that Pakistan faced during 1947-58.

Pakistan's political leaders did not realize that a political party like the Muslim League or its successor would have to be restructured in such a way that it would develop, on the one hand, grass-roots support throughout the country and, on the other, the skills and the machinery to run the government. This meant that besides being a well-knit organization at the governmental level, the party would have to provide leadership both at the religious and ethnic levels. The Muslim League leaders simply did not have either the imagination or the resources to develop such a party.

The challenges they faced were indeed formidable. West Pakistan for another decade or so would continue to be dominated by the landlords with periodic religious outbursts of a serious nature. The social structure in East Bengal, on the other hand, was of a vastly different nature. Despite its economic backwardness, the lower-middle-class groups — lawyers, traders, merchants, schoolteachers, and small farmers — were emerging to challenge the domination of both the old traditional landowning groups and even urban-based leaders. Another major problem was the growing ethnic and regional conflict between the Punjabis and Bengalis and the Punjabis and other ethnic groups like the Sindhis and the Pakhtuns. As a result of these internecine conflicts, the civil and military leaders emerged dominant, but they could not provide a clear sense of direction and national unity because the domination of civil and military bureaucracies in effect meant the dominance of the Punjabi or West Pakistan groups.

Before all the provinces, states, and other areas in West Pakistan were integrated into the province of West Pakistan in 1955, there were in all four provinces in Pakistan. In the eastern region, there was East Bengal. In the west, there were West Punjab, Sind, and the North-West Frontier. There were also states like Bahawalpur and Khairpur in West Pakistan. In addition, there were areas like the Tribal Areas in the North-West Frontier Province, Baluchistan, and Karachi, which were under the jurisdiction of the central government. The population of East Bengal in 1951 was 41.9 million and that of West Pakistan 33.7 million. In terms of area, West Pakistan was slightly more than five times as large as East Bengal.

In 1953, in the constituent assembly of 79 members, the Muslim League Parliamentary party had 60 members, 33 of whom were Bengalis. In addition, there was a Dacca-Karachi-Peshawar axis. Bengalis had been able to win the support of the Frontier and Sindhi groups because of the resentment that they often displayed toward Punjabi domination. The Punjabis dominated the civil service, and in the army, next to the Punjabis, the Pakhtuns were influential. Under the quota system in civil service recruitment, East Bengalis could hope to occupy some of the key positions in the future, whereas in the army West Pakistani domination was so complete that East Bengalis could not hope to alter the situation for a long time to come. The Bengalis pointed out that it was because of the preponderance of West Pakistanis in the army and the civil service that there was economic disparity between the two wings. Economic policy, formulated under the influence of West Pakistani civil servants, had been such that industrialization in West Pakistan had forged ahead, leaving East Bengal far behind.

In addition, central government expenditure, because of the location of Karachi and the concentration of the army in West Pakistan, was much greater than in East Bengal. East Bengal contributed much more to foreign exchange earnings of the country than the west and yet it was lagging behind West Pakistan in economic development. The center's plea was that scarce resources were being invested in West Pakistan because its developed economy would yield higher returns than that of East Bengal. The only course open to Bengalis was to use their majority in the constituent assembly in such a way that government decisions with regard to allocation of economic resources were not unduly influenced by the West Pakistani groups. Bengali Muslim Leaguers knew that it was not easy for them to build a united Bengali front because there were 11 Congress (Hindu) members in the Bengali group. Therefore they were eager to form an alliance with the Sindhi and Frontier groups.

The conflict between the Punjabi and the Bengali elites should be understood in the political, social, and institutional settings. Some of the landlord politicians from Punjab, Sind, and the Frontier shared similar cultural and political outlooks with the Urdu-speaking Bengali prime minister, Nazimuddin (1951-53), and his associates or even the later Bengali prime minister, Muhammad Ali Bogra (1953-55). But these similarities soon dissolved into differences when one considered that the Punjabi landowning politicians were much closer in both outlook and interest to the Punjabi civil servants and military officers than the Bengalis could ever be.

Behind the various versions of the Basic Principles Committee Report set up to formulate the principles of the constitution there lay the basic political and economic conflicts that existed between the Punjabi and Bengali elites. An attempt to resolve these conflicts was made through the principle of parity of representation to satisfy the fears of the Punjabis about the Bengali majority and the ability of the Bengalis to exploit the anti-Punjabi feeling that existed among the Sindhi and the Pakhtun representatives. But even such formulas could not dispel their differences and suspicions. The Punjabis felt that the Bengali front should be confronted by an integrated West Pakistan in the constituent assembly. The Bengalis, on the other hand, complained bitterly that even their slight majority position was being undermined through the principle of parity. This meant that the Punjabi domination of Pakistan's economy through their dominant position in the civil services and the army would continue relatively unchallenged for a long time to come.

Politicians from Bengal found that their political support had disappeared after the defeat of the Muslim League in the provincial elections of 1954 in Bengal and the emergence of new political groups committed to asserting a strong measure of Bengali autonomy. The first climacteric in this continuing conflict was reached in April 1953 when the Punjabi governor-general, Ghulam Muhammad (a former civil servant and later finance minsiter, 1947-51), dismissed the Bengali prime minister, Nazimuddin, and his cabinet. The charges were that the government had proved itself incapable of maintaining law and order and of arresting the deteriorating food situation. It was apparent to the political circles that the reference to law and order meant the anti-Ahmadi riots that had erupted in Punjab in February-March 1953 when Nazimuddin had replaced the

Punjabi chief minister. Even though Nazimuddin enjoyed majority support in the assembly, he was dismissed, presumably because a civil servant like Ghulam Muhammad felt national considerations as viewed by his faction were more important than adherence to parliamentary practices.

The new prime minister, Muhammad Ali Bogra, in deference to the growing militancy in Bengal, was able to get the assembly to approve both Urdu and Bengali as state languages. In the new version of the Basic Principles Committee Report he produced a formula under which in a joint sitting each of the two wings would have equal representation. The Punjabi group was keen to unite all the provinces of West Pakistan under a zonal subfederation, but was being opposed by the Bengalis and the smaller provinces. The prime minister, anticipating dismissal from the governor-general, tried to reduce the powers of the governor-general through an amendment. The governor-general struck back in October 1954 when he dissolved the constituent assembly itself. *Dawn's* colorful comments were not too far off the mark:

> There have indeed been times — such as that October night in 1954 — when, with a General to the right of him and a General to the left of him, a half-mad Governor General imposed upon a captured Prime Minister the dissolution of the Constituent Assembly and the virtual setting up of a semi-dictatorial Executive.[1]

DISINTEGRATION OF THE MUSLIM LEAGUE IN THE PROVINCES

So far political infighting at the central level has been discussed. One of the reasons why the central politicians could not offer much resistance to the governor-general, the civil servants, and the military was because they often tended either to lose total control over their constituencies, as in the case of Punjab, or had lost virtually all support, as in the case of East Bengal. In order to explain this phenomenon, this analysis will concentrate on the political situation in the two major provinces of Punjab and East Bengal. Later in the discussion of the One Unit issue, the other provinces of West Pakistan, Sind and the North-West Frontier, will be considered.

The main instruments of political organization in the rural areas in Punjab where the great majority of the population lived were the landlords who controlled their tenants and the pirs and sajjada nashins who could be used to mobilize support through the Islamic appeal. In Bengal as well, the Muslim League during 1947-54 relied mainly on the more conservative Bengali landowners and lawyers, some of whom were Urdu-speaking, but most of whom were losing touch with the lower-middle-class groups. The latter were mobilizing support by demanding that Bengali should be recognized as one of the state languages and that Bengal should opt for maximum provincial autonomy so that its economic discrimination under the West-Pakistani-dominated center should end.

In Punjab, Muslim League governments without suffering any electoral defeats were replaced, dismissed, and set aside through central intervention brought about by the civil-military oligarchy. Muslim League politicians in Punjab were found to be inept in handling problems like the anti-Ahmadi demonstrations and the One Unit issue. In East Bengal, on the other hand, the Muslim League found itself virtually decimated in the provincial elections of 1954, but the United Front politicians — members of the Awami League, the Krishak Sramik (Peasants and Workers) party, and other parties — had aroused so much ethnic consciousness and anticenter feeling that provincial governments were often dismissed or suspended by the central government.

If landowning politicians were the main instruments of the Muslim League in Punjab, and if some form of Islamic polity was the central issue that generated the political and emotional support of the Muslim League, in what state were these two factors in Punjab during the early 1950s? As emphasized in the first chapter, most of the landlords in Punjab were mere creations of the British and could not claim ancient aristocratic origins dating back to Mughal or early periods. They had been nurtured by the British on the principle that if they remained loyal to the Raj, the Raj would look after them and preserve the privileges that the British had conferred upon them and thus let them exploit and fleece their peasants. No lofty principles of loyalty to a state or religion or king animated their political behavior.

From the very inception of Pakistan they had become noted for their intrigues and feuds. In a personal communication, Sir Francis Mudie, the British governor of Punjab in 1947-49, wrote to the author that Jinnah as governor-general had become so disgusted with the performance of the Muslim League ministry in Punjab that he told the governor that he would wash his hands of them and that his policy was to let the ministry "stew in its own juice" of intrigues and feuds. Some of the landlords were involved in feuds with each other dating back several decades. These disputes had originated in cases involving cattle stealing and claims against each other's landed property.

One of the principal actors in this feudal infighting was Mian Mumtaz Daultana, who emerged as the chief minister after the provincial elections in Punjab in 1951. The 1951 provincial elections in Punjab were won by the Muslim League not because it offered a coherent political program but because Daultana, as the leader of a government-backed party, could attract the support of the leading landlords in each district. The normal practice in Punjab on the part of a winning coalition was to prepare a list of leading notables in each district and offer party tickets to the most influential of them, thereby ensuring their success even before the elections were held. These notables were feudal landlords who in districts like Multan, Muzaffargarh, and Dera Ghazi Khan also held the titles of pirs and sajjada nashins. This meant that the landowning notables commanded almost complete monopoly of political support through their tenants and even smaller landlords who were tied to them through bonds of land and religion.

Daultana was a superb craftsman in compiling lists of notables who had political support in each district. Prior to the elections of 1951 he had been able to entice the notables through a highly intricate network of pacts and alliances. Thus pacts like the Daultana-Gilani pact and the Gardezi-Gilani pact were promoted by Daultana in order to maximize his support in an important district like Multan. In order to lend solemnity and religious sanction to these pacts, they were calligraphed on a leaf of the Qur'an and the signatories declared they would support each other as God-fearing Muslims.[2] Daultana eventually acquired considerable notoriety for breaking these pacts and letting down his friends. The trouble was that he entered into so many intricate pacts and alliances that it was difficult for him to satisfy everyone and he sometimes got caught in the coils of his own intrigues.

Islam had served as the unifying link between Muslims belonging to various sects like the Sunnis and the Shiahs or ethnic groups like the Punjabis, Sindhis, and Pakhtuns, and even in rallying Muslims from the Hindu-majority provinces of India who could not expect to profit much from Pakistan. Now that Pakistan had been formed, it was not as easy through the Islamic appeal to overcome the differences that arose between the various sects and ethnic groups as a result of the normal policies of the government in the matter of allocation of resources or creation of new jobs and opportunities.

If the Muslim League had developed its grass-roots organization and had not allowed the mullahs and maulanas to continue to exercise almost total influence in religious matters, the anti-Ahmadi movement might not have erupted with the same ferocity as it did in the early part of 1953. Beneath the facade of overall Islamic unity there lay deep fissures in the Islamic polity. On the basis of evidence that was furnished by the ulama belonging to various schools and sects to the court of inquiry set up to investigate the anti-Ahmadi disturbances of 1953, the court felt that in the eyes of certain Sunni leaders all Shiahs were kafirs (unbelievers) and some of the Shiah leaders were inclined to pay the same compliment to the Sunnis.

> The net result of all this is that neither Shias nor Sunnis nor Deobandis nor Ahl-i-Hadith nor Barelvis are Muslims and any change from one view to the other must be accompanied in an Islamic State with the penalty of death if the Government of the State is in the hands of the party which considers the other party to be *kafirs*.[3]

The community that provoked an intensely hostile attitude of the ulama belonging to different schools of thought and political parties during early 1953 was that of the Ahmadis, who numbered about 200,000 and were concentrated in the central and eastern parts of Punjab. They believed that their prophet, Mirza Ghulam Ahmad (1835-1908), had appeared to reform and renovate the original religion of Islam. Ever since Mirza Ghulam Ahmad proclaimed his faith toward the end of the nineteenth century, Muslims felt outraged that one of the cardinal doctrines of Islam, namely, the finality of the Prophethood under Muhammed, who had brought the best and most perfect faith, was being challenged. Therefore, in the eyes of the great majority of the Muslim community, Ahmadis were apostates.

Some of the religious leaders started not only attacking the Ahmadis but also the government of Pakistan, which had appointed a well-know Ahmadi like Muhammad Zafrullah Khan as the foreign minister. It was felt that he and other Ahmadis, besides propagating their faith, had established themselves in positions of importance in the civil service and military. In addition to the anti-Ahmadi feeling, toward the end of 1952 there emerged growing resentment against the government because of the deteriorating food situation. In Pakistan there usually is a reservoir of resentment against every government that needs to be fueled and focused. This was provided by the animosity that existed against the Ahmadis, and they became the targets of most violent demonstrations in Lahore, Sialkot, Gujranwala, Rawalpindi, Lyallpur, and Montgomery in late February and early March 1953.

The pattern of violence was similar. Crowds numbering between 5,000 to 10,000 would attack the police and burn public property and shops. Every time the police tried to take action against the demonstrators, they would seek shelter in mosques where sermons would be preached against the Ahmadis and the people would be urged to demonstrate against the government. By March 6, 1953, the situation in Lahore had deteriorated to such an extent that shops in certain areas of the walled city were ablaze and railway tracks had been cut. The city and the government offices faced the prospect of a total blackout and mobs were busy looting commercial buildings.

It was at this crucial moment that the chief minister, Daultana, issued a statement virtually capitulating to the demands of the demonstrators that the Ahmadi community should be declared a minority and that Ahmadi leaders like Zafrullah should be dismissed. However, on the same day martial law was declared and it was reported that the army restored law and order in a matter of six hours. Imposition of martial law was followed by the visit of Prime Minister Nazimuddin to Lahore. By the end of March, Daultana had resigned and had been replaced by Firoz Khan Noon, who was then the governor of Bengal. As noted earlier, Nazimuddin himself was dismissed by the governor-general in April 1953.

Martial law in Lahore gave an opportunity to both the army and the public to see what could be accomplished by strong and speedy measures. It was reported that the streets of Lahore for the first time in many years looked clean and that essential commodities were available to the public at controlled prices.

This was the first time that martial law was introduced in Pakistan. During subsequent years the common man became increasingly aware of the fact that while politicians intrigued and feuded, his problem remained neglected. He could also see the strong man, General Ayub Khan, standing behind these shaky governments, biding his time for that moment when there would be so much confusion in the country that important groups like civil servants, the land-lords, the big merchants, and the new industrialists would be willing to support a regime led by a strong man.

Thus the political and ethnic conflicts at the center had their basic roots in the provinces. In Punjab economic discontent among the common people enabled certain religious groups to give vent to their pent-up antigovernment attitudes, and the anti-Ahmadi movement became a legitimate and natural outlet for this resentment. All this exposed the inability of the Muslim League politicians to control the situation and the center had to intervene.

The center had to intervene in Bengal as well in 1954, but the social landscape in that province was different and so was the challenge that the center was confronted with. Even under the British, East Bengal was not as completely under the grip of the civil servant and the landlord as Punjab had been. After independence a number of landlords who were Hindus fled to India and the remnants, both Hindu and Muslim, were further weakened by the East Bengal State Acquisition and Tenancy Act of 1950. Under this act, all rent-receiving interest between the cultivating tenant and the state was abolished and a ceiling of 33 acres was placed on individual ownership of land.

The first glimmerings of what one writer has called the rise of the vernacular elites during the first decade of independence[4] could be discerned even during the preindependence period in East Bengal. Even at that time Bengali Muslims resented the commercial prosperity and domination of certain Urdu-speaking non-Bengalis.[5] The vernacular elites of lower-middle-class groups came from rural areas or small towns and were mostly lawyers, lower-level civil servants, shopkeepers, and schoolteachers. They could be distinguished from the more prosperous landlords like Nazimuddin or Muhammad Ali Bogra or even Suhrawardy, who identified himself closely with the Bengalis. The leader of the vernacular elites since the prepartition period was Fazlul Huq.

After Pakistan the misgivings or suspicions of the vernacular elite were converted into open hostility toward the non-Bengali ruling elites of Pakistan whose most visible representatives were the civil servants. In the Indian central services and particularly the powerful Indian Civil Service, the representation of Bengali Muslims was behind that of Punjabi Muslims or Muslims from Indian provinces. The result was that when Pakistan came into being, out of the 83 Muslim members of the Indian Civil Service who were given top positions in the central and provincial governments, there was only one Bengali Muslim. The government tried to rectify this imbalance through special quotas allotted to provinces, but in 1954 the imbalance that persisted was such that even in their own province there were hardly any Bengalis in the East Bengal secretariat and there was not a single Bengali occupying the top position of a secretary in a government department.[6] In the eyes of the Bengali lower middle classes who came in contact with the civil servants, the dominance of the non-Bengalis was matched by their arrogance and ethnic superiority. "You go and see the I.C.S. from Western Pakistan or the minority provinces in Bengal and they are hardly on meeting terms with any of the Bengali officers."[7]

This growing resentment of the lower middle class against the civil servants was further compounded by the declaration of Prime Minister Nazimuddin in January 1952 that Urdu alone would be the state language of Pakistan. This triggered student demonstrations in February 1952 and several students were killed. Since then, students became some of the most militant participants in the movement for maximum autonomy for Bengal. Similar hostility toward non-Bengali domination could be detected among Bengalis in the new industrial centers like Narayanganj, Chittagong, and Khulna, where most of the unskilled workers tended to be Bengalis working in factories owned and managed by non-Bengalis. The Bengali vernacular elites were also watching with growing apprehension the various attempts made in the constituent assembly to draft the constitution. They could sense that in the various formulas attempts were being made to undermine or weaken the Bengali majority at the center and also leave East Bengal with a quantum of autonomy that would continue to keep East Bengal as a "colony" of West Pakistan.

During the provincial elections that took place during early March 1954, the various parties representing the vernacular elite or the lower middle and middle classes like the Awami League, the Krishak Sramik party, the Nizam-i-Islam, and others combined and fought the election as the United Front party under its 21-point manifesto. The main planks in the manifesto were recognition of Bengali as an official language and complete autonomy for East Bengal in all matters except defense, foreign policy, and currency. The manifesto also demanded that the headquarters of the navy be located in East Bengal and that an armament factory be established in the province. Other demands relating to financial autonomy and East Bengal's complete freedom from the center with regard to export of jute were bound to create apprehension both among the central elites and business interests.

The rout of the Muslim League in the elections, which obtained only 10 seats in an assembly of 309 members, and the triumph of the United Front, which won 237 seats, were followed by serious disorders in the industrial centers of Chittagong, Narayanganj, and Khulna. Riots in the government-owned paper mill at Chandragona involved clashes between Bengalis and non-Bengalis, resulting in the killing of several non-Bengali executives. Even more serious disturbances took place during May in which there were armed clashes between Bengali and non-Bengali workmen at the Adamjee jute mills at Narayanganj, the largest jute mill in the world, which employed 18,000 men. The death toll was 400.

During this time, when delicate negotiations were going on between the center and East Bengal, the new prime minister, Fazlul Huq, created a stir by challenging the very logic that created the state of Pakistan. He said that with the help of the people of India he hoped "to remove the artificial barriers that had been created between the two Bengals" because the Bengalis were "bound by a common language and heritage and they have had age-long traditions." In another interview he asserted, "Independence will be the first thing to be taken up by my Ministry" at the negotiations between the center and East Bengal.[8] The prime minister, Muhammad Ali Bogra, when dismissing Fazlul Huq as the chief minister and placing East Bengal under central control, called the chief minister a "self-confessed traitor." Referring to disturbances in industrial centers, the prime minister pointed out that they had created so much panic among industrialists that there was a wholesale flight of capital from East Bengal. "We realized that the clock of the economic development and progress of the province was being set back by at least two decades and we were not prepared to allow this. . . ."[9]

In May 1954, the government of East Bengal was handed over to the centrally appointed governor, Major General Iskander Mirza, who at that time was the secretary of defense at the center. Thus the same pattern of central intervention had taken place in East Bengal as in Punjab, the difference being that it was the Muslim League politicians who could not control the situation arising out of religious disturbances in Punjab who had been removed. In East Bengal, politicians of the United Front, who had won an overwhelming majority in the provincial elections and who had been able to mobilize massive ethnic support in the province, were dismissed. In both cases there was military intervention except that martial law was imposed in Punjab, whereas a defense official was put in charge of the civil administration in East Bengal.

Beneath these patterns, there lay even more serious differences. Except for the law and order situation in Punjab, there was no fundamental conflict of interest between the landowning politicians and the central elites nor was there one between the landowning politicians and the emerging mercantile and industrial interests. In East Bengal, on the other hand, the vernacular elites represented not only the middle and lower middle classes of East Bengal but also the fierce, anticenter, and anti-West Pakistan Bengali consciousness. The new elites in Bengal through their activities were also challenging the West Pakistani industrialists and entrepreneurs who dominated the economy of East Bengal. It was noteworthy that the prime minister in his speech to the central legislature condemning the East Bengal disturbances referred to the growing communist menace in the province.[10]

The civil-military oligarchs in the center, who until this time were only partly aware of the dangers that more radical representatives from Bengal armed with a new mandate for maximum provincial autonomy could pose for them, were jolted into making some quick calculations. Until this time they had talked of a subzonal federation of West Pakistan. A more united Bengal delegation would exploit the ethnic and political divisions in West Pakistan and mobilize enough support for a constitution that would weaken the center by offering the alluring prospect of maximum provincial autonomy for Bengal and the smaller provinces of West Pakistan. The net result of such an outcome would be a weak center, which would threaten national unity, retard economic development, and deal a crippling blow to national security by weakening and dividing the armed forces.

It was for this reason that the ruling elites in Pakistan had to devise the One Unit plan integrating West Pakistan. General Ayub in his autobiography has disclosed that he conceived of the One Unit plan on October 4, 1954, while he paced the floor of his hotel room in London. It was there that all his ideas jelled into one grand design for the future of Pakistan. What endless confabulations of the Basic Principles Committee of the constituent assembly had failed to produce he could set forth in one simple document entitled "A Short Appreciation of Present and Future Problems of Pakistan."[11]

To a military strategist who thought in terms of defense in depth, political and economic divisions of West Pakistan did not make any sense. Similarly, accelerated economic development could only take place in an integrated West Pakistan and such a development was necessary for providing resources for a higher living standard and an adequate defense of the country. The creation of such a united province, however, depended upon the large-heartedness of the biggest constituent, namely, Punjab. General Ayub suggested that Punjab should be persuaded into accepting 40 percent representation in the West Pakistan legislature, which was less than what was due to it in proportion to its population, whereas other provinces should be accorded representation in proportion to their population. The author of this plan was also a member of the central cabinet during 1954-55 when he "initiated the process of merger of the provinces."

Thus the military leaders and the administrators were completely convinced that both military strategy and sound economics demanded that the provinces of West Pakistan should be integrated into one unit. They were aware that politicians, provincial civil servants, and the intelligentsia from the provinces of Sind and the North-West Frontier would offer resistance. The One Unit documents prepared by Daultana for the integration of West Pakistan suggested the use of skillful propaganda, but the army leaders and the bureaucrats were in a hurry. They knew that "the real merit of the present regime is that it can hold a pistol to achieve political constitutional agreement," and they went about brandishing and using their weapons of arbitrary dismissals in Sind, the Frontier, and even in Punjab.[12] Through such methods the ruling oligarchs demonstrated the working of a new dictum that absolute power leads to absolute coercion. In Sind the chief minister, Pirzada, was able to produce a statement opposing the One Unit scheme signed by 74 of the 110 members of the Sind assembly.[13] He was dismissed and replaced by Muhammad Ayub Khuhro. Khuhro was appointed chief minister on November 8, 1954, and by December 12, 1954, the same assembly that had opposed One Unit under Pirzada reversed itself and passed a resolution approving the One Unit by 100 votes to 4.[14] Such quick and efficient methods of extracting the desired decisions from the assembly or the electorate were characterized as "Khuhroism."

> It is very interesting to know what Khuhroism means . . . that members of Legislative Assemblies shall be arrested; their relatives will be put under detention; officers will be transferred who will not carry out the behests against inconvenient persons; elections shall be interfered with and members of legislatures shall be terrorized.[15]

The integration of West Pakistan was brought about soon after the dissolution of the constituent assembly on October 4, 1954. Thus there was no democratic check at all on methods like dismissals and installation of pliable regimes in the provinces. Governor-General Ghulam Muhammad issued an ordinance in March 1955 to amend the Government of India Act of 1935 and invest himself not only with the power to establish legally the new province of West Pakistan but also to provide a constitution for the entire country. The governor-general was debarred by the federal court from assuming such powers. The federal court made it clear that the constitution could only be formulated by a constituent assembly and acts like the integration of the provinces and territories of West Pakistan into the province of West Pakistan could only be validated by the new constituent assembly.

The composition of the second constituent assembly was quite different from that of the first, owing to the overwhelming defeat of the Muslim League in East Bengal in 1954. Indeed, Muslim League representation from that province was reduced to two. All the other Muslim Leaguers in the assembly were from West Pakistan. As a result of this change, the East Bengali, Muhammad Ali Bogra, was replaced by Chaudhri Muhammad Ali, a West Pakistani and former head of the Civil Service of Pakistan, as prime minister in August 1955 and the governor-general, Ghulam Muhammad, gave way to Iskander Mirza.

DISINTEGRATION OF THE POLITICAL PROCESS

Elsewhere a detailed account of the kind of squabbles and intrigues that riddled and rendered unworkable the political process and the 1956 constitution has been given.[16] The *Economist* described the internecine feuding among the West Pakistani and East Pakistani politicians as something that ranged "between the grotesque and the macabre."[17] It was clear that no major political group either in West or East Pakistan was capable of uniting and running a government in pursuit of a clear and coherent political program. The Punjabis were hopelessly divided, and to make matters worse the president, Iskander Mirza, with his civil service background, divided them further by floating a political party called the Republican party to counteract and disrupt the Muslim League. Civil servants who had worked in the districts and the provinces had mastered all the methods of manipulating the feudal, ethnic, and political factions, thus dividing and ruling the politicians. Only a few Pakhtun and Sindhi politicians, who had mobilized support in their respective areas, remained united behind their demand for the breakup of the integrated province. Even though Punjabi politicians belonging to either the Muslim League or Republican parties were committed to maintaining the One Unit plan, when tempted with the possibility of seizing or clinging to power, they would align themselves with a party like the National Awami party drawn principally from the Pakhtun and Sindhi areas and that was determined to undo the One Unit. Because the central government and the civil servants could always intervene to frustrate such efforts, the behavior of the politicians became increasingly contemptible and laughable in the eyes of the public.

One may ask that as the great majority of the West Pakistani politicians belonged to the landowning class, why couldn't such politicians unite on class lines? Because class consciousness increases in a class struggle and because the landowning groups faced no immediate or possible threat of any opposition from their small peasants, tenants, or landless laborers, there was no compelling need for class solidarity. Similarly, the Bengali politicians displayed an equal incapability in the face of constant central interference to unite behind their demand for maximum regional autonomy. It was significant that these politicians had won a massive victory in the 1954 elections by persuading the electorate that they would be able to arrest or reverse the gross economic disparities between East and West Pakistan by asserting maximum autonomy of their province in matters relating to economic development. In September 1958, however, when the legislative process in the East Pakistan assembly broke down completely, with one party moving a motion to declare the speaker to be insane and with the other party assaulting the deputy speaker, East Pakistan was in the grip of acute food shortages, floods, and epidemics.[18]

General Ayub, who was watching the situation very closely, wrote: "The President had thoroughly exploited the weaknesses in the Constitution and had got everyone connected with the political life of the country utterly exposed and discredited."[19] However, President Mirza could not have pursued his Machiavellian policies without the backing of the military. Indeed, General Ayub as commander-in-chief had been the most powerful member of the central government during 1954-55 when the integration of West Pakistan had been brought about through outright coercion. This policy had set in motion a chain reaction that President Mirza was trying to control through further central and bureaucratic manipulation. To quote a perspicacious comment on these developments, "It is well, however, to remember the role of men in creating the necessities by which they profess to be compelled."[20] Mirza and Ayub were the two dominant leaders of the civil-military oligarchy that had decided that Pakistan could be governed best by tightening the grip of these two institutions on its government and people.

Among the major political leaders of that period, Suhrawardy was perhaps the only leader who was firmly committed to freeing the political process from the clutches of the civil-military oligarchy. Suhrawardy, who was prime minister during September 1956-October 1957, tried to build a coalition between his Awami League party and the West Pakistan Republican party. By supporting the One Unit plan, he had won considerable support among the Punjabi politicians, both Republicans and Muslim Leaguers. Even though his party, the Awami League, had campaigned for maximum provincial autonomy in the 1954 elections, after assuming office as prime minister he once dubbed the demand for autonomy as a "stunt" because East Pakistanis had already attained most of their demands for provincial autonomy. This must have reassured the West Pakistanis that even though he was a Bengali leader, he would not allow national unity and the national economy to be undermined by extreme forms of Bengali regionalism. Mirza, fearing that a coalition between the Awami League party and the Republican party would weaken his own position, succeeded in pressuring Suhrawardy to resign.

Even after his resignation, when Firoz Khan Noon of Punjab became the prime minister, Suhrawardy pursued his plan of forging an alliance between Bengal and Punjab, something that had not been attempted before. Formerly the Muslim League leaders from Bengal used to combine with Sind and the Frontier against Punjab. Suhrawardy, however, was shrewd enough to realize that political stability at the federal level was not possible without some kind of an understanding between the two major areas of Pakistan. In class terms, Suhrawardy's plan involved an alliance between the lower-middle-class groups of East Pakistan represented by the Awami League and the landowning groups of Punjab represented by the Republican party. In fact, this alliance could have easily been extended to include the cooperation of the big mercantile and industrial groups. Some of the members of the mercantile and industrial groups had already started working for the Awami League.[21] Suhrawardy's government, by granting import licenses to Bengali business interests, also tried to create a new class of prosperous businessmen in East Pakistan. It was clear that such broad-based and interregional political support would have helped Suhrawardy to win a majority in the forthcoming elections and thus become the prime minister.

The fatal flaw in Suhrawardy's plan was that the Punjabi leaders were hopelessly divided. An almost insurmountable obstacle that Suhrawardy also faced was the opposition of President Mirza and probably General Ayub because his plan ran counter to their interests. If his plan had succeeded and the general elections held, political parties supported by the class interests of the big bourgeoisie, the landed interests, and the lower middle class would have not only cut across ethnic divisions but might have outflanked the military and civil service oligarchs.

It was significant that the two leading figures during September-October 1958 — Suhrawardy, who represented the political forces, and Ayub, who represented the military — were being supported by the United States. United States backing of Ayub was perhaps more obvious because as a military leader he had been mainly instrumental in Pakistan joining the U.S.-sponsored defense pacts in the Middle East and Southeast Asia. Suhrawardy, on the other hand, represented the political alternative with his attempts to create a political coalition between East and West Pakistan. Charles Burton Marshall, who was functioning in Pakistan as an adviser to prime ministers during 1955-57,[22] was an ardent supporter of Suhrawardy. Commenting on Mirza's action in removing Suhrawardy as prime minister, Marshall wrote: "It sent out of office the only available man with aptitude as a politician and giving reasonable promise of national leadership."[23] The author was present at a conference on Pakistan held at Duke University during September 27-29, 1974, when Marshall in an address pointed out that he was working for the Central Intelligence Agency in Pakistan during the time of Suhrawardy's resignation. This suggests that the United States was probably backing both contenders.

Ayub succeeded in seizing power because he had the support of the military and could control the actions of Mirza, who abrogated the constitution of 1956 and ushered in martial law in Pakistan. There is evidence to suggest that "a broad tactical outline" to impose martial law in the country was being prepared and that it received the final approval of General Ayub on September 20, 1958.[24] Later, even when Iskander Mirza was still president, General Ayub disclosed that it was at his initiative that the president imposed martial law. "I said to the President: 'Are you going to act or are you not going to act? It is your responsibility to bring about change and if you do not, which heaven forbid, we shall force a change.' "[25]

CAPITALIST DEVELOPMENT UNDER MILITARY PROTECTION

So far in this analysis of the ruling power elites, the discussion has concentrated mainly on the civil-military oligarchs. The growing influence and importance of the merchant industrial groups during the 1950s needs to be shown more clearly. Under the Ayub regime, which is dealt with in the next chapter, these groups became the principal instrument of Ayub's development policies. Most of the big industrialists were drawn from certain trading communities like Memon, Bohra, Khoja, and Chinioti.

It may be seen from Table 2.1 that these four trading communities controlled 35 percent of investment in all firms, that is, both private and corporate. Of

TABLE 2.1
Approximate Percentage of Industrial Assets, by Community, 1959

Community	Private Muslim Firms Only		All Firms	
Private Muslim enterprises			100	67.0
Memon	26.5 }		18 }	
Khoja	10.5 } 41.5		7.5 } 29.0	
Bohra	5 }		3.5 }	
Chinioti	9		6	
Other Muslim trading communities (including Chakwali, other Bohra, Delhi, Saudagar)	5.5		4	
Syed and Sheikh	18.0		12	
Pakhtun	8		5.5	
Bengali Muslim	3.5		2.5	
Other Muslim (including unknown)	14		8.5	
Private Hindu and foreign enterprises				21.5
Bengali Hindu			8.5	
Marwari			2	
Other Hindu and Sikh			1.5	
Parsi			1	
British			7.5	
U.S., other foreigners			1	
Public enterprises				12.0
Pakistan Industrial Development Corporation			7	
Government			5	
Total			100.5	100.5

Note: According to Papanek, these are rounded and approximate percentages, and explain why the totals are more than 100 percent.

Source: Derived from Gustav F. Papanek, *Pakistan's Development: Social Goals and Private Incentives* (Cambridge, Mass.: Harvard University Press, 1967), p. 42. Reprinted by permission.

these, all except the Chiniotis, who belonged to a small town in Punjab, came from India. The most important community was the Memons, who in 1959, controlled over 25 percent of investment in privately owned Muslim firms. Syed and Sheikh communities controlled 18 percent of private Muslim firms and 12 percent of all firms. The local indigenous Pakistani Muslim communities like the Chinioti, Pakhtun, and Bengali Muslims controlled 20.5 percent of private Muslim firms and 14 percent of all firms. Owing to declining profits in international trade and with profits ranging between 50 to 100 percent of invested capital in a single year in manufacturing, these trading communities became industrialists.

They were also encouraged by the industrial policies of the government that clearly stated that public ownership would be confined to only three groups of industries: arms and ammunition, hydroelectric power, and railway, telephone, and wireless equipment. The government set up the Pakistan Industrial Development Corporation (PIDC) to pioneer industries neglected by private investors, but its activities did not in any significant way hamper the expansion of the private sector. By 1953-54, the corporation's cumulative expenditures amounted to Rs. 170 million, or about 7 percent of total industrial assets. From Table 2.1, it may be seen that by 1959 the PIDC had floated only 7 of about 100 firms. The number of firms that the government had set up in the public sector was no more than 5.

Table 2.2 indicates how the private sector had expanded in 12 of the largest industries in terms of capital investment. This expansion of the private sector and the growing concentration of wealth in the hands of certain families or groups of merchant capitalists belonging to certain ethnic communities came about because of the deliberate policies that the government followed. The policy not only to tolerate but to create inequalities of income and wealth in the commercial and industrial sectors was followed because the government's considered view was that these were absolutely essential for the economic development of the country. Thus the first five-year plan, 1955-60, recommended

TABLE 2.2
Increase in Investment for the Top 12 Major Industries, 1955-60
(in millions of rupees)

Industry	Capital Invested, 1955	Capital Invested, 1960	Rank in Group, 1955	Rank in Group, 1960
Cotton textiles	530	912	1	1
Jute goods	186	286	2	3
Cotton ginning	134	151	3	6
Edible vegetable oils	105	116	4	10
Medium and light engineering	104	151	5	7
Jute baling	88	90	6	12
Sugar	87	369	7	4
Gas transmission	84	298	8	5
Cement	66	145	9	8
Printing, writing, and wrapping paper	60	604	10	18
Fertilizer	56	388	11	2
Shipyards	35	145	14	9

Source: Derived from National Planning Board, Government of Pakistan, *The First Five Year Plan 1955-60* (Karachi, December 1957), pp. 424-25.

certain radical reforms in the land ownership and tenure system in West Pakistan, but argued that:

> The inequalities of income and wealth . . . in the commercial and industrial sectors present a *different problem* [emphasis added]. The businessmen and the industrialists play a useful role in the development of the country and the functioning of its economy, though they often extort an unduly high price for their services. Their incomes nevertheless serve a social purpose insofar as they lead to increased savings and investments.[26]

With this increasing industrial wealth concentrated in a few families or groups, there should have been a corresponding increase in the political influence and power of the big business groups. There was an increase in political influence but not in power. For a nongovernment group to become powerful, it must have certain social bases of support in the country and it should also, because of the smallness of its numbers (in the case of business groups), combine with other influential groups like the landlords. This did not happen in Pakistan during the 1950s. First of all, a number of merchant communities who became industrialists came from India and thus had no social base in Pakistan. Similarly, in terms of population they represented 0.26 percent of the population, but controlled 41.5 percent of Muslim private firms and 29 percent of all firms.

This section primarily shows how the military, by manipulating the external variable, made itself the most powerful political group in Pakistan. The power it acquired was so dominant that the military could use the civil service as its policy advisers and the capitalists as the instrument of Pakistan's economic development. The military under Ayub Khan acquired this power because of the special military relationship that developed between Pakistan and the United States during 1954.

Pakistan became a member of the Central Treaty Organization and the Southeast Asia Treaty Organization. Because political institutions had proved to be fragile in most of the Asian countries, one of the factors that influenced the U.S. decision makers in extending military aid to a country like Pakistan was that the army with its monolithic unity was much more capable than traditional political parties of serving as a bastion against the quasimilitary organization of communist parties. Indeed, a U.S. president's committee had approved military intervention in developing countries in times of political crises and concluded "that the military officer corps is a major rallying point of the defense against Communist expansion and penetration."[27]

Ayub's contacts with Pentagon officials were very close; they had been profoundly impressed by his ability as a military leader and as an advocate of pro-Western military alliances for Pakistan. When he was involved in military negotiations during 1953-54, it was reported that the U.S. officials were reluctant to let the governor-general, Ghulam Muhammad, enter into negotiations with President Eisenhower regarding military aid.[28] It was clear that in such negotiations the only man who mattered was the commander-in-chief, General Ayub.

It seemed that Ayub as a soldier knew what kind of logic would appeal to the Pentagon generals. He couched his arguments in terms of global strategy and pointed out that the United States as the superpower needed the services of the Pakistan army in the Near East as the British Empire had once needed the services of the British Indian army. In July 1958, Ayub made it clear that Pakistanis were prepared to fight on behalf of the West and put forward the idea of "lend-lease," which he defined as "we provide the manpower and you provide us with the means to do the fighting."[29] Addressing the U.S. Congress in 1961, Ayub declared: "The only people who will stand by you are the people of Pakistan." It was pointed out in the House of Representatives that one of the advantages the United States derived from its military alliance with Pakistan was this: "In its relations with other Moslem states and with other members of the Afro-Asian bloc, Pakistan can be an efficacious advocate of Western policies and can exert a moderating influence on the extreme nationalism and anti-Western attitudes of some of the members of these groups."[30]

Thus Ayub was the supreme architect of the special relationship that developed between Pakistan and the United States. It also seemed that in this special relationship Pakistan under Ayub had been able to forge an even more special relationship with the Pentagon so that there were times when the government in the United States or the State Department was not responsive to certain requests of Pakistan, but Ayub had a feeling "that the armed forces in the United States were more sympathetic to our point of view."[31]

The dividends that accrued to Pakistan from this special relationship not only helped Pakistan to develop its military capabilities but also launch its economic development plan. In terms of the badly needed military hardware, the total assistance extended to Pakistan from 1954 to 1965 amounted to between $1.2 to $1.5 billion.[32] Economic assistance in the form of U.S. Public Law 480 and other agricultural commodity programs, grants for economic development, technical assistance development grants, and loans of various kinds was much larger. From 1947 through June 30, 1965, economic assistance of this nature amounted to $3 billion. As compared to U.S. aid of $3 billion to Pakistan, India, which had nearly four times the population of Pakistan, received $6 billion during the same period. This demonstrates the capabilities of the Pakistani military regime in attracting economic aid of such magnitude. It may also be noted that out of a total development outlay of $5.5 billion during the second five-year plan, 1960-65, the United States contributed $1.7 billion in the form of loans, grants, and other assistance, or about 30 percent of the total outlay.[33]

Economic assistance and the way it was channeled to Pakistan also produced certain desired political consequences from the U.S. point of view.

The Planning Commission, which had attached to it an advisory team from Harvard University, played a crucial role in using commodity aid as a leverage to persuade the bureaucracy to dismantle the detailed import controls. Thus decontrol, on the one hand, led to some diminution of the power of the bureaucracy, and on the other, through liberalization of imports and the availability of raw materials through commodity aid, to the growth of the private sector.

Thus the military regime in Pakistan was able to persuade U.S. policymakers that military assistance should be linked with economic assistance. The political consequences of economic assistance were that Pakistan's economic development should not only proceed at an accelerated pace but that economic development should be along capitalist lines leading to the strengthening of the private sector. Pakistani capitalists themselves did not play a significant role in the formulation and implementation of these policies. They functioned mostly as the beneficiaries of such policies. It was the military regime that propped them up and pampered them with the help of the external support that they acquired principally from the United States. It has been argued by Hamza Alavi that the bureaucratic-military oligarchy mediated between the competing demands of the three propertied classes — the indigenous bourgeoisie, the neocolonial metropolitan bourgeoisie, and the landowning classes — and in playing this role the bureaucratic-military oligarchy represented the relative autonomy of the postcolonial state of Pakistan.[34]

It is being suggested here that it is not enough to describe the role of the bureaucratic-military oligarchy as a mediator only. A careful analysis of the role of the military regime in the context of Pakistani-U.S. relations would indicate that the military leaders probably emerged as the most "autonomous" group in this configuration. The military regime of Ayub Khan played a more positive (from its point of view) and an interventionist role than that of mere mediation. It imposed a pattern of capitalist development that was more efficient and speedier than that of the previous regimes dominated by the civil-military oligarchy. It was able to do this because it had brought the other member of the oligarchy, the civil service, under control and also classes like the indigenous bourgeoisie and the landlords.

Ayub first made sure as commander-in-chief that he established his control over the military during the years 1951-58. After he seized power as the head of the military regime in October 1958, by curbing the power of the bureaucracy and making it more amenable, by defusing the relative monopoly power of the Karachi-based capitalists and extending the benefits of the new capitalism to areas like Punjab, and by mobilizing the support of certain groups of landowners more interested in raising agricultural productivity and undermining the influence of certain other landowners, he restructured the power relationships and thereby produced a different power configuration for Pakistan.

NOTES

1. *Dawn,* August 11, 1957.
2. Photographic copies of these pacts have been reproduced in Syed Hassan Mahmud, *A Nation Is Born* (Lahore, 1958), pp. 20-21.
3. *Report of the Court of Inquiry Constituted Under Punjab Act II of 1954 to Enquire into the Punjab Disturbances of 1952* (Lahore: Government Printing, 1954), p. 219. This report is popularly known as the Munir report because the president of the court of inquiry was Justice M. Munir.
4. Rounaq Jahan, *Pakistan: Failure in National Integration* (New York: Columbia University Press, 1972), pp. 38-41.
5. Abu Husain Sarkar, who later became chief minister of East Pakistan, expressed this resentment. *Bengal Legislative Assembly Proceedings,* vol. LIV, Fifth Session (1939), pp. 29-30.
6. *Constituent Assembly (Legislature) of Pakistan Debates,* vol. 1, no. 26 (July 17, 1954), p. 1475.
7. Ibid., p. 1474.
8. *The Round Table,* September 1954, pp. 401-02.
9. *Constituent Assembly (Legislature) of Pakistan Debates,* vol. 1, no. 23 (June 28, 1954), p. 1367.
10. Ibid., p. 1363.
11. Mohammad Ayub Khan, *Friends Not Masters* (London: Oxford University Press, 1967), pp. 186-91.
12. There was a series of One Unit documents prepared by Daultana. See Khalid B. Sayeed, *The Political System of Pakistan* (Boston: Houghton Mifflin, 1967), pp. 76-78.
13. *Dawn,* October 24, 1954.
14. *Dawn,* December 12, 1954.
15. *Constituent Assembly of Pakistan Debates,* vol. 1 (September 10, 1955), p. 656.
16. Sayeed, op. cit., pp. 82-93.
17. *The Economist,* October 11, 1958, pp. 1-2.
18. The author was present in the house when these events took place.
19. Ayub Khan, op. cit., p. 56.
20. Charles Burton Marshall, "Reflections on a Revolution in Pakistan," *Foreign Affairs* 37 (January 1959): 252.
21. Y. V. Gankovsky, *A History of Pakistan 1947-1958* (Lahore: People's Publishing House, n.d.,), p. 248.
22. In the January 1959 issue of *Foreign Affairs* in which Charles Burton Marshall's article appears, he is announced as "Adviser to Prime Ministers of Pakistan 1955-57. Now Visiting Research Scholar at the Carnegie Endowment for International Peace. Author of *The Limits of Foreign Policy.*"
23. Marshall, op. cit., pp. 251-52.
24. Fazal Muqueem Khan, *The Story of the Pakistan Army* (Dacca: Oxford, 1963), p. 194.
25. *Pakistan Times,* October 10, 1958.
26. National Planning Board, Government of Pakistan, *The First Five Year Plan 1955-60* (Karachi, December 1957), p. 4.
27. *Supplement to the Composite Report of the President's Committee to Study the United States Military Assistance Program,* vol. 2 (Washington, D.C.: U.S. Government Printing Office, 1959), p. 79.
28. Mohammad Ahmed, *My Chief* (Lahore: Longmans, 1960), pp. 75-76.
29. Muhammed Ayub Khan, "Strategic Problems of the Middle East," *Islamic Review,* July-August 1958, p. 12.

30. *Mutual Security Act of 1958,* hearings before U.S., House, Committee on Foreign Relations, 2d sess., April 15-16, 1958, p. 1753.

31. Mohammad Ayub Khan, *Friends Not Masters,* p. 158.

32. The figures mentioned are usually $1.2 or $1.5 billion. According to Selig S. Harrison, *Washington Post,* August 12, 1965, it is $1.2 billion. According to *The New York Times,* August 29, 1965, it is $1.5 billion. Similarly, in *The Times of India,* November 29, 1965, it is $1.5 billion.

33. Figures regarding U.S. economic assistance to Pakistan have been furnished to the author by the Agency for International Development, U.S. Department of State.

34. Hamza Alavi, "The State in Postcolonial Societies: Pakistan and Bangladesh," in *Imperialism and Revolution in South Asia,* ed. Kathleen Gough and Hari P. Sharma (New York: Monthly Review Press, 1973). See particularly pp. 159-61.

3
DEVELOPMENTAL STRATEGY
UNDER AYUB KHAN

No other political leader in Pakistan before Ayub had formulated a political plan for his country. Karl von Vorys extolled Ayub for having formulated a course of action after examining "in minute detail the political structure of Pakistan" long before he actually seized power.[1] As Ayub paced the floor of his hotel room in London in October 1954, before sitting down to produce his famous plan, he said to himself, "Let me put down my ideas in a military fashion: what is wrong with the country and what can be done to put things right."[2]

There emerge from Ayub's speeches and particularly from his autobiography, *Friends Not Masters,* certain perceptions of what he regarded as the main malaise of Pakistan. Cultural and racial diversity of the country created divisiveness in spite of the unifying pull of Islam. To make matters worse, the political leaders had opted for parliamentary democracy, which created further divisions because of the presence of too many political parties, the lack of universal literacy, and the hold of traditional leaders like the big landlords and the pirs over the illiterate voters.

Cultural and linguistic diversity compounded by political divisions meant that no government had been able to mobilize adequate political power for national and developmental purposes. Therefore the remedies were both clear and desperate. The three provinces and other territories in West Pakistan had to

This chapter is taken from an article by the author with the same title in *Contributions to Asian Studies,* series #14, pp. 76-86, from E. J. Brill, Leiden, Netherlands.

be integrated into one. East and West Pakistan could only be kept together through a strong central government under a strong president. A strong central government reinforced by the cementing bond of Islam and rapid economic growth would give an enduring and increasing sense of unity to the country.

Under the new political system that Ayub created, there was a constitution that gave the president all the essential powers that he needed to keep the country firmly under his control and to pursue his developmental policies with a legislature constitutionally incapable of challenging the president's authority or suggesting alternative policies.[3] Maximum mobilization of political power and the docility of the legislature were ensured through indirect elections of the president and the assemblies through a system of Basic Democracies. The constituencies from which these local councillors were elected were small enough to be kept under the coercive control of the civil servants, and the Union Councils could again be managed and manipulated through the patronage and coercive powers that the central government could exercise through the deputy commissioners and their lower echelons. In this way the urban areas were out-flanked and the president's power came directly from the quiescent rural areas.[4]

This strategy won high praise from Samuel Huntington, for it created "the institutional link between government and countryside which is the prerequisite for political stability in a modernizing country."[5] For Huntington, this represented the hallmark of institution building. The concentration of governmental power in the hands of the president rested on the institutions of Basic Democracies with their links extending to every nook and corner of the country. Huntington was ecstatic when he discerned the architectonic design and strategy of Ayub. "More than any other political leader in a modernizing country after World War II, Ayub Khan came close to filling the role of a Solon or Lycurgus or 'Great Legislator' on the Platonic or Rousseauian model."[6]

The key to a military officer's thinking is that he reduces every complex problem to its bare essentials, and once the problem has been so simplified he has to reach firm decisions and carry them out relentlessly. Speaking to the cadets at Kakul Academy, Ayub exhorted them to follow the motto that he had followed, "I may be right, I may be wrong, but I have no doubts."

In this line of reasoning, growth was the key variable. Economic growth taking place under the aegis of a strong central government would take care of all other problems. Growth rates computed in terms of broad aggregates like gross national product, per capita income, and industrial and agricultural production were truly impressive, particularly in comparison to the previous decade. Gross national product, in terms of 1959-60 factor cost, had grown at 2.5 percent during 1949-50 to 1959-60, but had gone up to 5.6 percent during 1959-60 to 1969-70. Per capita income at 1969-70 prices had gone up from Rs. 253 in 1949-50 to Rs. 567 in 1969-70. Increase in agricultural output in the first decade was 1.4 percent, which was below the annual increase in population of 2.3 percent. In the second decade, agricultural output increased at a rate of

3.9 percent, that is, ahead of the annual increase in population during that decade of 3.0 percent. In large-scale manufacturing, the average growth rate throughout the two decades was 14 percent, estimated as one of the highest in the developing world. This meant that the industrial growth rate had started registering impressive increases in the first decade as well. In the 1960s, growth in large-scale manufacturing was at the rate of 12 percent per year.[7]

The developmental or growth strategy of the Ayub regime has to be examined in terms of both its normative and political objectives. Ayub took credit that, unlike his predecessors, he had been able to implement land reforms under which ceilings of 500 acres for irrigated and 1,000 acres for nonirrigated lands were fixed. However, the mere size of the ceilings suggested that certainly the medium-sized landowners whose scions were heavily represented in the army and civil services were not going to be adversely affected. In addition, there were so many loopholes in Ayub's land reforms that landlords could still own and cultivate up to about 2,000 acres of irrigated or 4,000 acres of nonirrigated land if they transferred some of their land to their legal heirs and converted some into orchards, nurseries, and game preserves. It has been estimated that no more than 2.3 million acres were acquired under the land reforms and of these, 930,000 acres consisted of waste, hills, and riverbeds.

The large landlords transferred another 5 to 6 million acres to middle farmers. Thus the main beneficiaries of these reforms were the middle farmers, whose average holding increased by 33.6 percent — from 34.8 acres in 1959 to 46.5 acres in 1969.[8] It would be difficult to argue that as a result of these reforms the class basis of Pakistan's power structure shifted from big landlords to medium-sized landowners.[9] As may be seen, the big landlords did not suffer any eclipse in political power, and they were able to transfer some of their wealth and savings to investment in industries.

When one examines the impact of the Green Revolution, that is, of improved seeds, fertilizers, and tubewells, one is again struck by the fact that the benefits were confined not only to big and medium-sized landowners in West Pakistan but that the benefits were further concentrated in Punjab. According to the Survey of Farm Mechanization in 1968, the biggest landowners (more than 500 acres) accounted for 52.3 percent of the land (area owned) and 43 percent of the area operated of all mechanized farms. As for owners of mechanized farms with holdings of more than 100 acres, they represented over 80 percent both in area owned and area operated categories.[10]

In terms of regional distribution of the prosperity resulting from the Green Revolution, Punjab was the main beneficiary. According to the Farm Mechanization Report, 91.2 percent of the 75,700 tubewells were located in Punjab, with 2.7 percent of private tubewells in the Peshawar division of the Frontier and 1.7 percent in the Khairpur division of Sind. Concentration of tubewells in Punjab was matched by concentration of tractor ownership. Of the 16,600 tractors in West Pakistan in 1968, 13,800 were in Punjab.[11] In terms of both tubewells and tractors, it was also estimated that 80 to 90 percent of the tube-wells and tractors were to be found on farms of over 25 acres.

In its defense, the government could argue that mechanization in agriculture was profitable mostly on large farms. As for the concentration of tubewells in Punjab and their relative scarcity in the Frontier and Sind, it could be argued that tubewells could not be easily installed in areas where there was a shortage of accessible supplies of groundwater or, as in the case of Sind, where there was a high degree of salinity of groundwater. An equally important factor was the lack of peasant unrest in West Pakistan, which meant that the government, guided both by growth considerations and its political interests, could continue to invest most of its resources in big farms.

Pakistan was perhaps one of the few developing countries that openly and officially advocated the capitalist doctrine of "functional inequality" on the familiar plea that government should tolerate "some initial growth in income inequalities to reach high levels of saving and investment."[12] A more outspoken champion of this doctrine was Pakistan's Harvard adviser to the Planning Commission, Gustav F. Papanek, who espoused the concept of the "social utility of greed" by pointing out that income inequalities not only contributed to the growth of the economy but also made possible a real improvement for the lower-income groups.[13]

The results of this policy of encouraging industrial concentration were twofold. First, by 1968, the 22 largest families controlled 66 percent of industrial assets, 70 percent of insurance funds, and 80 percent of bank assets.[14] In regional terms, this policy implied that in order to maximize growth, resources should first be invested in West Pakistan where the return was much higher than in East Pakistan where, because of a relatively less developed economic infrastructure and relatively uncertain political conditions, returns were expected to be lower.

Thus a policy of income inequality between classes was pursued simultaneously with a policy of regional inequality in terms of West and East Pakistan and, as it would be seen later, in terms of the regions within West Pakistan itself. During the decade 1959-60 to 1969-70, per capita gross domestic product in terms of 1959-60 constant prices grew only by 17 percent in East Pakistan, but by 42 percent in West Pakistan.[15] The central government also conceded that disparity measured by the difference between per capita incomes in West and East Pakistan expressed as a percentage of the per capita income of all Pakistan had increased from 38.1 percent in 1964-65 to 47.1 percent in 1969-70.[16]

Ayub was aware that certain areas like Karachi had reaped most of the benefits of rapid industrialization during the 1950s. He did initiate policies to extend the industrial belt from its original concentration in Karachi-Hyderabad to other centers in Punjab like Lahore, Lyallpur, and Multan. Similarly, he tried to extend this class of nascent capitalists or merchants-cum-industrialists to areas of East Pakistan as well. He probably felt that in this way economic growth would be dispersed to other areas. But he wanted the benefits to be confined to the upper-income entrepreneurial groups because growth could be sustained only through their efforts.

One of these policy instruments was the bonus voucher scheme under which exporters were given vouchers that represented a certain proportion of the value of goods sold abroad. These vouchers could be sold in the open market with the result that exporters could accumulate capital and importers could use them to obtain foreign exchange for importing goods that were placed on the bonus list.

During the 1950s, industrial imports were licensed in such a way that only Karachi-based merchant-industrialists could import machinery and raw materials. Under the bonus voucher scheme, such restrictions were eliminated and new-comers from Punjab and other areas could enter the industrial sector. In addition to these newcomers from Punjab, big landlords, mostly from Punjab but some from Sind and a few from the Frontier, who had been compensated for surrendering some of their lands under the land reforms, also became industrialists.

Bengali merchants and contractors were also encouraged to join this growing class of the bourgeoisie or merchant-cum-industrialist. They were granted permits and licenses that had a ready marketable value. Small businessmen were also awarded construction contracts. The policy was to encourage these merchants and contractors to become industrialists. The Industrial Development Bank of Pakistan would advance about two thirds of the investment funds with half of the remaining third being financed by the East Pakistan Industrial Development Corporation. The remaining one sixth was expected to be provided by the prospective industrialist. In some cases he needed no more than 10 percent of the required capital because a part of the final one sixth could be subscribed by the state-sponsored National Investment Trust and the Investment Corporation of Pakistan.[17] Thus a new Bengali bourgeoisie had emerged who identified their interests with that of the Ayub regime and who were increasingly apprehensive of the growing militancy in the industrial and rural areas of East Pakistan.

The basic questions that keep arising in a discussion of the developmental strategy of the Ayub regime are what kind of development was being pursued and for whose benefit was this development being promoted. It has been pointed out that according to the spokesmen of the regime it was development mostly in terms of economic growth. This growth was to be achieved through a system under which income inequalities were to be tolerated for a long time until the benefits of such a system would trickle down to the disadvantaged groups at a later stage. Because economic growth could best be brought about through the efforts of the merchants-cum-industrialists and because their exertions depended upon how much of their rapacity could be satisfied, it was imperative that others like the peasants and the industrial proletariat tighten their belts so that the surpluses they produced would be offered as inducements to the new industrialists.

The industrialists had recently been merchants and therefore were used to profits ranging between 50 to 100 percent and were not likely to be satisfied with anything less in their new ventures.

The strategy that emerged from this reasoning was crystal clear. Industrialists needed foreign exchange to import machinery and industrial raw materials for setting up import substitution industries. In addition, they wanted food, which was the most important wage good, to be available at cheap prices so that wages could be kept low. All this meant that the surplus that the industrialists needed in the form of foreign exchange and food could only be extracted from agriculture given the nature of Pakistan's economy.

Jute was the largest foreign exchange earner and it was grown by peasant farmers in East Pakistan on an average holding of under three acres. The foreign exchange that the jute grower earned was surrendered to the government in return for Pakistani rupees at the official rate. As the rupee was overvalued to the extent of 50 percent, it meant that for each dollar the peasant received only Rs. 4.25, whereas the dollar was actually worth Rs. 8.61. In this way the government extracted 50 percent surplus from the Bengali peasant and handed over the same dollar to the Gujarati or Punjabi merchant or industrialist who could import goods worth Rs. 8.61.

In addition, the merchant or the industrialist was operating as an importer or as a manufacturer in a market where he received enormous protection. The same was not true of agricultural goods. Through compulsory procurement of agricultural products, the government kept their prices below world market prices. This was a subsidy, particularly from the West Pakistan farmer who produced surplus food, to urban incomes and the industrialists who benefited from cheap food prices. In order to benefit the merchant capitalists who were becoming industrialists overnight, the government had to exploit not only the East Pakistan jute grower and the peasants of West Pakistan but the Pakistani consumer as well, who ended up paying an average of two and a half times the world market prices for the full range of Pakistan's consumer manufactures.[18]

It was apparent that this system of functional inequality involving disparities among the various regions and classes could operate with far fewer checks under an authoritarian system like that of Pakistan. Highlighting its main features, Angus Maddison wrote:

> In Pakistan, income tax is considerably lower than in India, and direct taxes are only 2 per cent of national product. Total public sector spending on social services such as health, education, housing, water and sewerage is only about 3 per cent of national product, and most of the benefits of this go to the upper income groups. In education only a third of expenditure goes to the primary level, in health most expenditure is for urban areas; nearly all public housing projects and housing subsidies are for middle and upper income groups, nearly all spending on amenities is for urban areas.[19]

This is a "heads I win, tails you lose" kind of developmental process so far as the industrialists were concerned. The so-called entrepreneurial classes were being pampered, protected, and mollycoddled through tax benefits, cheap credit, import permits, and availability of foreign exchange because they had the initiative, industry, capacity to save, and willingness to plow these savings into investment. Similarly, surpluses were being extracted, particularly from the Bengali peasants through the foreign exchange earnings of jute, and to a lesser extent from the West Pakistani peasants through wheat procurement at less than world market prices.

All these surpluses were offered to the industrialists because only they could convert these surpluses to socially productive and useful economic and industrial growth. After receiving all these benefits, the well-to-do classes continued to clamor for more. They paid lower income taxes than their counterparts in India. They wanted to enjoy more and better health and educational facilities. The mansions in which they lived were not enough. They wanted more of them. In other words, the propertied classes were saying, give us more not only because we produce more but also because we want to keep more and more of it for ourselves.

In order to determine what benefits or disadvantages the developmental process produced for people living below the poverty line in rural and urban areas, one has to rely on the few sample surveys of consumer expenditure patterns that are available. Table 3.1 shows that the percentage of people in rural areas having a per capita income consumption of less than Rs. 250 per year (or Rs. 21 per month) declined from 43.1 percent in 1963-64 to 26.0 percent in 1969-70. However, if the poverty line were set at Rs. 300 per capita, that is, an increase of only Rs. 4 per capita or Rs. 20 per household per month, the percentage of people who existed below this poverty line was around 60 percent during the years 1963-70.

TABLE 3.1
Estimates of Persons Below the Poverty Line in Rural Areas

Year	Below Rs. 300 per Year (Rs. 25 per month)		Below Rs. 250 per year (Rs. 21 per month)	
	Percentage	Number (in millions)	Percentage	Number (in millions)
1963-64	60.5	23.46	43.1	16.7
1966-67	59.7	24.80	32.0	13.3
1968-69	61.5	26.72	25.1	10.9
1969-70	59.7	26.51	26.0	11.5

Source: S. M. Naseem, "Mass Poverty in Pakistan: Some Preliminary Findings," Pakistan Development Review 12, no. 4 (Winter 1973): 322.

It is true that these results are based on sample data that cannot be regarded as very precise. On the other hand, it must be emphasized that the data also tend to underestimate the level and growth of income of the highest income groups. However, the researcher who produced these data pointed out that the data reveal certain clear patterns: "About 25-40 per cent of the people in the 1960s — the decade of development — lived in abject poverty and another 25-30 per cent, perhaps, lived a little better, but not much above the subsistence level."[20]

As regards urban poverty, Table 3.2 shows the percentage of urban people with a per capita expenditure below Rs. 300 per year and below Rs. 375 per year for 1963-64, 1966-67, and 1968-70. Again, it depends at what level of income the poverty line is set. If it were set at Rs. 375 per month, the extent of urban poverty during the developmental decade was inexcusable. "As many as 70 per cent of the urban population, according to this criterion, will be categorised as poor in 1963-64. Although the percentage of urban poor declines in the late sixties to around 59 per cent, the number increases to about 1 crore in 1969/70."[21]

TABLE 3.2
Estimates of Persons Below the Poverty Line in Urban Areas

Year	Below Rs. 375		Below Rs. 300	
	Percentage	Number (in millions)	Percentage	Number (in millions)
1963-64	70.0	8.65	54.8	6.78
1966-67	59.3	8.60	47.0	6.81
1968-69	57.9	9.33	34.7	5.59
1969-70	58.7	9.98	25.0	4.25

Source: S. M. Naseem, "Mass Poverty in Pakistan: Some Preliminary Findings," *Pakistan Development Review* 12, no. 4 (Winter 1973): 325.

At a time when the Ayub regime was facing urban militancy largely as a result of the decline in real wages and the growing awareness among urban groups of industrial and economic concentration, the Planning Commission reiterated in November 1968 the basic premise of the government's developmental strategy: "We cannot distribute poverty. Growth is vital before income distribution can improve."[22] However, the commission admitted that in spite of rapid growth, Pakistan continued to be one of the poorest and most illiterate societies. It failed to admit that the strategy that it had followed implied that because growth was vital before income distribution, the poor had to remain poor for a long time so that growth might continue at an accelerating pace. This vicious circle of more and more growth with poverty increasing or remaining the same or improving very little could only be broken if the poorer groups were to acquire political power.

The question is the same as was raised by Karl Marx in his "Critique of the Gotha Program."[23] Distribution was linked to a given system of production. If the power and interests associated with a given production system were in the hands of propertied classes, how and why would they agree to a system of distribution that would diminish their power and improve the conditions of the poor? The usual answer is that such concessions have been made by the capitalist classes in Western societies. This logic ignores the unique conditions under which Pakistan's developmental strategy was fashioned and pursued. The alliance between semifeudal landowning interests and those representing merchant capital was such that these groups could not be satisfied, given their social background and mode of production, with anything less than ruthless exploitation and therefore exorbitant profits. They were not only greedy but wanted to maintain their living styles of conspicuous consumption.

Ayub has been described as a political planner and it has also been seen how he tried to concentrate political power in his hands to maintain national unity and promote maximum economic growth. But it has also been shown that the concentration of political power in his hands and the emphasis on economic growth, per se, resulted in concentration of economic and industrial power in the hands of a small section of the private sector. Through concentration of political power, he antagonized certain important middle-class urban groups like lawyers, students, and political leaders. By allowing and even encouraging economic and industrial concentration, he created the distinct impression that his regime was devoid of concern for social justice and the economic deprivations of the poor. Thus the unintended consequences of his developmental strategy turned out to be more important than the intended or planned consequences. If he deserves praise, it is not for what he actually tried to accomplish but for unwittingly setting in motion certain trends and social forces of historic consequence in Pakistan.

Ayub represents a watershed in the history of Pakistan. It was in his regime that one saw a clear unfolding of certain trends and developments that represented what may be described as an ideological change in Pakistan. Under him there was economic change through industrialization, improved agriculture, and modest land reforms spreading to areas other than Karachi, particularly to Punjab and a few urban centers in Sind and the Frontier.

It may be suggested that as a result of these changes the masses in many parts of West Pakistan could no longer be aroused by appeals to vague and emotional notions of Islamic unity. The role of an ideology in the last resort is to justify or explain the rationale for a particular social order. If the ruling elites in Pakistan were not very religious, and at the same time created an economic and social system that was inegalitarian and the knowledge of such social and economic inequities was spreading, there arose a serious credibility gap when the ruling elites continued to preach that Pakistan's polity was Islamic. This explains why during the 1970 elections Bhutto's Pakistan People's party made such serious inroads in the semiprosperous areas of Lahore division, eastern Multan division, and all along the Grand Trunk Road where lay areas of industrial development and agricultural prosperity. It offered a new but vague ideological program under the name of Islamic socialism, or Masawat. *equality*

Ayub, by not being able to satisfy Bengali expectations that he had aroused through his constitutional assurances that disparity would soon be removed and by his policies of coercion of urban elements in East Pakistan, laid the foundations for the dismemberment of Pakistan in 1971. It was in Ayub's regime that in both East and West Pakistan there was a growing skepticism as to whether the appeal of Islam could continue to keep the two disparate wings together.

This represents the other side of ideological change, that is to say, Islam could neither be used to justify nor explain the increasing inegalitarian society that had emerged in Pakistan, nor could the Islamic factor serve any longer as the only cementing force between the two disparate wings of the country.

How does one encapsulate this ideological change that took place during the Ayub era? It has been suggested that the existential base had changed, creating in its wake certain social conflicts. The gross national product went up, *GNP* but inequitable distribution of these increases in the gross national product stared the people in the face. Expectations had been aroused both in the urban and rural areas. Islam as the cementing force between the two wings did not seem to be working, and it was clear that Bengali aspirations could never be satisfied within the existing framework if the economy had to satisfy the increasing expectations of the West Pakistanis as well. There were regional conflicts in West Pakistan itself. Class conflict in the urban areas of Punjab and Sind was increasing. Under Defense of Pakistan Rules instituted during the Indo-Pakistan war of 1965, it was a criminal offense to create disaffection among the people of Pakistan against the established government. It was ironic that one of Pakistan's great promoters of political stability and economic growth had done precisely that.

NOTES

1. Karl von Vorys, *Political Development in Pakistan* (Princeton, N.J.: Princeton University Press, 1965), p. xi.

2. Mohammad Ayub Khan, *Friends Not Masters* (London: Oxford University Press, 1967), p. 186.

3. Khalid B. Sayeed, *The Political System of Pakistan* (Boston: Houghton Mifflin, 1967), pp. 108-09.

4. This was done through the ingenious system of Basic Democracies under which, given the composition of Pakistan's population, the majority of constituencies were in the

rural areas. For the direct election of local councillors, called Basic Democrats, the constituencies were small enough to be controlled or manipulated by civil and police officers. Basic Democrats, who elected the president and members of the national and provincial assemblies, could in turn be even more easily controlled through government coercion and patronage because the numbers involved in this electoral college were no more than 80,000 for the entire country. For details, see ibid., pp. 244-61.

5. Samuel P. Huntington, *Political Order in Changing Societies* (New Haven, Conn.: Yale University Press, 1968), p. 252.

6. Ibid., p. 251.

7. These figures have been taken from Planning Commission, Government of Pakistan, *The Fourth Five Year Plan 1970-75* (Islamabad, 1970), pp. 1-2, 5.

8. Shahid Javed Burki, "Economic Decisionmaking in Pakistan: An Overview" (typescript), p. 18; and Shahid Javed Burki, "Economic Policymaking: Pakistan, 1947-1969" (typescript), p. 25.

9. It was true that in the political game of musical chairs that the government played with the landlords some of the big landlords associated with former regimes like Daultana in Punjab or Khuhro in Sind lost political power. But others like the Nawab of Kalabagh in Punjab or Hoti in the Frontier wielded enormous political influence both at the central and provincial levels and big landlords belonging to both in and out factions were finding new outlets for their wealth in industrial investments.

10. Figures taken from Hamza Alavi, "Elite Farmer Strategy and Regional Disparities in the Agricultural Development of West Pakistan" (typescript), p. 5.

11. Ibid., p. 19.

12. Planning Commission, Government of Pakistan, *The Second Five Year Plan (1960-65)* (Karachi, 1960), p. 49.

13. Gustav F. Papanek, *Pakistan's Development: Social Goals and Private Incentives* (Cambridge, Mass.: Harvard University Press, 1967), p. 242.

14. *Business Recorder* (Karachi), April 25, 1968, p. 1.

15. Planning Commission, Government of Pakistan, *Reports of the Advisory Panels for the Fourth Five Year Plan 1970-75,* vol. 1 (Islamabad, 1970), p. 22.

16. Ministry of Finance, Government of Pakistan, *The Budget in Brief 1970-71* (Islamabad, 1970), p. 78.

17. Hamza Alavi, "The State in Postcolonial Societies: Pakistan and Bangladesh," in *Imperialism and Revolution in South Asia*, ed. Kathleen Gough and Hari P. Sharma (New York: Monthly Review Press, 1973), pp. 169-70.

18. For the above analysis the author has relied on Richard Nation, "The Economic Structure of Pakistan and Bangladesh," in *Explosion in a Subcontinent*, ed. Robin Blackburn (Harmondsworth: Penguin, 1975), pp. 260-62; and Stephen R. Lewis, *Economic Policy and Industrial Growth in Pakistan* (Cambridge, Mass.: MIT Press, 1969), pp. 20-37, 65-84.

19. Angus Maddison, *Class Structure and Economic Growth: India and Pakistan Since the Moghuls* (London: Allen & Unwin, 1971), p. 142.

20. S. M. Naweem, "Mass Poverty in Pakistan: Some Preliminary Findings," *Pakistan Development Review* 12 (Winter 1973): 322.

21. Ibid., p. 325.

22. Planning Commission, Government of Pakistan, *Socio-Economic Objectives of the Fourth Five Year Plan (1970-75)* (Karachi, 1968), p. 17.

23. Karl Marx, "Critique of the Gotha Program," in *The Marx-Engels Reader*, ed. Robert C. Tucker (New York: Norton, 1972), pp. 383-99.

4
CAUSES FOR THE SEPARATION
OF EAST PAKISTAN

Political scientists often talk about how a political system functions, but they seldom tell us how a system breaks down. They speak of how a system maintains itself, adapts itself, integrates its different tasks and functions, and, finally, attains its major goals and objectives. They refer to the basic and relevant units of a political system, the interdependence that exists between the inter-action of such units, and the stability that exists or emerges in the interaction of these units. However, their analyses almost always center around the concept of an ongoing political system. Although David Easton does refer to the stresses that a system may undergo through the erosion of support and speaks of how cleavages become major sources of stress on a system, he is mainly concerned with "output" failure: "Major tendencies to output failure will be set in motion as a result of the degree of internal dissension and conflict to be found among the members that they find themselves unable to cooperate, negotiate, or com-promise their differences even to the minimal extent necessary so as to discover some kind of acceptable output resolution."[1]

It would seem that the political system in Pakistan broke down in 1971 largely because of output failure arising out of dissension and conflict among East and West Pakistanis. Further the author would support the view that this dissension arose largely because the power elites of West Pakistan formulated

Used with permission from *International Journal* 27 (Summer 1972): 381-404, which is published by the Canadian Institute of International Affairs.

certain policies that provoked so much opposition and bitterness from the East that the system was brought to the verge of collapse. It might have been saved in March 1971, but the power elites were not prepared to let the system be transformed into one more acceptable to the East. Apart from an unwillingness to share their policy-determining power with the elites of the East, the elites of West Pakistan were convinced that, should a new constitutional arrangement be constructed on the basis of the Awami League's Six Points, the system would not be able to maintain itself or it would be so radically transformed that the raison d'etre of the state itself would disappear.

The question is thus: If the breakdown of the system did not come about solely because the economic policies chosen failed to achieve even marginally acceptable results, in what way and to what extent were the basic ideological and political policies and postures of the dominant groups[2] in Pakistan contributing factors? Was Pakistan a coherent political system when it came into being despite the cultural and linguistic differences of East Bengal and the various regions of West Pakistan? Few political systems have completely complementary political and cultural units. Leaders and governments must try, through their various policies and actions, to integrate the parts or at least to reduce their incoherence. Could one say that the dominant groups in Pakistan pursued political and ideological policies such that the differences among the units increased instead of diminished? This is not to suggest a deliberate policy to this end but rather that so far as East Bengal was concerned the instruments of integration, such as Islam and a fear of Indian, were probably counterproductive.

The principal leaders and groups representing East Bengal in the Muslim League came from the upper-class, landowning, Urdu-speaking families of Dacca or the mercantile groups of Calcutta. Even Jinnah, the Quaid-i-Azam, had been criticized by Bengali leaders for paying heed to the wishes and representations of these groups. However, under Suhrawardy, Abul Hashim had organized the Muslim League at the grass-roots level with some left-wing support, and it appeared that the leadership had been wrested from the conservative groups led by Khwaja Nazimuddin. It may be recalled that it was Abul Hashim who raised the demand for a separate Bengal state in the Council session of the All-India Muslim League in 1946 on the plea that the Lahore resolution could be interpreted as an endorsement of two separate states.[3] But these forces, including Suhrawardy himself, were passed over by the Quaid and Khwaja Nazimuddin was installed as the chief minister of East Bengal in 1947. However, soon after the formation of Pakistan, the conflict between those who claimed to represent popular and more radical forces in Bengal and these more conservative elements began.

The central leadership adopted the view that a significant number of influential Bengali Muslim leaders were probably not completely loyal Pakistanis. It was suspected that such leaders not only believed in retaining the Bengali language and culture but admired Tagore and were not opposed to the steady and surreptitious influx of Hindu ideas and other cultural influences from across the border. Muslim nationalism in the subcontinent was almost completely dominated by the Urdu language and literature and the other cultural strands emanating from north Indian Muslims, Punjabi Muslims, and possibly Muslims from other parts of West Pakistan. This conception, laced with the orthodox or Jamaat-i-Islami view that even Muslims in these parts of the subcontinent were not really pure and strict Muslims, led many to regard Bengali Muslims as an inferior breed who needed to be purified even more rigorously. This is a monolithic and an unrealistic view of Islam. It veers towards some utopian, ideal conception of Islam and moves away from the more catholic, flexible, and tolerant view advocated by the Mughals. The author believes that Pakistani leaders should have leaned heavily on the broader Mughal concept and even extended it to encompass a multicultural and multilingual Islam rather than advocating the narrower (purer) view, thereby antagonizing the emerging social forces in Bengal. However, it can be argued that the Pakistanis were merely reacting to what they felt was the aggressive attitude of India and particularly to the fact that India had never reconciled itself to the existence of a separate, stable Muslim state of Pakistan. Without this fear, it is conceivable that men like Suhrawardy would have been successful in charting the course of Pakistani politics along more liberal lines.

In fact, the collision course on which the Pakistani leaders embarked was disastrous and disruptive from the beginning. The author was teaching political science in Dacca University in 1951 and could sense the wave of hostility set in motion by Khwaja Nazimuddin's statement that Urdu alone, as the Quaid had once said, should be the language of Pakistan. In social gatherings, one could hear West Pakistani and other Muslims from Urdu-speaking provinces of India referring with scorn to the Bengali's devotion to his language and to his inability to pronounce correctly Muslim names. Even after Bengali was adopted as one of the two state languages, Governor Monem Khan attempted during the Ayub era to ban the broadcast of Tagore's songs or poems over Dacca radio and to prevent the import of Bengali books from Calcutta. In opposition to this official view, the majority of influential East Pakistani leaders subscribed to secular politics and joint electorates. East Pakistanis were not prepared to be ashamed of the profound impact that Bengali literature (particularly Rabindranath Tagore) had exercised on their way of life and thinking. To establish a majority in the Pakistan legislature, they had to unite with their fellow Bengali Hindus and therefore a man like Suhrawardy was a consistent advocate of joint electorates. Statesmanship demanded that Pakistanis should think of Islam in broader, confederal terms. Even the father of the nation had advocated that his Pakistan would have many mansions.

In the political and constitutional sphere, repeated attempts were made to strengthen the center and resist the East Pakistani demands for what were termed extreme forms of autonomy bordering on secession. When the army established its total ascendancy under Ayub, a highly centralized and autocratic presidential system was imposed on the country. It was obvious that such a system would arouse the antagonisms and deep-seated suspicions of East Pakistanis in that they would no longer have the advantages that their numbers would have given them in a strong parliamentary system. A parliamentary system could have at least partially offset the West Pakistani dominance in the civil and military services. Again, the same mistake was made. Instead of opting for a looser confederal form of government and a consociational type of executive, the power elites decided in favor of a highly centralized presidential system. Canada, Switzerland, and Belgium should have been the models, but the power elites settled for a government of the president, by the president, and for the president.

It should have been apparent that each time West Pakistani power elites along with some associates from the East tried to set up a highly centralized or even a quasi-federal system, the opposition from East Pakistan was intense and unequivocal. One could even argue that there was a progressive increase in the amount of autonomy that East Pakistanis demanded. Pakistan is not unique in this respect, for there are other countries where efforts to bring about rapid integration or to minimize diversity have exacerbated the problem. Pakistan would have been wiser to have followed the opposite course and to have reassured the regions that the cultural and other forms of autonomy would be respected and even encouraged. As Easton has written: "Greater success may be attained through steps that conduce to the development of a deeper sense of mutual awareness and responsiveness among encapsulated cultural units."[4]

Of course, the demand for maximum autonomy from East Pakistan was unique in that it was not merely a demand for maintaining a cultural identity. The fact of physical separation had always meant economic separation at least in the sense that there was no easy and free mobility of capital and labor. Given these hard economic realities and the growing antagonism between the two regions, hikmat-i-amali (judicious management) suggested that transactions and contacts between the two regions should have been kept at a minimum. As Walker Connor has observed: "It is a truism that centralized communications and increased contacts help to dissolve regional cultural distinctions within a state such as the United States. Yet, if one is dealing not with minor variations of the same culture, but with two quite distinct and self-differentiating cultures, are not increased contacts between the two apt to increase antagonisms?"[5]

Karl Deutsch has noted that in a solidarity system, like that of the United States, the components are linked by the "covariance of rewards" in the sense that all the individuals or groups involved in certain social or economic transactions derive positive advantages. In conflict systems, however, it is likely that some groups or partners will find such transactions rewarding but others will feel penalized. Such transactions are described as negative covariance.[6] Clearly, East Pakistanis regarded some of their transactions with West Pakistan in this light.

In an interview with the author in Dacca in February 1971, Tajuddin Ahmad, who later became a prominent Bangladesh minister, constantly referred to the economic deprivations that East Pakistanis were suffering as a result of the suspension of trade relations with India:

> We have to resume trade relations with India. . . . We are being forced to import coal from China which costs us Rs. 172 per ton. We can import the same coal from India at Rs. 53 per ton. We used to produce our own cement in Sylhet but the raw material, limestone, used to come from Assam. That has been suspended since the war. West Pakistan industrialists sell cement to us at Rs. 12 to Rs. 16 per bag of cement. Our cement, ex-factory, used to retail at Rs. 7 to 8. Indian cement is Rs. 8.50 per bag. India was the only buyer of low-quality jute. We can't sell that to India. . . . Hundreds of thousands of problems have been created in this way. . . . Any standard cloth from Japan would cost Rs. 2 per yard whereas West Pakistani cloth is sold in the protected market at Rs. 6 per yard. They play havoc with the bonus scheme.

One may well ask why no compromise position emerged that would have lessened the conflicts that existed in Pakistan during the early part of 1971. It seems to the author that the Six Points of the Awami League offered such a middle position. Points 3, 4, and 5 of the Six Points conferred powers regarding currency, taxation, utilization of foreign exchange earned by a federating unit, and foreign trade to the regional governments. These were interpreted by West Pakistanis as designed to bring about the disintegration of the country. The Awami League's view, which was supported by 75 percent of the electorate in East Pakistan who voted in the national elections,[7] was that these vital areas of economic policy should be transferred to the regional governments. They argued that the domination and determination of such vital policy areas by the West Pakistani power elites had resulted in increasing economic deprivation of East Pakistan. Since such policies had embittered the relations between the two regions and brought the country to the verge of disintegration, a transfer of such powers to the regions would considerably reduce the areas of conflict and allow the two regions to develop a more workable relationship with the powers of the center confined almost exclusively the defense and foreign affairs. Even the most pessimistic observer would have said that under the Six Points the union would have lingered for several years, and an optimist might have predicted that such a union might have flowered into a stable consociational system and an example for other pluralist societies.

It seems, then, that attempts to impose certain unitarian cultural-religious concepts and a centralized constitution brought Pakistan to the verge of disintegration. What was the role of the power elites in shaping and determining the economic policies whose impact was also destabilizing and disequilibrating for the political system of Pakistan? The author's concept of the power elite is derived from C. Wright Mills, who believed that the U.S. power elite exercises its power through the "many interconnections and points of coinciding interest" of the corporations, political institutions, and military services.[8] The questions that arise when examining this concept are: Was the power or ruling elite a well-defined group? Did it make all or most of the major decisions, so that its preferences prevailed against those of other groups? Assuming that such elites shaped and determined the major policy decisions, what was the impact of such decisions on the political system? Did such decisions tend to stabilize or destabilize the political system? Did they integrate or disintegrate the political system?

In Pakistan the power or ruling elite was an easily defined group comprising the top echelons in the civil service and military hierarchy. Their clear ascendancy as a ruling group had long been established, particularly since the military coup of Ayub in 1958. This group made all the major decisions in terms of economic and defense policies, decisions that were on the whole dysfunctional toward the stability and maintenance of the political system. The civil services played a decisive role in determining economic policies and the military monopolized the formulation of defense policies.

Members of the civil service of Pakistan who held command positions in the central secretariat formed the majority of the civil service elites, but it also included some individuals from the Pakistan audit and accounts service and other services and some economists working with the Planning Commission. Civil servants who occupied top positions such as those of secretary of a ministry or managing director of a government-sponsored corporation exercised a dominant influence in policymaking. Significant inputs usually came from joint secretaries, while the incumbents of positions such as deputy secretaries were usually influential only in implementing policies and not in their formulation. In the formulation of economic policies, decisive roles were played by secretaries of ministries such as those of finance, industries, commerce, and possibly agriculture, the deputy chairman, secretary, and senior economists of the Planning Commission, and the chairmen or managing directors of such institutions as the State Bank of Pakistan, the Industrial Development Corporations and Water and Power Development authorities of the two regions, and the Pakistan Industrial Credit and Investment Corporation. Associated with civil service officers in the directorates of important government-sponsored corporations like the Pakistan Industrial Credit and Investment Corporation were managing directors and directors of various private industrial and commercial corporations. In addition, leading businessmen and industrialists representing chambers of commerce or important business firms were not only members of advisory bodies attached to various ministries but through informal and direct channels they were close to civil servants with high policy leverage.

East Pakistanis often bitterly complained that there were few East Pakistani officers at the highest levels of the civil service. In some of the key ministries associated with economic policymaking, particularly at the secretary level, all the officers until 1969 were from West Pakistan or had emigrated from the Muslim-minority provinces of India. In 1969, after the imposition of the second era of martial law under General Yahya, some kind of parity in the secretariat was brought about by giving accelerated promotions to East Pakistani officers. Even then, the complaint was that the *key* positions were still held by West Pakistanis. An equally persistent complaint of both Bengali and other non-Punjabi officers was that all the key points of leverage in the policymaking structure were occupied by Punjabi officers. It would not be fair to say that the power elite in the civil service hierarchy came entirely from Punjab. A random sample of some of the officers of high policy leverage includes officers like Ghulam Faruque, former chairman of the PIDC and a commerce minister (Frontier); Ghulam Ishaq Khan, former finance secretary and cabinet secretary (Frontier); Abbas Khaleeli, former secretary of industries and originally from Madras; Muhammad Shoaib, former finance minister, originally a civil servant from the Uttar Pradesh; S. S. Jafri, former secretary of industries and also originally from the Uttar Pradesh. However, insofar as these officers identified themselves with West Pakistan and as nearly all of them were from Urdu-speaking areas, they really belonged to the West Pakistani power elites. Table 4.1 indicates the backgrounds of the civil service officers holding positions of power and influence in the central secretariat from 1965 to 1970.

Although ministries like finance, industries, and commerce and the Planning Commission were important in the economic policymaking structure, the secretaries of the Cabinet Division, the Establishment Division, and also a ministry like that of information and broadcasting are included because these officers, particularly the latter, were considered to exercise high leverage in the entire policymaking process. Sometimes the position of the secretary of commerce or another ministry is missing because such positions were not always held by officers belonging to the elite cadre of the civil service of Pakistan.

The Pakistan army was almost entirely recruited from four districts of northern Punjab (Rawalpindi, Campbellpur, Jhelum, and Gujarat) and two districts of the Frontier Province (Peshawar and Kohat). Sixty percent of the army were Punjabi and 35 percent were Pakhtun.[9] Generals, admirals, or air marshals occupying positions such as the presidency, the deputy commander-in-chief of the army, chief of the general staff, the commanders-in-chief of the navy and air force, the director of interservices intelligence, the military governor of a province, and the command of certain divisions constituted the military elite.

Is it possible to describe the power elite of Pakistan in class terms? In 1957, Philip Mason observed: "It is no doubt a chance association, but if you speak of the ruling class in Pakistan today, I think of men watching the polo in Lahore, the kind of people you'd see at point-to-point races in England, with check caps pulled down over their eyes and horsey coats with slanting pockets."[10] This description probably referred to the civil and military officers drawn from the

TABLE 4.1
Background of Civil Service Officers in Influential Positions, 1965-70

Year	West Pakistan	Urdu-Speaking Indian Provinces	East Pakistan	Others	Positions Held
1965	9 Punjab	4	0	1	Foreign affairs; agriculture and works; cabinet; establishment division; home and Kashmir; economic affairs; communications; industries and natural resources; defense; secretary to president; finance; investment promotion bureau; WAPDA; information and broadcasting
1966	9 Punjab	3	0	1	Foreign affairs; agriculture and works; defense; home and Kashmir; economic affairs; communications; secretary to president; cabinet; industries and natural resources; finance; investment promotion; WAPDA; information and broadcasting
1967	8 Punjab 1 Frontier	3	0	0	Secretary to president; communications; cabinet; foreign affairs; industries and natural resources; deputy chairman, Planning Commission; agriculture and works; economic affairs; investment promotion; planning division; finance; information and broadcasting
1968	7 Punjab 1 Frontier	2	0	0	Foreign affairs; agriculture and works; deputy chairman, Planning Commission; cabinet; industries and natural resources; planning division; finance; information and broadcasting; economic affairs; defense
1969	7 Punjab 1 Frontier	2	1	0	Foreign affairs; agriculture and works; deputy chairman, Planning Commission; cabinet; economic affairs; industries and natural resources; planning division; finance; communications; information and broadcasting
1970	5 Punjab 1 Frontier 1 Sind	0	2	0	Chairman and managing director, Steel Mills Corporation; deputy chairman, Planning Commission; defense; cabinet; planning division; industries and natural resources; finance; communications; agriculture and works

Source: Gradation lists of the civil service of Pakistan for 1965 through 1970.

landowning classes of Punjab and the Frontier. In institutional and professional terms, the ruling elites remained the same, but in class terms they expanded to include a number of those who were originally lower middle class and, as noted earlier, certain of the business groups. The heads of business firms may not be included in the hard-core ruling elite, but they had gained access to those with high-policy leverage, even if they could not themselves determine policy decisions.

Another significant development was the emergence of interlocking business and family relationships between the civil service, the military, and the business groups. In the years 1965 and 1966, the secretary of foreign affairs, Pakistan's ambassador in Washington, and the secretaries of Home and Kashmir Affairs and the Economic Affairs Division were related. Similarly, some of the senior civil servants were linked by family ties to members of the military hierarchy. And civil service, military, and business families were becoming interrelated through new matrimonial alliances. It was also significant that when Ayub introduced martial law in 1958, 13 civil service officers were dismissed or asked to resign and some of the business firms that had dealt with these officers were asked to pay their taxes and surrender their foreign exchange holdings. Again, when martial law was imposed in March 1969, over 300 officers belonging to the central civil services were dismissed or retired and business firms called upon to pay their taxes and surrender their foreign exchange holdings.

Elites in every society tend to be exclusive, but to maintain themselves in power and legitimize their policies they have to draw on resources such as ideology and political support. To do so involves political institution building. In Pakistan, bureaucratic elites did not have these advantages and were not much concerned about lack of ideological and political support. Thus Pakistan's bureaucratic and military elites were not only separated from the majority of their population who lived in East Pakistan but their regional exclusiveness was such that they were separated in both social and regional terms even from the people of regions like Sind, Baluchistan, and the Frontier.

T. B. Bottomore has pointed out that in underdeveloped countries the elites, being "widely separated from the rest of the people, by their Western education, by their origins in higher castes, in landowning or business families, or in the families of tribal chiefs, and by their whole style of life," have often set up authoritarian regimes. Even countries like India, where democracy prevails, have not been fully successful in "eliciting popular participation in development activities."[11] Some people go so far as to argue that lack of adequate representation of civil servants from regions like the Frontier, Sind, and Baluchistan explains to a considerable extent why the integrated province of West Pakistan had to be broken up into its former constituent units.

Recently several scholars have tried to explain the decision-making process with models derived from cognitive psychology. This model is particularly applicable to a decision-making process dominated by bureaucratic power elites.

It has four basic components:

1. The formative images that a bureaucrat acquires during his training period in academies and in his early life in the districts are crucial and leave a profound and permanent impression on his thinking and behavior. In the context of Pakistan, a civil servant's dealings with the people in the districts, how he controls law and order situations, the cynical attitudes that he develops toward politicians and also toward business groups whom he regards as interlopers or traders interested in quick and questionable profits, are of great significance.
2. When dealing with complex situations for which solutions or decisions are not easy, the bureaucrat tends to select from all available information those pieces that tend to confirm the images that he has already acquired or has stored in his memory.
3. Particularly when faced with crisis situations, the bureaucrat tends to depend very much on the images and categories of thought acquired from experiences gained during his formative years. Because his colleagues have similar images, there is a fundamental agreement among the bureaucrats about how to tackle a given crisis situation.
4. Bureaucrats in all systems tend to cling to such images even as they become increasingly invalidated by new events and changed circumstances. However, this tendency is even more pronounced under autocratic systems.

The formative years of the senior civil servants who made the major policy decisions regarding political, religious, and law and order problems in Pakistan coincided with the heyday of the British Raj. They learned that law and order provided a basic framework without which government could not be carried on and, as a corollary, that political activity tended to be a threat to law and order. The famous Munir report, after waxing eloquent about the intellectual inability of the political leaders in providing a rational and modern interpretation of Islamic ideology, observed: "And it is our deep conviction that if the Ahrar had been treated as a pure question of law and order, without any political consid- erations, one District Magistrate and one Superintendent of Police could have dealt with them."[12] The author came across the same emphasis on law and order in interviews with senior civil servants, who pointed out repeatedly that develop- ment could never become a substitute for law and order. A former home secre- tary of the central government observed that the government from time to time had followed a simple rule-of-thumb method for dealing with political and other demonstrations: that the killing of one man in Karachi and two in Lahore could bring an unruly situation under control. When one considers these statements within the context of the Pakistani situation where upper-class civil servants had to control unruly mobs drawn from lower and illiterate classes, one cannot help thinking that there was a thinly concealed contempt for the common man. A similar point emerges in the regional context. A senior civil servant who had spent almost all his early career in Bengal wondered what had gone wrong with the Bengalis when their language demonstrations could not be brought under control through normal coercive methods. In a government house meeting, he turned to a Bengali newspaper editor and asked: "What has gone wrong with the Bengalis? I simply cannot understand why they are reacting in this fashion."

General Ayub, who had served in East Pakistan soon after independence, had also formed certain impressions about the Bengalis, their attitudes, and their culture. In October 1954, when Pakistan was faced with a political crisis, he wrote a note entitled "A Short Appreciation of Present and Future Problems of Pakistan," including this considered judgment of the Bengalis:

> It would be no exaggeration to say that up to the creation of Pakistan, they had not known any real freedom or sovereignty. They have been in turn ruled either by the caste Hindus, Moghuls, Pathans, or the British. In addition, they have been and still are under considerable Hindu cultural and linguistic influence. As such they have all the inhibitions of down-trodden races and have not yet found it possible to adjust psychologically to the requirements of the new-born freedom. Their popular complexes, exclusiveness, suspicion and a sort of defensive aggressiveness probably emerge from this historical background.[13]

Later, when he became president, his fundamental approach and basic policies toward East Pakistan were influenced by these early images. Faced with growing resentment of East Pakistanis toward his government, he appointed Governor Monem Khan, who was known for his ruthlessness toward his political opponents and who believed that coercion was the only answer to political opposition. Faced with Sheikh Mujibur Rahman's demand for regional autonomy, Ayub threatened his political opponents with resort to the "language of weapon" and a civil war. General Yahya, who had also served in East Pakistan, was equally receptive to the policy of ruthless coercion recommended to him by Major General Umar, chairman of the National Security Council, and Major General Akbar, chief of the Inter-Services Intelligence Committee. The advice was that "the Bengali nationalists would quickly collapse, then tamely conform after one violent military assault."[14]

It has been argued that the exclusiveness of the power elite and the kinds of policies it pursued are interdependent variables and that these had a dysfunctional impact on Pakistan's political system. Given the regional and economic interests of the power elite, one could see what kind of economic doctrines and strategies would appeal to them. The policies of the elites were also influenced by economists who thought that because economic growth was of paramount importance, inequality of income and encouragement of the private sector were necessary to stimulate savings. More than a modicum of investment in social justice would mean a reduction in economic growth. Thus West Pakistani elites, in pursuing policies of development favoring the growth of West Pakistan, could reassure themselves that these policies could also be justified in terms of certain respectable economic doctrines and by the support of advisory groups of Western economists for their policies.[15]

The specific policies that increased the disparity between East and West Pakistan at an ever faster rate during the 1950s and 1960s have been described and documented elsewhere. The policy of industrialization through the encouragement of the private sector dates back to 1948. One could see that the scales were tipped against East Pakistan from the beginning because most of the private sector (centered on the mercantile groups who had migrated from India) was located in West Pakistan. In addition, East Pakistanis felt that since the central policymaking structures were dominated by West Pakistani civil servants, most of the lucrative import licenses were given to West Pakistanis. This meant that prior to the Korean War boom, West Pakistani traders could reap fortunes when imports were being encouraged. During the boom and after the decision of the government not to devaluate the Pakistani rupee, West Pakistani traders, who dominated the external trade of both East and West Pakistan, were able to capitalize on the exports of jute and cotton, which were being sold at higher prices because of the overvaluation of the Pakistani rupee. These profits enabled West Pakistani mercantile groups to turn to manufacturing, particularly when the government was prepared to develop the infrastructure facilities in West Pakistan and offer maximum scope to the private sector in industries like cotton textiles. Later, West Pakistan's industrial growth was further facilitated by the support of the government-sponsored Pakistan Industrial Development Corporation for such industries as woolen cloth, sugar, food canneries, chemicals, telephones, cement, and fertilizer.

The economic disparity brought about by government policies was accentuated by the investment policies pursued during the three plan periods. It has been estimated that the share of East Pakistan was about 26 percent of total investment (public and private) during the first plan period, 1955-60. The total revenue expenditure in East Pakistan during this time was Rs. 2.5 billion as against Rs. 8.9 billion in West Pakistan.

Disparity in development increased during the second and third plan periods because the policies that had created this disparity also continued unchanged. It is a strange but understandable commentary on the unresponsiveness of policymakers to the demands and grievances of East Pakistanis that even though the wave of resentment in East Pakistan against this disparity had been rising ever since the 1954 elections, there was no significant change in these policies. In an autocratic regime where political forces were not allowed to articulate their demands, why should West Pakistani civil servants have paid administrative heed to the pious declarations regarding attainment of parity found in the 1962 constitution and the statements of the president? Thus, during the second plan, in terms of actual implementation, the share of East Pakistan in the total public and private sector expenditure (including that of the Indus Basin) was about 32 percent. During the third plan, the share was 36 percent. The figures of development and nondevelopment expenditure in per capita terms are even more graphic. During the third plan (1960-65) the per capita development and revenue expenditures in West Pakistan were Rs. 521.05 and Rs. 390.35, respectively, whereas the expenditures for East Pakistan were as low as Rs. 240 and Rs. 70.29, respectively.[16]

Commenting on this disparity, the East Pakistani panel of economists in its report to the Planning Commission pointed out:

> The administrative effort for plan implementation was basically limited by the absence of East Pakistanis at the top executive positions both in Central and Provincial Governments. The former was responsible for the lack of the right kind of motivation of the central administration toward the development of East Pakistan. The latter was responsible for the lack of requisite leadership in the Provincial administration for the initiation of economic development in East Pakistan. And it is well-known that in Pakistan the initiation, formulation, and the implementation of development projects and policies were primarily undertaken by the bureaucrats in the top executive positions.[17]

Even when East Pakistani civil servants could influence policy, it was extremely difficult for them to be effective because the West Pakistani civil servants dominated the policymaking structures to such an extent that East Pakistani civil servants could either be overruled or transferred. The frustrations and obstacles against which East Pakistani civil servants worked from 1960 to 1965 were poignantly related by A. F. Rahman, one of those officers, when he was being tried in the Agartala conspiracy case. He spoke of his difficulties when, as secretary of the Department of Health, Labor and Social Welfare of the East Pakistan government, he tried to send East Pakistani doctors abroad for higher education and was opposed by his director of health services, a military officer from West Pakistan. As deputy financial adviser to the Health, Labor and Social Welfare Department in the central government, he found that his West Pakistani colleagues were interested in handing over factories built by central funds to the West Pakistan Industrial Development Corporation without any payment being made by the latter and in making grants to West Pakistani institutions in areas such as welfare and education even though these subjects had been allotted to the provincial jurisdiction. Similarly, as deputy secretary of development in the central Ministry of Finance, he found that the central government departments were submitting a large number of projects located in West Pakistan relating to provincial subjects like health, agriculture, and education for financing, even though the central government was not expected to execute such schemes. He recorded: "The intentions of the departments manned mostly by West Pakistani officers were to develop institutions in West Pakistan with the Central Government's money though the subjects were provincial."[18]

Table 4.2 illustrates how the disparity between East and West Pakistan grew steadily and at an accelerating pace between 1959-60 and 1969-70. As well, the central government conceded that the disparity measured by the difference between per capita incomes in West and East Pakistan expressed as a percentage of the per capita income of all Pakistan, excluding 3 percent for unallocable items, increased from 38.1 percent in 1964-65 to 47.1 percent in 1969-70.[19]

It is not surprising that East Pakistani and West Pakistani economists disagreed over the factors responsible for the growth in disparity. To East Pakistanis, it seemed that their interests had been systematically neglected by a government that was dominated by West Pakistani policymakers. West Pakistani economists seemed to think that East Pakistan enjoyed twice the public sector outlays of West Pakistan throughout the 1960s; therefore it was not the policy-makers who were to be blamed but certain economic factors over which they had very little control: "During this period considerable difference in private sector investment between East and West Pakistan and a dramatic break-through in agriculture in West Pakistan based on the new seed-based technology were the major factors resulting in the growth of disparity. Institutional arrangements

TABLE 4.2
Per Capita Gross Domestic Product in East and West Pakistan, 1959-60, Constant Prices

	Per Capita GDP East	Per Capita GDP West	West-East Disparity Ratio	Index of Disparity
1959-60	269	355	1.32	100
1960-61	277	363	1.31	97
1961-62	286	376	1.31	97
1962-63	277	393	1.42	111
1963-64	299	408	1.36	113
1964-65	293	426	1.45	141
1965-66	295	427	1.45	141
1966-67	290	448	1.54	169
1967-68	307	468	1.52	163
1968-69	312	490	1.57	178
1969-70	314	504	1.61	191
Growth over the decade	17%	42%		
Growth in third plan period	7%	18%		

Source: Planning Commission, Government of Pakistan, *Reports of the Advisory Panels for the Fourth Five Year Plan 1970-75,* vol. 1 (Islamabad, July 1970), p. 22.

for implementing large development programmes in the public sector remained weak in East Pakistan despite considerable improvement."[20] What is striking in this debate is that the central Ministry of Finance endorsed the West Pakistan point of view: "Despite the best efforts, which have no doubt helped accelerate the growth rate in East Pakistan, it has not been possible to reduce the disparity between per capita income of East and West Pakistan. . . . The increase was essentially due to the faster growth of West Pakistan than East Pakistan. . . . The major factor responsible for the slower growth of East Pakistan, or inversely the faster growth of West Pakistan, has been the behaviour of the agriculture sector."[21]

The policymakers in the central government did not seem to realize that in a heterogeneous society like that of Pakistan with most of the policymakers drawn from one province of West Pakistan (Punjab), they could not hope to carry much conviction among East Pakistanis by explaining away disparity in terms of economic factors beyond their control. When resources were scarce and when their own society was by no means prosperous, it was natural that policymakers would tend to pursue and implement policies designed to develop their own areas first. It may also be argued that if West Pakistani policymakers could not maintain balanced ongoing development for all the provinces in West Pakistan itself, how could they be expected to be so fair and just as to promote the development of East Pakistan at an accelerated pace to make up for the years of neglect?

Regional economic disparity provoked, particularly in East Pakistan, bitter opposition and resentment toward the central government. This opposition had begun during the early 1950s. Why was such economic disparity allowed to continue? Mahbub ul Haq, the former chief economist of the Planning Commission, suggested that such regional disparities were a direct outcome of a policy that allowed the free market forces to work in an unhindered fashion.

It shows that if there are wide economic disparities between two regions, the pull of free market forces will tend to aggravate them. Economic growth will tend to become concentrated in the relatively richer region, with its better infra-structure, more aggressive entrepreneurs, and known opportunities for investment. Private saving from the poorer region will also go to the richer region in search of profitable opportunities. Foreign investment will tend to flow to the richer region where some dynamism has been built up and returns seem to be safer and larger. Foreign aid and loans will be distributed more in favour of the richer region where those "sound" projects are located, on the basis of which foreign assistance has been negotiated. The Government becomes an unconscious ally in this process of concentration of economic forces — or "polarization process" as Myrdal has called it — by creating more infrastructure where bottlenecks are more obvious, by distributing scarce resources like foreign exchange where demand for them is higher, and by concentrating its administrative personnel in the more dynamic region where the problems of control are more keenly felt. It is clear that this is what has happened in the case of East and West Pakistan. This was but a natural sequence of events in the absence of a clearly defined, regional policy.[22]

One may well ask why the regional disparity between East and West Pakistan was allowed to grow at an accelerated pace after a clear policy declaration by the Ayub regime that definite steps would be undertaken to eliminate it. A commitment to the progressive elimination of disparity was made in the constitution of 1962 itself. However, mere declarations could not have altered the situation unless two major changes had been brought about in Pakistan's political and economic system. Because West Pakistani civil servants continued to dominate the structure, declarations of policy without alteration in the power structure could not produce the desired changes. An equally important factor was the commitment of the Ayub regime to certain clear economic doctrines and principles.

The doctrine that at least in the beginning economic inequality was essential for rapid economic growth was expounded with considerable eloquence by both Pakistani and Western economists. Mahbub ul Haq, probably the most influential adviser of his government and drafter of several of the plan documents, pointed out that "the underdeveloped countries must consciously accept a philosophy of growth and shelve for the distant future all ideas of equitable distribution and welfare state. It should be recognized that these are luxuries which only developed countries can afford."[23] Gustav Papanek, an adviser to the Pakistan Planning Commission, also subscribed to this view. In his book he wrote: "The problem of inequality exists, but its importance must be put in perspective. First of all, the inequalities in income contribute to the growth of the economy, which makes possible a real improvement for the lower-income groups."[24] These policy recommendations were accepted in toto by Pakistan's policymakers. In his foreword to the third plan President Ayub wrote: "There have been no grand experiments in nationalisation, no fancy slogans about socialism, no undue intervention in the private sector. In fact, the government has gradually removed most of the administrative and bureaucratic controls which hampered progress of the private sector."[25] Mohammad Shoaib, the finance minister, and the secretaries of the Ministries of Finance and Industries were equally eloquent in praising the virtues of private enterprise.

Therefore, in addition to the continued dominance of West Pakistani power elites in the policymaking structure of Pakistan, the problem of regional inequality was further accentuated by the commitment of policymakers to the doctrine that income inequalities were necessary for rapid economic growth of the country. This entrepreneurial approach to development, in which certain advanced class and regional groups were given further help in the belief that their prosperity would spill over to less favored groups and regions, suggested that growth would take place largely through the provision of maximum incentives to the private sector, with the ruling civil service elites pursuing appropriate fiscal and monetary policies. This strategy, as seen, created regional inequalities throughout Pakistan and class inequalities within the favored region itself. According to Mahbub ul Haq, 66 percent of the nation's industrial assets, 80 percent of the banking assets, and 79 percent of the insurance assets were controlled by only 22 families. Also, the tax structure in Pakistan was extremely regressive with only 2 percent of the gross national product being realized as direct taxes as compared to an average of 6 percent for developing countries and 17 percent for developed countries. The result was that a widespread sense of social injustice in West Pakistan created support for a party with socialist orientations like the Pakistan People's party. The defeat of the Islamic orthodox groups in West Pakistan in the elections in 1970 showed that the appeal of Islam was declining. All this suggests that regimes in which civil servants determine major economic policy decisions tend to be influenced by such business criteria as efficiency and returns on capital and considerations such as the equitable distribution of wealth and the welfare state are deliberately given a lower priority. In the long run, pure economics at the expense of social and political factors is bad economics and explosive politics.

An attempt has been made here to show that the political system of Pakistan could not cope with the stresses and strains generated by the nation's economic policies and so eventually broke down. It is clear from the Six Points of the Awami League that it was these economic policies that, in the view of East Pakistani leaders, hurt East Pakistan most significantly.

Given the heterogeneous base of a country like Pakistan, the more exclusive its power elite is, the more dysfunctional in terms of its political system the policies produced by such an elite are likely to be. To appreciate how exclusive the power elites of Pakistan were, one has to bear in mind that the bureaucratic power elites were drawn only from West Pakistan's civil service cadres. One may go so far as to say that the "coalition of brains and guns" in Pakistan was not only against the numbers of East Pakistan but also against the brains of East Pakistan. By and large, bureaucratic and military elites tend to hold the political process in disdain and often they suspend or suppress the political process. This was the case in Pakistan. Given the heterogeneous social and regional base, the political process tends to be more receptive to regional and other pressures than the bureaucratic process or a political process dominated by an exclusive bureaucracy. Third, an entrepreneurial development strategy tends to heighten not only regional conflicts throughout the country but also class conflict even within the favored region itself.

The beginning of this chapter explored the unitarian and simplistic approach to building an ideological consensus and making a constitution among Pakistan's power wielders. If there was a consistent and tragic pattern during the first 24 years of Pakistan's history, it seemed to be that the more the power elites tried to preserve the unity of the political system, the more certain did its eventual disintegration become. We have not gone into the gruesome details describing the reign of terror and killings unleashed by the Pakistan army in East Pakistan during March-December 1971 nor have we highlighted the precipitous factor that dismembered Pakistan, namely, the intervention of the Indian army in the civil war during December 1971. Our attempt all along has been to analyze some of the long-term factors that brought about the separation of East Pakistan in December 1971.

NOTES

1. David Easton, *A Systems Analysis of Political Life* (New York: Wiley, 1965), p. 233.
2. Power elites in the context of this chapter encompass the top echelons in the civil service and military hierarchy. Dominant group is a more inclusive term that embraces old Muslim League politicians and ministers as well as civil service and military leaders.
3. Later he changed his views and became an ardent spokesman for an Islamic polity. His son is a former political science teacher and probably a pro-Peking political worker.
4. Easton, op. cit., p. 250.
5. Walter Connor, "Self-Determination: The New Phase," *World Politics* 22 (October 1967): 49-50.
6. Karl W. Deutsch, *Politics and Government* (Boston: Houghton Mifflin, 1970), pp. 120-24.
7. Of the electorate in East Pakistan 55.8 percent voted in the national elections according to figures obtained from the Election Commission. However, this figure excludes nine cyclone-affected national constituencies of East Pakistan.
8. C. Wright Mills, *The Power Elite* (New York: Oxford University Press, 1956), p. 19.
9. Khalid B. Sayeed, "The Role of the Military in Pakistan," in *Armed Forces and Society,* ed. Jacques Van Doorn (The Hague: Mouton, 1968), p. 276.
10. Philip Mason, "India and Pakistan After Ten Years," *The Listener,* September 5, 1957, p. 336.
11. T. B. Bottomore, *Elites and Society* (London: Watts, 1964), pp. 102-03.
12. *Report of the Court of Inquiry Constituted Under Punjab Act II of 1954 to Enquire into the Punjab Disturbances of 1953* (Lahore: Government Printing, 1954), p. 387. This report is commonly known as the Munir report.
13. Mohammad Ayub Khan, *Friends Not Masters* (London: Oxford University Press, 1967), p. 187.
14. Nicholas Tomalin, "Far from the Holocaust," *Sunday Times,* April 18, 1971.
15. The most important was the Harvard Advisory Group of economists. This view of the author regarding the ideological biases of the economists is supported by Gunnar Myrdal, *The Challenge of World Poverty* (New York: Pantheon, 1970), Chap. 3.
16. All these figures have been taken from "Report of East Pakistan Economists," which is included in Planning Commission, Government of Pakistan, *Reports of the Advisory Panels for the Fourth Five Year Plan 1970-75,* vol. 1 (Islamabad, July 1970), pp. 27-28.
17. Ibid., p. 27.
18. *Pakistan Observer,* February 3, 1969.

19. Ministry of Finance, Government of Pakistan, *The Budget in Brief 1970-71* (Islamabad, 1970), p. 78.

20. *Reports of the Advisory Panels for the Fourth Five Year Plan 1970-75,* op. cit., p. 107.

21. *The Budget in Brief 1970-71,* p. 78.

22. Mahbub ul Haq, *The Stretegy of Economic Planning* (Karachi: Oxford, 1963), p. 113.

23. Ibid., p. 30.

24. Gustav F. Papanek, *Pakistan's Development: Social Goals and Private Incentives* (Cambridge, Mass.: Harvard University Press, 1967), p. 242.

25. Planning Commission, Government of Pakistan, *The Third Five Year Plan 1965-70* (June 1965), p. iv.

5
BHUTTO'S POPULIST MOVEMENT
AND THE BONPARTIST STATE

The dents made by Ayub's industrialization policy in the predominantly feudal and rural social structure of West Pakistan had generated a series of changes that have often been characterized by political and social scientists as social mobilization.[1] Social mobilization has been defined "as the process in which major clusters of old social, economic and psychological commitments are eroded or broken and people become available for new patterns of socialization and behaviour."[2] This is how social scientists, with their concern and claim to be value free and objective, have characterized clusters of changes in third world countries.

These changes happen to people who undergo modernization or who move from traditional to modern ways of life. When these changes happen, a political scientist like Karl Deutsch would urge that the governments concerned should improve their capabilities to provide better housing, more jobs, and other amenities to cushion or absorb the unsettling experiences of "uprooting or breaking away from old settings, habits and commitments." While the governments of Western Europe and the United States took many generations to accomplish these tasks, the governments of the third world countries are being called upon to skip the intermediate stages of transition and laissez-faire and set up modern welfare states.

What appeared to Deutsch as basically the task of improving the capabilities of governments so that they might keep "abreast of the burdens generated by the processes of social mobilization"[3] was identified and diagnosed as essentially that of political institutionalization by Samuel Huntington.[4] However, neither of these political scientists nor many others who have followed their line of reasoning have appreciated that one of the major problems generated by economic development promoted largely through state-promoted capitalism in these countries is a heightened consciousness of social injustice because of growing class and regional inequalities. This lack of appreciation was particularly startling in the case of Huntington, who had followed so closely the political and economic developments under the Ayub regime.[5]

This lack of appreciation, sometimes amounting to even a gross misunderstanding on the part of certain Western political scientists of the nature and totality of social change in the third world, largely arises from the fact that such social scientists think that the relatively backward countries of the third world would go through the same stages of political and economic development as did the Western countries. Because the problem has been reduced to such simple historical terms of growth and development, the task of political theory, according to Deutsch, is "to make this image [of social mobilization] more specific; to bring it into a form in which it can be verified by evidence; and to develop the problem to a point where the question 'how?' can be supplemented usefully by the question 'how much?' "[6]

How can a political theory that is not broad enough to mirror the overall process of social change in these countries capture its image in more specific terms? There are two basic flaws in such a political theory. The first one has already been referred to, namely, the inability of such theorists to appreciate that social mobilization has created new conditions of social injustice and therefore heightened the consciousness among the people of such inequities. Second, this political theory has not paid enough attention to the resilience of certain belief systems like that of Islam.

It looked as if Bhutto, who had watched first as a minister and later as a political leader the changes that had been generated by Ayub's policies of economic development, had a much better grasp of the overall process of social mobilization than many social scientists. First of all, he could see the deepening ideological crisis that Pakistan faced. Islam and the fear of India could no longer be taken for granted as cementing forces to bind the two disparate parts. An equally serious crisis was the economic crisis in which the "development decade"[7] under Ayub had become a decade of exploitation and deliberate promotion of inequality between classes and regions with the 22 big industrial families amassing most of the wealth. There was also the national or military crisis partly accentuated by the political propaganda of leaders like Bhutto himself, who had created the widespread belief that Ayub and his government through their supine incompetence had bungled the 1965 war and thereby caused damage to Pakistan's prestige and even security.

Thus Bhutto could appeal to a number of groups and classes. There was the disgruntled industrial labor whose real wages had gone down after the 1965 war. There were migrants from rural areas coming to the urban areas who were faced with a lack of job opportunites, poor housing, and rising prices. There were military and civil officers at various levels who were apprehensive that the government could neither prosecute its war effort against India nor promote national solidarity by satisfying the demands and aspirations of East Pakistanis. Students represented another explosive force. They had often borne the brunt of Ayub's repression of political and urban opposition.

It is in this context that one has to see the emergence and development of a populist movement like Bhutto's Pakistan People's party (PPP). The fourfold motto of the party reflected the demands and aspirations of the various disgruntled groups in Pakistan. The ringing declaration of the party was: "Islam is our faith. Democracy is our polity. Socialism is our economy. All power to the people."

This was populism par excellence. David Apter, while discussing regimes of third world states, observed: "Few are totalitarian. Almost all are populist, and in a real sense, mainly predemocratic rather than antidemocratic."[8] Even though Apter thinks that almost all the political regimes of third world states are populist, he does not elaborate or analyze the content of the term populism. There are different views regarding populism. Even though reference to the people occupies a central place in populism, questions have been raised as to whether populism is a class movement or a coalition of divergent classes or groups that a leader, often with the help of an ideology, organizes against the state or the status quo. Therefore the appeal is to the people and not to classes.

Many theorists regard the populist movement as a transitional phenomenon generated by the process of economic development. It is claimed that in England and in other Western countries the transitional stage did not create any explosive problems because of the gradual mobilization of an increasing proportion of the population through multiple mechanisms of accommodation or integration. These mechanisms were trade unions and political parties. Similarly, education, social legislation, and mass consumption also became vehicles of mobilization and integration. Thus democracy, starting with limited franchise, finally emerged as democracy with total adult franchise. Capitalism with its big corporations and the consumer society and the welfare state were also accepted as legitimate norms by West European and U.S. societies.

The question arises: Can populism in a third world country like Pakistan also be regarded as a transitional phenomenon that would serve as an intermediate stage between the problems of a changing transitional society and the needs of the emerging modern or industrialized society? The Pakistan People's party under the leadership of Bhutto claimed to be a dynamic, progressive movement, and with its espousal of nationalization of key industries and land reforms, had gone far beyond the stage reached by other political parties in Pakistan. It was not only successful in defeating religious and traditional groups like the Muslim League and the Jamaat-i-Islami in the national elections in Pakistan in

1970 but also in persuading the urban and rural masses that Islam had certain collectivist doctrines and traditions. Other political parties like the Muslim League and the Jamaat-i-Islami, on the other hand, tried to propagate the idea that Islam and socialism were antithetical. The author's interviews with some of the PPP leaders also suggest that they had been successful in driving home the point that Islam supported a socialist order and that Islam from the very beginning had put forward the notion of nationalization of all landed property and an interest-free monetary system.[9] Thus, in this sense, Bhutto was not using the populist movement so much as a bridge between a traditional and industrialized society but as a launching pad to move Pakistan from nascent capitalism combined with a semifeudal agrarian system to nascent socialism with an agrarian economy in which land reforms would diminish considerably the influence of feudal interests.

There is a tendency on the part of certain social scientists to think that third world countries are always moving from their present state of backwardness to a state of industrialization and capitalist development that Western countries have already reached with some of them having moved into a post-industrial state. Therefore, associated with this view is the view that through populist movements some of the third world countries would be able to make the transition from a traditional society to a more developed industrialized and capitalist society. There are writers like Ernesto Laclau, on the other hand, who advance the view that some of the third world countries through a populist movement could move in a more advanced and different direction than the traditional path followed by Western countries. Laclau has pointed out that the role of the migrant in urban centers in populist movements of Latin America is both dynamic and forward looking.

> Superficially this would seem to be the survival of old elements but in reality, behind this survival is concealed a transformation: these "rural elements" are simply the raw materials which the ideological practice of the new migrants transforms in order to express new antagonisms. In this sense, the resistance of certain ideological elements to their articulation in the dominant discourse of older urban sectors can express exactly the opposite of traditionalism: a refusal to accept capitalist legality which in this sense − reflecting the most radical of class conflicts − expresses a more "advanced" and "modern" attitude than European-style trade unionism.[10]

During the election campaign of 1970, Bhutto presented himself as a fairly radical socialist. To the charge that his socialism was foreign and against Islam, he replied with the slogan of Islamic socialism and constantly emphasized that the latter was the same as Masawat-i-Muhammadi (equality as preached by the Prophet Muhammad). In the early stages the party emphasized its leftist leanings. In a Mochi Gate meeting in Lahore, the slogans displayed were

> Who is the destroyer of the temples of capitalism and landlordism? Zulfikar Ali Bhutto. East is Red and Left. Every man is demanding food, clothing, and shelter. Arise and awaken the poor people of my world. American imperialists, stop your war in Vietnam. Islam zindabad [long live Islam]. Islamic massawat zindabad [long live Islamic equality].[11]

However, during the campaign itself certain differences between the left and moderate factions of the party had emerged over questions like how radical the land reforms should be and the desirability or otherwise of giving party tickets to Sindhi and Punjabi landlords. In the eyes of certain leftist radicals in the party, Bhutto was willing to curb capitalism but was somewhat averse to the idea of curbing landlordism unduly and particularly the influence of landlords in politics.

After the election, when told that his opponents attributed his political success to the financial support of Peking, Bhutto laughed off the allegation and said:

> The most angry people in Pakistan today are the communists for they know I have stopped the tide of communism by introducing Islamic socialism in this country. . . . In fact I have done more to combat communism in Asia than the Americans in spite of all the resources and the money they have piled into this part of the world. Before these elections the choice in Pakistan was a straight one between communism and capitalism. . . .
>
> But don't think I am watering my socialist concepts down. I am a true socialist — a democratic socialist who believes in socialism on the Willy Brandt or British pattern.[12]

Thus, Bhutto was aware from the beginning that the political expectations and consciousness that his movement had aroused could create problems for his government later on. In December 1972, nearly a year after assuming office, one finds him complaining that communist cadres were trying to mislead the workers in Pakistan.[13] Industrial labor was not the only major problem and, in any case, was not so powerful that it could not be controlled by the vastly expanding police force, the Federal Security Force.

After the dismemberment of the country in December 1971, when East Pakistan broke away to become the state of Bangladesh, Bhutto must have felt that he needed even a more powerful state apparatus than that of his predecessor, Ayub, under whom he had served as foreign minister. Both Pakistan's military and the police machinery had to be expanded considerably in order to suppress all threats to the security of the state arising either from urban unrest or separatist forces in the Frontier and Baluchistan.

In order that his own policies and directives should be carried out without any delay or challenge to his authority, a powerful instrument like the Civil Service of Pakistan should be eliminated insofar as its monopolistic hold over certain jobs and positions was concerned. He abolished its separate and prestigious cadre, and its officers were to be treated in the same manner as any other central civil servants. In order to establish his control over the economy, he undermined the influence of the big landlords through his land reforms and the economic power of the big industrialists through his nationalization of 31 industrial concerns in 10 basic industries.

THE BONAPARTIST STATE

Every since Ayub seized power in 1958, Pakistan was being governed by a Bonapartist regime. By this is meant not just the rule of an arbitrary dictator but the rule of a leader who derived his power and authority from a well-established institution like the army, in the case of Ayub, or from a political movement, in the case of Bhutto. However, the source of power and authority like the army or the movement does not explain fully the nature of such a Bonapartist state. The effectiveness of such a state depends upon how the leader manipulates or brings under control certain institutions like the bureaucracy and the army and mobilizes and controls the economy and some of the nascent classes represented in it by altering or modifying the dominant modes of production, like the capitalist mode, in the case of industry, and the feudal mode, in the case of agriculture. Based on such an analysis, Table 5.1 compares the characteristics of the less advanced Bonapartist state of Ayub with the more advanced Bonapartist state of Bhutto.

Various theories have been put forward regarding the nature of the postcolonial state. One such theory is that of Hamza Alavi, who draws his data almost exclusively from Pakistan in support of his theoretical propositions. He states:

> The central proposition I wish to emphasize is that the state in the postcolonial society is not the instrument of a single class. It is relatively autonomous and it mediates between competing interests of the three propertied classes — the metropolitan bourgeoisies, the indigenous bourgeoisie, and the landed classes — while at the same time acting on behalf of all of them in order to preserve the social order in which their interests are embedded, namely the institution of private property and the capitalist mode as the dominant mode of production.[14]

According to Alavi, the postcolonial state was relatively autonomous and mediated between competing interests of the various propertied classes. One cannot describe the role of Bhutto's Bonapartist state principally in terms of

TABLE 5.1
Comparison of State Government Under Ayub and Bhutto

Less Advanced Bonapartist State (Ayub)	
Economy	*State Instruments*
Industry — Expansion of the capitalist mode of production. Industrial concentration. 22 big industrial families.	Management of the army by its former commander-in-chief. Considerable autonomy of the Civil Service of Pakistan.
Agriculture — Slight modification of the feudal mode of production through highly conservative land reforms and the Green Revolution. Some penetration of the Feudal mode by the capitalist mode.	Classes that support the regime are the capitalists and the big landlords. Public policies are influenced by these two classes.

More Advanced Bonapartist State (Bhutto)	
Industry — The dominance of capitalists checked slightly through the development of the public sector and nationalization of some of the basic industries. Capitalist mode of production has not been altered. Remains intact in the private sector and is also present in the nationalized sector. Managers in public sector think like capitalists. What has emerged under the nationalized sector is a form of state capitalism	Greater political control and management of the army than under Ayub because the controller is a political leader.
More rights and facilities accorded to trade unions, but their militancy curbed by the considerably expanded police apparatus.	Autonomy of the civil service undermined.
Agriculture — Further dose of land reforms weakens the big landowners. Emergence of middle farmers who through subsidized inputs become rich and prosperous.	Expansion of the police force and the creation of the Federal Security Force.
Nascent class consciousness among the tenants and landless laborers who receive minor benefits from the Bhutto regime.	The Bonaparte wants to dominate the state structures rather than being dominated by the landowning and capitalist classes.

mediation between the various competing interests or classes. Bhutto was primarily motivated by animus dominandi, that is, through the aggrandizement of his own power, he wanted to control every major class or interest by weakening its power base and by making it subservient to his will and policies. He nationalized a number of major industries with the purpose of setting up not socialism but a kind of state capitalism. In this way he thought that he had weakened the power base of the industrialists. Through labor reforms, he granted certain benefits to labor but virtually took away their right to strike or any form of industrial action by setting up a police force like the Federal Security Force. He introduced what he termed radical land reforms and conferred other benefits on the tenants and poorer peasants so that all the agricultural interests like the landowners, the small peasants, the tenants, and landless laborers might look up to him as the source of all benefits. Through greater control over the civil services, the expansion of the police forces, and the political management of the army, the Bonapartist state had mobilized more effective and coercive power. It was true, as shall be seen later, that Bhutto failed to mobilize the full potential of the political power that he had through his control of a populist movement like the PPP.

One also needs to analyze how Bhutto came to terms with the external variable. Through his adroit policies he used unfavorable external developments like the oil price increase to his own advantage. It was true that Pakistan's balance of payments suffered as a result of the increase in oil prices, but the economic boom that the Middle East experienced in the wake of the oil price increase was capitalized on by Pakistan through its policy of increasing the outflow of Pakistani labor to the Middle East countries. Bhutto could also claim credit for having been successful in attracting Arab and Iranian investments.

Before an attempt is made to evaluate fully Bhutto's Bonapartist regime, an assessment will be given of some of his major policies such as those relating to land reforms, industry, and labor. Policies designed to increase central control over the regions are assessed in the next chapter.

AGRARIAN REFORMS

Under Bhutto's land reforms, landholdings were limited to 150 acres of irrigated land in the first phase (1972) and later to 100 acres in the second phase (1977). For unirrigated land, the ceiling was 300 acres in 1972 and 200 in 1977. The power and influence of the big and medium-sized landlords did not undergo any drastic change because of these land reforms. The limits were fixed in terms of the individual and not family holdings, with the result that many landlords managed to get around the limitations on ceilings by transferring land to relatives. According to one of the charges framed by the martial law against Bhutto, he and his family owned 2,200 acres of agricultural land. This became possible because Bhutto transferred part of his land to some trusted and dependable persons, making sure that the transfer remained no more than a paper transaction.

Similarly, it has been estimated that if allowances like tractor and tubewell allowances, in terms of produce index units allowable under the land reforms of 1972, were taken into account, a family of five members could possess irrigated land well above the fixed ceilings of 150 acres in the following districts:[15]

District	Number of Acres
Lyallpur	1,000
Multan	1,240
Saliwal	1,088
Lahore	765
Sukkar	2,620
Thatta	2,818
Muzzafargarh	2,000
D. G. Khan	1,550
Bhawalpur	1,240
Peshawar	765
Mardan	850
Larkana	1,973
Nawabshah	2,480

Thus the way the big and medium-sized landowners had been allowed to get around the matter of land ceilings explains how Bhutto was able to maintain their support. Bhutto was also shrewd enough to realize that because a large number of small peasants and tenants, particularly in Sind, continued to look up to their landlords as their political leaders, it was not in his interest to enforce the land reforms rigorously.

However, in Bhutto's political strategy all effective levers of political power should remain in his hands. He was prepared to use the landlords as his political agents but at the same time he wanted to make it very clear to the small peasants and the tenants that he, as the prime minister, was the source of all benefits and rights that had accrued to them under the new reforms. In November 1975, the prime minister announced that small landowners owning up to 12 acres of irrigated land or 25 acres of unirrigated land would be exempted from the payment of land revenue, local rates development cess, and all other assessments relating to land revenue. It was obvious that such a decision would confer automatic benefits on millions of farmers throughout Pakistan. It has been estimated that this decision would exempt 5 million farmers in Punjab, 1.74 million in the Frontier, and 0.53 million in Sind.[16] Thus, by this decision alone the prime minister must have won the support of as many as 7.27 million farmers in Pakistan. In addition, Bhutto offered 5 marlas of land for building houses to all those who were artisans, farm laborers, or tenants who did not own houses.

According to a government survey as many as 1.2 million people were eligible for allotment of such residential plots but the actual number of persons who applied for such plots was slightly over 800,000. In Punjab, according to government sources, over 600,000 plots were allotted to such applicants.[17] Thus, if the 7.27 million cultivators who had been exempted from land revenue and roughly 700,000 artisans, farm laborers, and tenants who had been given residential plots are added together, one could say there were over 8 million direct beneficiaries from these two measures.

It is not being suggested that because of these benefits the peasants, tenants, and other groups had become totally committed supporters of the Bhutto regime. What is being implied is the extent of support that Bhutto had created for himself. It may also be pointed out that a mere exemption from land revenue or the allotment of residential plots or lands made available to some thousands of farmers under the land reforms had not made any major dents in the poverty that existed in the rural areas. But Bhutto's great contribution was that he had aroused both a new hope and political consciousness among these classes that, given certain decisive policies on the part of the government, their lot could improve. According to the evidence produced by the supporters of the Bhutto regime, in a province like Sind the combined result of land reforms and other provisions under which the landlord was required to pay the tenant's share of land revenue besides providing seeds to the tenant was such that the cultivator's income had doubled.[18]

Table 5.2 indicates the number of families who benefited from the various agrarian reforms. It may be noted that when land was allotted to the peasants under the land reforms or residential plots under the 5-marla scheme, each such grantee was given an official certificate that clearly stated that these benefits had been conferred on him because Zulfikar Ali Bhutto, as chairman of the Pakistan People's party and as prime minister of Pakistan, had fulfilled the promises that he had made to the peasants of Pakistan. The certificate also read that after

TABLE 5.2
Estimated Redistribution of Cultivable Land

	Acres (millions)	Benefiting Families
Land reform, 1959 and 1972	1.4	130,000
Tribal area regulations, 1972	0.4	40,000
Land reform, 1977	0.4	40,000
Peasants charter, 1976	2.0	100,000

Source: These figures have been obtained from Federal Land Commission reports during 1976 and 1977.

centuries of servitude, the peasant was able to enjoy such rights and benefits in dignity and honor.[19] The parallel between this situation and that described by Karl Marx in *The Eighteenth Brumaire of Louis Bonaparte* is revealing.

> They [the peasants] are consequently incapable of enforcing their class interest in their own name, whether through a parliament or through a convention. They cannot represent themselves, they must be represented. Their representative must at the same time appear as their master, as an authority over them, as an unlimited governmental power that protects against the other classes and sends them rain and sunshine from above.[20]

Bhutto's plan was to bring the entire network of the agrarian economy under the control of the government. Between the flour milling, cotton ginning, and rice husking mills, which numbered nearly 2,000 throughout the country, and the millions of cultivators stood the arti (middleman), who made his profit in collecting such products and passing them on to the mills. The big landlords could send their products directly to the mills. The great majority of the mills were owned by private capitalists, though some were also owned by the landlords. In the eyes of Bhutto, all such middlemen should be eliminated. In July 1976, he announced that the government would nationalize cotton ginning and paddy husking mills and those flour milling operations that distributed flour to the consumer through the provisioning system. Bhutto declared that this extension of the public sector was "far larger than that of the nationalization of certain undertakings in the industrial sector in 1972" with a turnover of nearly 14 billion rupees.[21]

What sort of broad conclusions emerge from this analysis of Bhutto's agrarian policies? The first conclusion is that Bhutto was trying to ensure that, whether it was the landlord or the small peasant or the tenant or the artisan, everyone looked up to the supreme benefactor. It was from him that all benefits were received and to him all support should be given. Second, his policies were pursued in such a manner that every class, whether it was the landlord or the small peasant or the tenant or the landless laborer, received some benefits. Thus the antagonisms that might have been aroused between these classes because of his rhetoric were modified or kept under control by the way his land reforms were implemented. As seen, even though the size of the landholdings had been drastically reduced, the landlords were allowed to retain most of their lands within their families through various loopholes and evasions. It was true that not many peasants, tenants, and landless laborers had benefited directly from these land reforms, but they could find some satisfaction in the new benefits that were made available in the form of residential plots and the exemption of land revenue.

NATIONALIZATION OF INDUSTRIES

In January 1972, 31 industrial concerns in 10 basic industries were nationalized and placed under a Board of Industrial Management (BIM) chaired by the federal minister of production. Further streamlining took place in 1973 and 1974 and 10 sector corporations emerged out of such measures:

Federal Chemical and Ceramics Corporation (FCCP)
Federal Light Engineering Corporation (FLEC)
National Design and Industrial Services Corporation (NDISC)
National Fertilizer Corporation of Pakistan (NFCP)
Pakistan Automobile Corporation (PACO)
Pakistan Industrial Development Corporation (PIDC)
Pakistan Steel Mills Corporation (PASMIC)
State Cement Corporation of Pakistan (SCCP)
State Heavy Engineering and Machine Tool Corporation (SHE & MTC)
State Petroleum Refinery and Petrochemical Corporation (PERAC)

This meant that basic industries of a capital-intensive nature like iron and steel, basic metals, heavy engineering, electrical equipment, automotive assembly and manufacture, tractor assembly and manufacture, chemicals, petrochemicals, and natural gas were placed beyond the purview of the private sector. The private sector was thus restricted mainly to textiles, light engineering, manufacture of paper, and consumer goods industries such as sugar and cigarettes.

It may be seen from Table 5.3 that the public sector industrial investment constituted only 7 percent of total industrial investment in 1971-72, but by 1976-77 in percentage terms it had increased by more than 10 times and constituted 71 percent of total industrial investment. Private industrial investment

TABLE 5.3
Private and Public Sector Industrial Investment (in millions of rupees, current prices)

Year	Private	Public	Total	Public Investment as Percentage of Total
1971-72	1,235	99	1,334	7
1972-73	1,019	111	1,130	10
1973-74	1,023	391	1,414	28
1974-75	1,437	1,065	2,502	43
1975-76	1,818	3,182	5,000	64
1976-77	1,795	4,315	6,110	71

Source: Data obtained from Statistics Division, Ministry of Finance.

starting from as high as 93 percent of total industrial investment in 1971-72 declined to 29 percent of total industrial investment in 1976-77. This decline in private investment was largely caused by the continuing fear of further nationalization. In spite of government assurances to the contrary after the first spurt of nationalizations in 1972, other sectors like shipping, banking, and vegetable ghee were nationalized in subsequent years. Another constant complaint of the private sector was the rapid cost inflation brought about by higher wage demands and lower labor productivity. Following these national-izations and the erosion of confidence on the part of the private sector, there took place a considerable flight of capital to the Middle East and Britain.

Explaining the objectives of the first major nationalizations of basic industries in 1972, Bhutto declared:

> My Government is committed to eliminate the concentration of economic power in order that no single entrepreneur or a group of entrepreneurs should obtain control of the strategic heights of the economy and use this dominant position against the public interest.[22]

It was significant that Bhutto's declaration was couched in negative terms, that is, he was thinking mainly in terms of denying to the private sector the control of the strategic heights of the economy. He was not thinking in terms of the public sector occupying the commanding heights of the economy with a view to determining the direction of the rest of the economy along certain developmental lines.

His pronouncements often created the impression that he and his advisers had not thought the strategy through. As has been suggested earlier, the Bona-partist regime was more interested in amassing power and denying it to its opponents than in thinking what it should do with the amassed power. From the kind of industries that were assigned to the 10 sector corporations, one could see that they were all heavy, capital-intensive industries and therefore not likely to generate much employment. By the end of December 1976, the total employ-ment of the 10 sector corporations belonging to the BIM group was 61,731. One could see the relatively insignificant contribution that the corporations made to the overall employment situation in Pakistan when the annual increase in the country's labor force was supposed to be around 600,000. Similarly, it has been estimated that the biggest public sector project, the Karachi Steel Mill with a capital cost of $1.4 billion, and fertilizer projects costing $200 million each, were so capital intensive that the investment cost per job amounted to $100,000 to $300,000.

One would also expect that one of the major social benefits created by the public sector industries would be the provision of inexpensive consumer goods for the common man. The private sector in a country like Pakistan was not likely to initiate or invest in industries producing inexpensive consumer goods that figured prominently in the budget of the poorer sections because of the relatively low profit margins in such industries. Therefore it was incumbent on the public sector and a government committed to the promotion of socialism that such goods were made available for the betterment of the living standards of the lower-income groups. One could see that with its concentration on heavy industries, the public sector was not likely to pay much attention to this objective. In fact, promotion of heavy industries and the overriding concern about developing an industry like steel created the impression that the government, dominated by middle- and upper-class values and interests, was largely interested in using state power to enhance Pakistan's national prestige and power and create jobs for professional and middle-class groups like lawyers, engineers, and other technicians.

Bhutto's rhetoric was often directed against the follies of capitalism. As a pragmatic politician, he would also extol the virtues of a mixed economy under which the public and private sectors would coexist harmoniously. However, even the public sector in several respects tended to be a confusing mixture of capitalist practices and principles with a strong overlay of bureaucratic control. Even though the boards of directors of enterprises nationalized in 1972 were abolished, shareholders still continued to have their investments in 23 of the 53 units in production under the BIM group. The highest concentration of private shareholding was in the light engineering sector where 40 percent of the shares was in the hands of private investors. It may be noted that the government tried to create the impression that because BIM was making dividend payments to the shareholders, the public sector enterprises were being managed efficiently and on sound business principles. In 1973, even though the enterprises had lost money to the tune of Rs. 37 million, BIM distributed Rs. 19 million as dividends. For subsequent years, dividends paid as a percentage of net profits after tax were 69 percent in 1974, 39 percent in 1975, and 72 percent in 1976.

One could see that the kind of socialism introduced under the Bhutto regime was designed not so much to usher in a socialist society as it was to bring in state capitalism. State capitalism would obviously enhance the power of the Bonaparte and would not lead to any structural changes either in the economy or the society. From the very beginning it was stated that the state enterprises would be run along sound commercial lines under which there would be decentralized management and the management control tools would be built around budgets and corporate planning. In the early stages, with the exception of matters pertaining to labor and employment, managers tended to enjoy considerable autonomy. It was significant that many managers from the private sector were keen to serve under this kind of state capitalism. The former chairman of the National Fertilizer Corporation expressed his views on how managers should be trained to develop both technical expertise and at the same time the capacity to maximize decentralization and delegation of authority in an enterprise.

You take an academically qualified trainee, you make him a specialist, i.e. one who knows more and more about less and less; then you gradually enlarge his scope and vision and develop him into a manager of a department or a division and then finally into a top manager, one who knows less and less about more and more.[23]

Later this state capitalism became riddled with state bureaucratic practices and tight controls resulting in the erosion of decentralized management. Matters like day-to-day operations relating to expenses and spare parts replacements could no longer be administered by the operating units and decisions for these matters had to be referred to the higher authorities in the sector corporations.

All this suggests that under this system of mixed economy, the public enterprises had not developed any unique or special management system. In matters of administration and management, they tended to rely almost completely on the norms and practices of the private enterprise system. The underlying assumption was that the private sector almost always operated on sound business principles and therefore was efficient, whereas the public sector could only be efficient if it conformed to the norms and practices of the private sector. It was conveniently forgotten that the BIM inherited both from the private sector and the Pakistan Industrial Development Corporation a number of enterprises that were by no means highly efficient or profitable. Above all, the dynamism and high profits that the private sector took credit for in the 1960s were largely the result of the government policy of protection and subsidies that had been designed to pamper such enterprises. One could say that almost all the manufacturing value added by the private sector in Pakistan during the 1960s could be attributed to protection. It has been estimated that the manufacturing share in the gross national product in Pakistan in 1963-64 would drop from 7 percent at domestic prices to only 0.4 percent if it were measured in terms of world prices.[24]

It was clear that the state capitalism that developed in Pakistan in the form of public enterprises was neither fully fledged socialism nor efficient capitalism. It was not socialism in the sense that it had not basically changed the structure of the economy or raised the living standards of the lower-income groups by setting up new industries for the manufacture of basic consumer goods. Similarly, the employment that it generated was insignificant as compared to the overall needs of Pakistan. The complaint of the business groups, on the other hand, was that with very few exceptions most of the chairmen of the public corporations were civil servants without any business experience. The managing directors were also bureaucrats "who have not served in factories in their entire practical lives."[25] However, on balance, it must be said that as a result of the policies and measures initiated by the Bhutto regime, public sector enterprises had become an integral part of Pakistan's economy and polity. In the future the debate could only be about the degree of public control over industry and economic life that was consistent with national interests and economic efficiency.

In a way, Bhutto had tilted the political balance in favor of socialism and nationalization of industries. If socialism and nationalization of industries had not brought about many tangible benefits to industrial labor and lower-income groups, at least expectations had been aroused that the state could take over certain sectors of the economy to ensure a more equitable distribution of resources and economic power. Again, as a result of the rhetoric of Islamic socialism and the discomfort the business and industrial groups faced following the nationalization of industries, there had taken place in Pakistan a polarization between the conservative parties like the Muslim League, the Jamaat-i-Islami, and the Tehrik-i-Istaqlal and other less conservative and even radical groups that existed within the PPP. The PPP was being attacked because it was not a genuine organization but a party that was coming under increasing influence of the landowning groups.

LABOR POLICY

Table 5.4 indicates the number of workers employed in the principal industrial areas of Pakistan in 1970-71. The table shows that workers were concentrated in the industrial cities of Karachi, Lahore, Faisalabad, Multan, and Peshawar.

In Karachi and Lahore, there were two areas — Landhi-Korangi in Karachi and Kot Lakpath in Lahore — that emerged as the main centers of both labor concentration and potential labor turbulence. It may be noted that there was a steep increase in both the number of trade unions and their membership during the Bhutto period, 1972-77. In 1972, there were 4,452 trade unions with 525,062 members, whereas in 1976 there were as many as 8,611 trade unions

TABLE 5.4
Employees in Major Groups and Industries in Pakistan, 1970-71

Number of Reporting Establishments	3,549
Number of Persons on Last Payroll (June 1971)	421,206
Average Daily Employment	427,411
City	
Karachi	132,953
Lahore	38,068
Faisalabad	45,699
Multan	27,517
Peshawar	12,964

Source: Data furnished to the author by the Planning Commission, Government of Pakistan, in 1976.

with a membership of 718,331. Some of the trade union leaders were left-leaning and nearly all of them had political links. It was well known that a number of trade union leaders through their links with certain leftist leaders in Karachi and Lahore had campaigned for the Pakistan People's party in the general elections of 1970 when Bhutto had been extremely generous in his promises to industrial labor.

The Bhutto government introduced labor legislation through which benefits like medical coverage, compensation for injuries at work, compulsory group insurance, and certain safeguards against arbitrary termination of employment were made available to labor during 1972-73. Under the Labor Law (Amendment) Ordinance of 1975, certain measures were introduced to check undue proliferation of trade unions, and additional protection to the worker was offered by allowing him or the collective bargaining agent to make representation to the employer and the labor court in the case of suspension, layoff, or other labor disputes.

During the anti-Ayub campaign of 1969, labor had played a prominent part, and during subsequent years, as a result of strikes and the PPP rhetoric, had become increasingly confident that they could extract acceptance for their demands through organized militancy. In addition, there were a number of explosive ideas in the air. There was the widely believed notion that the capitalist had been unduly protected and pampered by the government to fleece the consumer and exploit the worker. In interviews with some of the trade union leaders, it was constantly emphasized that the Pakistani industrialist had not amassed his wealth through hard work and ingenuity. He was a tax evader who had also indulged in wholesale pilferage of publically provided power and electricity. Bhutto, through his actions and rhetoric, had aroused the expectations of industrial labor. In January 1972, a number of industries were nationalized. In the same month the public watched on television a former general, a chairman of the Gandhara Industries (the plant that assembled GM cars), and a few other industrialists all handcuffed and being taken into custody on various charges. In May, Bhutto waxed eloquent on "the spirit of the Paris commune" and proclaimed May Day a national holiday.

With these exhortations and some of the concessions either already on the statute books or in the process of being enacted, labor launched their militant campaign of gherao (forcible confinement of owners and management in the factory by workers until they agreed to their demands) during May-June 1972. Under a well-disposed PPP government, the workers thought that militancy and threats to paralyze or even destroy factories and industrial property would be effective in ensuring the acceptance of their demands for higher wages and security of employment. They probably felt justified in adopting this course of action because the conspicuous consumption they had witnessed among their employers and the admission of the previous government that Ayub's industrial policies had resulted in increasing industrial and income concentration had led them to the conviction that the system was based on outright exploitation.

This kind of labor militancy and attack on private property sent shock waves not only among business circles but also among conservative newspapers supporting parties like the Jamaat-i-Islami. Some of the moderate and conservative members of the PPP were also alarmed by these developments. One of them, Chaudhri Muhammad Hanif Khan, read extracts from editorials of newspapers dated May and June 1972 during the budget discussions in the National Assembly. All the editorials deplored the extreme and violent forms of labor militancy. A Jamaat paper, the *Jasarat,* emphasized that industrial labor led by certain trade union leaders had indulged in destruction and plunder of property and resorted to callous and barbarous violence and killing. "The government should be just as concerned about the protection of lives and property of the management as it is about the rights of industrial labour."[26] In October 1972, the government unleashed both police and paramilitary forces in crushing this militancy. Fifteen workers were killed and several thousands arrested. Strikes, factory takeovers, and violence continued in a spotty and sporadic fashion throughout 1973-75.

The question that needs to be raised is, had industrial labor become so aggressive and militant that they provoked even a prolabor regime like that of Bhutto into taking strong measures against them? A white paper published by the martial law regime, while referring to the labor problem that existed in Karachi in June 1972, described the situation as follows:

> A typical example was the firing incident in an industrial establishment in Karachi in June, 1972 in which at least 12 workers were killed. All that the workers were agitating for was the payment, along with the wages, of the 2.5 per cent share of the profits to which they were entitled under Mr. Bhutto's own labour policy. The protest was a signal for arrests and firing.[27]

If the workers were agitating for something to which they were entitled under the government labor policy, why did the government resort to arrests and firing? This suggests that Bhutto did not want them to develop their own organizational power. He did not want to create the precedence of the trade unions successfully pressuring the government and management into accepting their demands through strikes and other forms of industrial action. In the Bonapartist state "all power to the people" flowed from the Bonaparte.

In the Kot Lakpath area of Lahore, industrial labor developed such a well-knit organization under the leadership of the well-known trade union leader Abdul Rahman, that it was often described as a state within a state. One of the trade union leaders reported to the author that the trade union organization administered justice, maintained law and order, and sometimes rendered the police organization ineffective in the area. When Abdul Rahman was killed on April 30, 1974, industrial labor organized such a mammoth procession on May

Day that the Federal Security Force was posted throughout Lahore. The processionists gave vent to their anger by raising slogans against the PPP and Bhutto. The Bhutto regime, however, was able to establish its firm control over industrial labor largely through a combination of coercion and economism. The Federal Security Force was used to suppress trade union militancy. In addition, many trade union leaders were pressured into joining the PPP.

The Bhutto regime used the pricing policy quite deliberately as an instrument of urban pacification. Bhutto, as a minister in the Ayub government, knew that as long as economic growth accompanied by stable prices continued, the Ayub regime did not encounter any social unrest. It was probably because of the inflationary conditions and the substantial fall in real wages that followed the Indo-Pakistan war of 1965 that the Ayub regime had to face urban unrest and was eventually overthrown. When Bhutto became head of the government in December 1971, Pakistan not only faced an inflationary situation resulting from the war in East Pakistan but also a steep devaluation of its currency of about 139 percent in May 1972. The consumer price index soared throughout 1972-75. Apart from the steep rise in the price of crude oil that hurt the middle-income groups, the Bhutto government had to be particularly mindful of increases in import prices of commodities like wheat (149 percent), edible oils (187 percent), and fertilizer (280 percent) because these prices had a more direct bearing on the consumption levels of the lower-income groups.

The government made a skillful use of the mechanisms of price control and stabilization in the sense that even though the Essential Commodities Control Order of 1971 empowered it to control prices of 40 different products, it relied more on the mechanism of price stabilization and less on direct price controls. Only about 10 percent of the value of products sold in Pakistan came under the purview of direct price control because price controls were too difficult to administer. The government also devised a system of wage-price packages in an attempt to link wages with prices in such a way that periodic adjustments were made in a number of taxes, in wage rates for different classes of workers, and price increases on products like kerosene, diesel oil, gasoline, vegetable ghee, gas, electricity, and sugar. Similarly, in April 1975, when the government increased the prices of wheat, vegetable ghee, and sugar, it announced an adjustment in wages as well.

Under the price stabilization program, the Trading Corporation of Pakistan imported certain products to expand domestic supplies and thus kept prices at relatively low levels. In addition, the government subsidized the domestic prices of some of these imported and essential products in such a way that their prices were maintained below imported costs. Subsidies on imported and essential products involved the government in enormous expenditures of Rs. 3.8 billion during the fiscal year 1975. It may be noted that 60 percent of the government's subsidies were offered on an essential product like wheat. Food subsidies, particularly those on wheat, increased steadily from 1972 to 1975, but were reduced in 1976. The government decided in April 1975 to increase the procurement price for wheat by 45 percent and that for rice by over 50 percent. Bhutto defended this decision by pointing out that continuation of heavy subsidies would have resulted in heavy deficit financing leading to increasing inflationary pressures.[28] It was significant that the government announcement of these price increases triggered a series of protests and demonstrations organized by industrial labor in Lahore and railway workers in Rawalpindi and Lahore.[29] These protests, though massive, did not continue too long.

One could see how potentially turbulent the industrialized urban areas had become in the Pakistan of the 1970s in that for the first time one of the main focal points of the government's pricing policy and subsidies was industrial labor. Material benefits combined with the threat to use the Federal Security Force to crush any organized or massive labor militancy kept industrial labor in a state of sullen resignation. The Sind labor secretary reported in February 1978: "There was complete industrial peace in the Sind province, no lock-out during 1976-77, the number of strikes declined from 68 in 1976 to 43 in 1977."[30] However, Bhutto had to pay a price for the unenthusiastic acceptance of his policies that he had extracted from industrial labor. When his government was faced with a massive onslaught from the demonstrations organized by the Pakistan National Alliance during the spring of 1977, industrial labor and the trade union organization that had benefited from his labor legislation and pricing were unwilling to come out in their thousands in his defense.

AUTOCRACY AND COERCION IN THE NAME OF NATIONAL INTEREST

In an interview granted to the well-known Italian journalist Oriana Fallaci, Bhutto admitted that he was often torn by many conflicts, which were a part of his mental makeup:

> There are many conflicts in me — I'm aware of that. I try to reconcile them, overcome them, but I don't succeed and I remain this strange mixture of Asia and Europe. I have a layman's education and a Muslim's upbringing. My mind is Western and my soul Eastern.[31]

If Bhutto had been more candid and laid bare his weaknesses further, he would have added that, with all his education and desire to promote public good, he had not been able to overcome some of the feudal habits that he had imbibed from his upbringing. Bhutto himself has provided glimpses of the paradox that lay at the heart of his personality. In his death cell Bhutto wrote:

> On my twenty-first birthday on 5th January 1948, I received in Los Angeles two birthday gifts from Larkana. One was an expensive set of

five volumes of Sloane's biography of Napoleon Bonaparte. The other
was an inexpensive pamphlet. From Napoleon I imbibed the politics
of power. From the pamphlet I absorbed the politics of poverty. The
latter ended with the words, "Workers of the world unite. You have
nothing to lose but your chains. You have a world to win."[32]

However, it seems that even though Bhutto was torn between his fascination
for personal power and the desire to render public service, he tended to resolve
this tussle in favor of greater and greater personal power because he was so
carried away sometimes by public adulation and sometimes by self-glorifiaction
that he believed that he had mobilized all this power for public good. Bhutto
was so enthralled by the exercise of power that it seemed that one of his main
motivations in promoting the public good was the expectation that this would
bring him greater power and a place in history. One cannot do better than to
quote him:

> Anyway look, you don't go into politics just for the fun of it. You go
> into it to take power in your hands and keep it. Anyone who says the
> opposite is a liar. Politicians are always trying to make you believe that
> they're good, moral, consistent. Don't ever fall in their trap. There's
> no such thing as a good, moral, consistent politician. . . . The rest
> is boy-scout stuff, and I've forgotten the boy-scout virtues ever since
> I went to school.[33]

Thus Bhutto became so absorbed in the remoreseless pursuit of power that
outwitting one's opponents or outright dissimulation and even coercion became
his stock-in-trade. "Have you ever seen a bird sitting on the eggs in the nest?
Well, a politician must have fairly light, fairly flexible fingers, to insinuate them
under the bird and take away the eggs. One by one. Without the bird realizing
it."[34] All this cunning, remorselessness, and inner irresponsibility turned out to
be his undoing, and the ultimate price he paid for it was his life.

Bhutto's desire for power was reinforced by two factors. First, as the first
Sindhi prime minister, he felt insecure because he was never sure whether the
Punjabis would continue to support him. Second, like his predecessor, General
Ayub, he was convinced that, given the social and political heterogeneous
conflicts of Pakistan, only a strong centralized government presided over by an
unassailable president or prime minister could keep the country united. In spite
of the denunciations that he often hurled against Ayub in his public speeches
and statements, one found that having spent the formative years of his public
and political life under the tutelage of and in the autocratic government of
Ayub, the political style[35] and system of Ayub continued to be his models.

The constitution of 1973 made it crystal clear that the kingpin of the entire
governmental structure, whether it concerned decision making in the central

government or whether it related to matters vis-a-vis the provincial governments, was the prime minister. As noted in Chapter 2, in 1953 the governor-general, exercising his discretionary power, dismissed the prime minister even though the budget presented by the same prime minister's government had been approved by the assembly. In 1954, the governor-general went so far as to dissolve the constituent assembly. Again, in 1957, the prime minister was removed by the president. The constitution of 1973 ensured that in the future no president would be able to act against the advice of the prime minister or issue any orders without the approval of the prime minister. The constitution made it clear that the advice of the prime minister was binding and all presidential orders relating to matters like dissolution of the National Assembly, the promulgation of ordinances when the National Assembly was not in session, and the declaration of a state of emergency in case of a threat to the security or financial stability or orders relating to other matters could only become valid if countersigned by the prime minister. Bhutto could argue that these provisions were not unusual. He was trying to ensure the unquestionable supremacy of the prime minister through the written constitution, whereas in other parliamentary governments these matters had been accepted through long-established conventions and traditions without being incorporated in the written constitutions.

It was in the matter of the dominance of the prime minister vis-a-vis the National Assembly that the constitution of 1973 departed fundamentally from the parliamentary norm. No other provision made the position of the prime minister impregnable against almost every eventuality that a parliamentary government was subject to as that which related to the motion of no-confidence in the prime minister. It was clearly stipulated in the constitution, Article 96 (5), that for a period of ten years from the commencing day of the constitution, that is, April 12, 1973, or from the holding of the second general election to the National Assembly, whichever occurred later, "the vote of a member, elected to the National Assembly as a candidate or nominee of a political party, cast in support of a resolution for a vote of no-confidence shall be disregarded if the majority of the members of that political party in the National Assembly has cast its votes against the passing of such resolution." This meant that as long as the prime minister enjoyed the support of the majority of the members of the Pakistan People's party in the National Assembly, he could not be ousted if a minority of the PPP members in the National Assembly decided to support a motion of no-confidence. Similarly, if another party supported the prime minister, its minority members could not support a motion of no-confidence against the prime minister because this would be considered as going against the wishes of the majority of that particular party. A motion of no-confidence could not be moved during a budgetary session and such a motion could not be reintroduced in the National Assembly until a period of six months had elapsed after its first rejection.

All this clearly indicated that the prime minister could neither be controlled by the president nor challenged by the assembly. The latter feature was extraordinary because the essence of parliamentary government was that a prime minister was both accountable to and removable by the assembly. As suggested in Chapter 3, and as it has often been remarked, the government of Pakistan under Ayub was that of the president, by the president, and for the president. Could it be said that in the Bhutto regime the prime minister's position was equally dominant?

It seemed that Bhutto was not satisfied even with the power of the prime minister that was available to him through the constitution. During 1975-76, he had started thinking of bringing the parliamentary system under still greater control of the prime minister so that he could push certain pieces of legislation through the parliament with practically no delay or obstruction. This was disclosed to the author by Leslie Wolf-Phillips of the Department of Government, London School of Economics and Political Science, who had been invited by the prime minister to advise him on how to change the constitution along these lines.

In January 1976, the prime minister told Wolf-Phillips that he had made up his mind about converting the present system into a presidential system. However, he expected that this would be brought about after the election. It may be noted that there was some speculation in Pakistan during the National Assembly elections of 1977 that Bhutto was eager to win these elections by a landslide because he wanted a two-thirds majority in the assembly for the purpose of amending the constitution along presidential lines.

One of the provisions discussed and explored by Wolf-Phillips related to a clause being inserted in the constitution under which a candidate standing for National Assembly election would have to announce his intention of supporting a particular candidate for the presidency. According to Wolf-Phillips, the report that he submitted to the prime minister was interpreted by the prime minister as one not very helpful to his contemplated efforts to convert the constitution into a presidential form.

Bhutto knew that Pakistan was no longer a predominantly feudal or rural society where autocratic governments drawing their support principally from the police and the feudal landlords could keep the country politically quiescent. As one of the major leaders of the anti-Ayub movement during 1968-69, he had had firsthand experience of how students and industrial labor could topple a powerful government like that of General Ayub. During his own tenure of office, his government was confronted with demonstrations in Karachi over the language issue in 1972. He was also aware that the government of Indira Gandhi in India had developed highly mobile and well-equipped paramilitary forces called the Border Security Force, the Central Reserve Police, and the Industrial Security Force. The clearest rationale for the creation of the Federal Security Force in 1973 was provided by Bhutto himself in a note to his chief security adviser:

> The people come out on the streets on the least pretext. They violently defy established authority. Many of them have now become experts in the art of guerilla tactics. Bloody clashes lead to more bloody clashes and the situation deteriorates so much that *it becomes necessary to call upon the armed forces to intervene. Once the armed forces intervene they play the game according to their own rules* [author's italics]. It is necessary for a civilian Government to avoid seeking the assistance of the armed forces in dealing with its responsibilities and problems. The police force in our country is terribly inadequate and badly equipped.... We must make provisions for a first class force.[36]

During the debate of the bill on the Federal Security Force in the National Assembly, the minister for the interior argued: "Efforts have been made all along to topple this Government by disturbances, by language riots, by spreading regional feelings, by growing hatred, sectarian hatreds."[37] During the National Assembly debate, some of the leaders from the opposition pointed out that they had been present in public meetings in Rawalpindi, Multan, and Lahore that had been disrupted by the Federal Security Force.[38] Later, during a National Assembly session in November 1975, when the opposition members voiced their bitter opposition to the way the government was pushing through a constitutional amendment limiting dissent, the Federal Security Force was brought in and several protesting opposition members were beaten and physically ejected from the assembly.[39]

Table 5.5 indicates that the expenditure on the Federal Security Force increased from Rs. 36.4 million during 1973-74 to Rs. 107.7 million for 1976-77, an increase of 296 percent. It may also be seen from the table that the expenditure on civil armed forces increased from Rs. 192.5 million during 1974-75 to Rs. 388.2 million for 1976-77, an increase of 202 percent. It should be noted that the total expenditure on police and security by the central government amounted to Rs. 521.8 million for 1976-77. This expenditure did not include expenditures on police and security incurred by the various provinces. As compared to the central government expenditure of Rs. 521.8 million on police and security for 1976-77, the entire allocation on education (which included both federal and provincial allocations) in the annual plan for 1976-77 was only Rs. 617.7 million. The allocation for both federal and provincial health programs in the annual plan for 1976-77 was Rs. 771.9 million.[40]

A popularly elected government committed to the rapid improvement of public well-being was spending only Rs. 95.9 million more on education than on police and only Rs. 250.1 million more on health than on police. This was a strange commentary on the system of social priorities that the government of Pakistan was pursuing, considering the fact that Pakistan had an adult literacy

TABLE 5.5
Police and Security Expenditure

	1973-74 (Rs.)	1974-75 (Rs.)	1976-77 (Budget estimate, in rupees)
Intelligence Bureau (Cabinet Division)		(1)	25,839,200
Federal Security Force	36,467,531 Civil armed forces		(2) 107,786,600
Police (Coast Guards and Rangers)		96,266,705	108,633,000
Frontier Watch and Ward		96,294,939	279,627,000
Total civil armed forces		192,561,644 (3)	388,260,000
Total expenditure on police and security (1, 2, and 3)			521,885,800

Source: For 1973-74 figures, see Finance Division, *The Budget 1975-76: Demands for Grants and Appropriations* (Islamabad: Government of Pakistan, 1975), p. 218. For 1974-75 and 1976-77 figures, see Finance Division, *The Budget 1976-77: Demands for Grants and Appropriations* (Islamabad: Government of Pakistan, 1976), pp. 5, 211, 215.

rate of only 21 percent, was 24 among 34 low-income countries of Asia and Africa in terms of literacy, and also occupied a similar rank in terms of life expectancy and percentage of population with access to safe water.[41]

It may also be noted that the defense expenditure for 1976-77 amounted to Rs. 8.1 billion, the great bulk of which was for defense services (slightly over Rs. 8 billion) and the rest for the ministry of defense and other items like aviation.[42] It must be borne in mind that this was not the total expenditure, as defense expenditures remained concealed under various other ministries like communications.

According to some of the Marxist writers, Marx designated Bonapartism as "the religion of the bourgeoisie" and regarded it as characteristic of all forms of the capitalist state. Because Bonapartism enabled the state to detach itself somewhat from the diverse factions of the dominant capitalist class, the state through this relative autonomy was better able to maintain and organize the hegemony of the capitalist class.[43] As noted earlier, Alavi applied this concept of the relative autonomy of the state to the neocolonial regimes in Pakistan. He argued that the state dominated by the bureaucratic-military oligarchy mediated between the competing demands of the three propertied classes — the metropolitan bourgeoisie, the native-comprador bourgeoisie, and the feudal land-owning class — and thus functioned in a relatively autonomous manner.

It was argued in Chapter 2 that General Ayub and his military organization, backed by enormous U.S. support through military and economic aid, were able to dominate the state apparatus as well as promote rapid economic development in the industrial and agricultural sectors in Pakistan. Thus one could see how a Bonapartist state emerged in a third world country like Pakistan that was not a developed capitalist state.

It has also been argued in the early part of this chapter that the Bonapartist state during the Ayub regime was less developed than it was during the Bhutto regime. In such an analysis not only the relative autonomy of the state apparatus as represented by the civil-military oligarchical institutions must be considered but also the relative autonomy of the Bonaparte as well. This relative autonomy of the Bonaparte was a more striking phenomenon of the Bhutto regime than it was in the case of the Ayub regime. First of all, Bhutto rode to power on the back of a populist movement at a time when the country was in a state of shock because of the military defeat at the hands of India and the separation of East Pakistan in December 1971. His relative autonomy was greater than that of Ayub because he had mobilized political support through a populist movement like the PPP, whereas Ayub had manufactured political support through his system of Basic Democracies. But in order to govern Pakistan, Bhutto thought he had to amass even greater power than what was available from his populist base. In fact, in order to keep his populist base under control he used both economism (wage and fringe benefits and subsidies) and police power. There were even more serious attacks from the rightist and Islamic forces through language and religious movements.

Bhutto organized the Federal Security Force not only to suppress such movements but also reduce his reliance on the army. Again, he was trying to increase his autonomy. He eliminated the monopoly of the Civil Service of Pakistan by throwing open top civil service jobs to all other civil servants and to those who had been brought in through lateral entry. In August and November 1973, the existing civil service cadres, including the CSP, were abolished and thousands of civil servants were amalgamated into the 22 pay grades of the new All Pakistan Unified Grades. Even though the CSP cadre was abolished, officers who belonged to this cadre were still occupying key positions in the center, the provinces, urban centers, and the districts. Bhutto weakened the power of these officers, particularly in the cities and the districts, by relying increasingly on police officers not only for the maintenance of law and order but also for coercing his political opponents and for rewarding the party faithfuls.

It has been discussed how Bhutto increased his hold over the agrarian sector through his land reforms and the various concessions like tax remission and residential plots that he offered to landless labor, tenants, and the small peasants. Even the big and medium-sized landowners were beholden to him because the land reforms could have been more radical and the legislation could have been much tougher in plugging the loopholes. It has also been indicated how, through nationalization of industries, he sought to break the economic power of the 22 families.

The fatal flaw in this grand design was that Bhutto, while retaining the majority of the mass support particularly in Punjab and Sind, failed to activate and mobilize the organizational support of the PPP. Being confident of the mass support, he tended to de-link his political power from the populist movement and became increasingly dependent on the coercive instruments of the state like the FSF and the army. He had not only antagonized significant sections of the trade union movement but also dismissed or imprisoned practically all the left-leaning leaders in his own party.[44] When his government was faced with a massive urban protest organized by mostly the petty bourgeoisie under the auspices of the Pakistan National Alliance during the spring of 1977, Bhutto had to rely primarily on the FSF and the army to suppress such a movement. In the kind of political polarization that Bhutto's policies and actions had brought about, the army threw its weight with the PNA and thus Bhutto was overthrown. These developments and their causes are analyzed at some length in Chapter 7.

NOTES

1. The term was put forward as a coherent concept by Karl W. Deutsch, "Social Mobilization and Political Development," *American Political Science Review* 55, no. 3 (September 1961).

2. Ibid., p. 583.

3. Ibid., p. 592.

4. Samuel P. Huntington, *Political Order in Changing Societies* (New Haven, Conn.: Yale University Press, 1968).

5. Ibid., pp. 250-55.

6. Deutsch, op. cit., p. 583.

7. The "development decade" was a self-glorification campaign launched by the Ayub regime to show what rapid economic strides Pakistan had made during the decade that Ayub was in power, 1958-68.

8. David Apter, *The Politics of Modernization* (Chicago: University of Chicago Press, 1965), p. 2.

9. Author's interview on February 9, 1971 with a leftist leader, Sheikh Muhammad Rashid, who later became a cabinet minister and also was made responsible for land reforms under Bhutto.

10. Ernesto Laclau, *Politics and Ideology in Marxist Theory: Capitalism, Fascism, Populism* (London: New Left Books, 1977), p. 157.

11. *Nusrat*, March 15, 1970, p. 15.

12. *The Times*, December 12, 1970.

13. Zulfikar Ali Bhutto, *Speeches and Statements, October 1, 1972-December 31, 1972* (Karachi: Government of Pakistan, 1973), pp. 197-98.

14. Hamza Alavi, "The State in Postcolonial Societies: Pakistan and Bangladesh," in *Imperialism and Revolution in South Asia,* ed. Kathleen Gough and Hari P. Sharma (New York: Monthly Review Press, 1973), p. 148.

15. *Al-Fatah*, May 25-June 1, 1972.

16. *Pakistan Economic Survey 1976-77* (Islamabad: Government of Pakistan, n.d.), pp. 191-92. The small number of farmers in Baluchistan have not been included.

17. *Pakistan Times,* April 30, 1977.

18. *Nusrat,* October 13-19, 1977.

19. The author has seen such certificates signed by the chief land commissioner, province of Punjab, dated October 28, 1974.

20. Karl Marx, *The Eighteenth Brumaire of Louis Bonaparte* (Moscow: Progress Publishers, 1972), p. 106.

21. *Prime Minister Zulfikar Ali Bhutto Address to the Nation on Take-Over of Large Flour Mills, Rice Husking, Cotton Ginning* (Islamabad: Government of Pakistan, 1976), p. 11.

22. Zulfikar Ali Bhutto, *Speeches and Statements,* April 1, 1973-August 13, 1973 (Karachi: Government of Pakistan, 1973), p. 3. Bhutto's phraseology is similar to that of Congress politicians in India except that they wanted their nationalized industries to capture the commanding heights to exercise countervailing power, whereas Bhutto seemed to be thinking first in removing the private sector from the heights that they had already occupied. For comments on Indian socialism, see Angus Maddison, *Class Structure and Economic Growth: India and Pakistan Since the Moghuls* (London: Allen & Unwin, 1971), p. 112.

23. S. Babar Ali, "Managers for the Public Sector," *National Seminar on Management of Public Enterprises* (Lahore: Pakistan Administrative Staff College, 1978), p. 2.

24. I. M. D. Little et al., *Industry and Trade in Some Developing Countries* (London: Oxford University Press, 1970), p. 5.

25. Khawaja Amjad Saeed, "Industrial Public Enterprises," *National Seminar on Management of Public Enterprises* (Lahore: Pakistan Administrative Staff College, 1978), p. 7.

26. *The National Assembly of Pakistan (Legislature) Debates,* vol. III, no. 22 (June 20, 1973), pp. 1585-89.

27. *White Paper on the Performance of the Bhutto Regime,* vol. III. *Misuse of the Instruments of State Power* (Islamabad: Government of Pakistan, 1979), p. 121.

28. *Pakistan Times,* April 10, 1975.

29. *Nasa-i-Waqt,* April 9, 11, 1975; *Pakistan Times,* April 10, 1975; *Lah-o-Qalam,* June 1975.

30. *Dawn,* February 4, 1978.

31. Oriana Fallaci, *Interview with History* (New York: Liveright, 1976), p. 202.

32. Zulfikar Ali Bhutto, *"If I Am Assassinated..."* (New Delhi, Vikas, 1979), p. 224. Bhutto had obviously read and reread William M. Sloane, *Life of Napoleon Bonaparte,* 4 vols. (New York: Century, 1896). Even though Bhutto was primarily a political leader, there were some striking similarities between Napoleon and Bhutto. Like Napoleon Bonaparte, Bhutto had also risen on the ladder of power through the support of certain patrons. Like Napoleon, Bhutto also found the country in disarray when he assumed charge. (For some of these striking similarities, see Sloane, vol. IV, pp. 220, 237.) Such similarities would always exist between two leaders, but what was significant was that Bhutto always seemed to admire Napoleon as a "complete man," and had probably one of the largest collections of books on Napoleon in the world.

33. Fallaci, op. cit., p. 206.

34. Ibid., p. 209.

35. One of Ayub's close advisers told the author that Ayub often referred to politicians and even some of his cabinet ministers as "pimps." Bhutto did not go this far, but the author has heard similar accounts of his contemptuous references to his cabinet ministers sometimes made in their presence.

36. *White Paper on the Performance of the Bhutto Regime,* vol. III, Annex 24, p. A-68.

37. *National Assembly of Pakistan (Legislature) Debates,* vol. III, no. 7 (May 31, 1973), p. 381.

38. Ibid., p. 390; ibid., vol. III, no. 9 (June 4, 1973), pp. 484-90; ibid., vol. III, no. 10 (June 6, 1973), pp. 635-38.

39. *The Guardian,* February 6, 1976.

40. Planning Commission, *Annual Plan 1976-77* (Islamabad: Government of Pakistan, 1976), pp. 181, 192.

41. World Bank, *World Development Report 1978* (Washington, D.C., 1978), pp. 108, 110.

42. Finance Division, *The Budget 1976-77: Demands for Grants and Appropriations* (Islamabad: Government of Pakistan, 1976), pp. 57-58, 60-64.

43. The statement that the author has paraphrased and tried to analyze is originally from Nicos Poulantzas, "Capitalism and the State," *New Left Review* 58 (November-December 1969): 74. Hamza Alavi also cites Nicos Poulantzas in "The State in Postcolonial Societies," in *Imperialism and Revolution in South Asia,* ed. Kathleen Gough and Hari P. Sharma (New York: Monthly Review Press, 1973), p. 160. Neither author cites the original work of Marx from which the remark that Bonapartism is the religion of the bourgeoisie has been taken.

44. Some of the noteworthy PPP leaders who fell from his favor were J. A. Rahim, a cofounder of the PPP and a cabinet minister was not only dismissed but assaulted by FSF personnel; Mukhtar Rana, a labor and peasant leader from Lyallpur remained in prison during most of Bhutto's tenure; Miraj Muhammad Khan, a well-known leader from Karachi who rose to be a minister of state, was imprisoned; and Mubashir Hasan, finance minister, and Khurshid Hasan Mir, minister for railways, were both removed from the cabinet.

6
PAKISTAN'S CENTRAL GOVERNMENT VERSUS BALUCHI AND PAKHTUN ASPIRATIONS

Chapter 2 described how the Muslim League and the force of Muslim nationalism under the charismatic leadership of Jinnah were not enough to overcome Pakhtun ethnic consciousness and therefore the Muslim League had to rely heavily on the Islamic armor to win the referendum in the North-West Frontier Province. In the second chapter it was found that in 1955 the civil-military oligarchy had to use outright coercive powers to impose the One Unit government on provinces like the North-West Frontier Province and Sind. And even after such tactics ethnicity intertwined with the economic factor continued to be a potent force resulting in the dissolution of the One Unit province of West Pakistan and the restoration of its separate provinces in November 1969.

In Chapter 4 there was an explanation of the causes that lay behind the steady and growing estrangement of East Pakistan and the eventual establishment of the independent state of Bangladesh in December 1971. The latter event cast such a traumatic spell on the government leaders that it was sometimes difficult for them to adopt a calm and statesmanlike attitude toward the problem of provincial autonomy. Bhutto, being himself a Sindhi, often claimed that he was sympathetic toward the aspirations for autonomy on the part of the provinces. However, Pakistan's Bonaparte with all his political adroitness could mostly think of what Karl Deutsch has called the muscle power of the state and had not sensitized himself to the nerves of Pakistan's diversity — the inchoate aspirations of the Baluchis or the more articulate demands of the Pakhtuns. As shall be seen, because of the lack of forbearance that Bhutto displayed in tackling the federal problem and the heavy reliance he placed on coercion rather than persuasion, Bhutto's contribution toward the resolution of the conflict between the center and the provinces turned out to be one of exacerbation rather than moderation.

In Chapter 1 the basic features of the Sandeman system as it operated in some of the Tribal Areas of the Frontier and in Baluchistan were discussed. This development of underdevelopment was brought about not primarily for economic reasons. Resurrection and bolstering of a decaying feudal system in the form of the sardari system were designed basically for military and geopolitical reasons. The Tribal Areas and Baluchistan should become a buffer zone between the British and other imperial powers like the Russians or the Germans who were inclined to cast their covetous glances at India.

Through the Sandeman or the sardari system, the British devised the lowest cost per unit of output method of pursuing and maintaining their imperial interests in that part of the world. The British could not afford to set up an elaborate civil administration with its deputy commissioners and a host of other officials in this vast area with its thin population. Therefore, the sardar was accorded almost absolute autonomy in the internal affairs of his area and tribe. The Khan of Kalat, who presided over the confederacy of Brahui sardars, was under the control of the political agent who arbitrated in all disputes that arose between the khan and the sardars as well as those among the sardars themselves. The sardars were responsible for raising their own levies for which they were paid salaries and allowances. The Sandeman system also guaranteed the presence of British forces in Baluchistan. This was, in brief, the system that Pakistan and the Bhutto government had inherited.

CONFLICT BETWEEN GROWING BALUCHI ASPIRATIONS AND THE CENTRAL GOVERNMENT

Baluchistan with its little over 134,000 square miles made up about 40 percent of the area of Pakistan. The population was 2.4 million according to the census of 1972. It was ethnically quite diverse. The majority of the Baluch people lived outside Baluchistan with most of them concentrated in Karachi and the western districts of Sind. Baluchi was spoken by nearly a third of the population of Baluchistan. The main Baluch tribes were Mengals, Marris, Bugtis, Mohammad Hasnis, Zehris, Bizenjos, and Raisanis. Brahui, which was a different language from Baluchi, was spoken by the Brahui tribes in Kalat division. Even if Brahui aspirations to maintain their linguistic and tribal identity were to converge with Baluchi nationalism, there were grounds for conflict between Pakhtun and Baluchi nationalisms. The indigenous Pakhtun tribes of Baluchistan, who spoke Pushtu and lived in the northern belt of Baluchistan, made up more than 60 percent of the population in Quetta division. This was the most settled part of the province. The Pakhtuns were active in commerce and more prosperous than the Baluchis.

Political and tribal diversity was matched by economic underdevelopment. In Kalat district there were hardly any literates among the Brahuis in 1951, and in the 1961 census only 4,000 out of nearly half a million were registered as literate. Prior to partition, rural Baluchistan was indescribably poor, while urban Baluchistan was dominated by the Sindhi and Punjabi merchants who monopolized the military contracts and the commercial life of a city like Quetta. After partition, when most of the Sindhi Hindu merchants left, others like the Pakhtuns moved into the commercial life. During the Bhutto period the overwhelming majority of the Baluchi workers were outside Baluchistan — more than 100,000 in Karachi and 50,000 or more in the Gulf states. In the well-known fertile Pat Feeder tract of Kalat, land belonging to the indigenous population was acquired by military and civil bureaucrats from Punjab during the Ayub regime.

During the 1970-71 provincial assembly elections, the Baluchi and Brahui sardars belonging to the National Awami party (NAP) won 8 out of 20 assembly seats, thus constituting the largest single bloc but not the majority in the provincial assembly. In the Pakhtun areas the conservative candidates of the Jamiatul Ulama-i-Islam (JUI) were successful.

During April 1972, when Bhutto appointed the NAP governor, Mir Ghaus Bakhsh Bizenjo, and installed the NAP-JUI government under Sardar Ataullah Khan Mengal as chief minister, in addition to the underdevelopment of Baluchistan another important factor had surfaced. According to Bhutto, when he visited Iran, he was shown maps of Greater Azad Baluchistan by the Iranian government, including "the Baluchistan of Pakistan and Iran and a small strip of another country." This irredentist movement was being supported by a number of foreign countries.[1] In his letter of appointment to Governor Bizenjo, Bhutto stated: "Therefore, movements like the Azad Baluchistan Movement, however nebulous, should be firmly put down, and not be permitted to affect our relations with foreign powers, particularly friendly neighbouring countries."[2]

Just before the removal of the governor and the dismissal of the provincial government in Baluchistan on February 14, 1973, it was announced that the government had seized a huge cache of arms in the Iraqi Embassy. Sardar Akbar Khan Bugti, who was appointed the new governor of Baluchistan, disclosed that he, along with Bizenjo and Mengal, had been involved in a separatist movement and that they had tried to bring about separation from Pakistan with the help of foreign arms.[3] The Iraqi Embassy announced that the arms had not been intended for use in Pakistan. However, it seemed that the government did not officially emphasize this factor as a cause for the removal of the NAP government.[4]

Could one say that it was not so much any immediate threat from the irredentist movement that precipitated the dismissal of the NAP government as pressure from Iran? According to Wali Khan, who made this charge in the National Assembly as well as during his trial in the supreme court, Bhutto was reluctant to install the NAP government in Baluchistan and said; "I cannot hand over Baluchistan to NAP, because the Shahinshah of Iran does not approve of it."[5]

The major causes for the dismissal of the NAP government in Baluchistan could be discerned from some of the fundamental social and political contradictions that existed in the Baluchistan situation. First, there was the contradiction between the emerging regional Baluchi elites and the national elites of Pakistan. This contradiction had been further heightened by the emergence of the PPP government under Bhutto in which he mobilized political support of the provinces of Sind and Punjab. The civil-military oligarchy of the central government was predominantly Punjabi. The second contradiction was one between the large rural and the small urban masses of Baluchistan and the regional Baluchi elites like the sardars. One could not expect the provincial government dominated by the Bizenjo and Mengal sardars to address itself to the latter contradiction. Its main interest as the new provincial government of Baluchistan was to try to tackle the first contradiction by strengthening the economic and political infrastructure of the provincial government. Whether Baluchistan remained a part of Pakistan or emerged as a separate state, it had to make up for the years of underdevelopment that the British and their successors, the Pakistani regimes, had imposed on them.

One of the principal ways of reversing this process of underdevelopment and promoting the maximum economic development of Baluchistan was to create a new Baluchi bourgeoisie through capitalist development. One clear indicator of the thinking of the Bizenjo-Mengal government was the Baluchistan Mining Concessions (Acquisition) Bill of 1972, which was passed by the Baluchistan provincial assembly in January 1973. Although a public mining corporation to be controlled by the provincial government was envisaged in this bill, one of the clauses clearly stated: "The mining concession acquired under the Act may be granted to Government in partnership with a private company." The opposition charged that the government was primarily interested in victimizing certain sardars who had acquired mining concessions and that after bringing these concessions under the control of the provincial government, the government planned to invite Karachi capitalists like the Adamjees to run the acquired mines. The minister for mineral resources pointed out that this form of capitalist development had been the normal practice in both Pakistan and Iran.

I think it is ashaming [sic] too much if Baluchistan Govt. ask an American firm or a German firm or a Japanese firm to invest in Baluchistan because that will be' for the lot of the people? I think the Baluchistan Government is justified in adopting this method because this will not only ameliorate the lot of the labourers, but will also benefit the Government and this is the democracy to give to every man — that is better life.[6]

The kind of bitter conflict that developed between the newly established provincial government and the central government arose largely out of the first contradiction, namely, the desire of the regional elites to assert themselves against what they regarded as the encroachment of the central government. Both the *White Paper on Baluchistan* and the affidavit of the then chief of staff, General Tikka Khan, emphasized that the NAP government in Baluchistan, soon after it came to power in April 1972, got rid of non-Baluchi technical and administrative personnel like the police, teachers, and engineers. They also organized bands of local guards. The same documents disclosed that at about the end of 1972 Marri tribesmen looted farms that belonged to non-Baluchi settlers (mostly civil and military bureaucrats) in the Pat Feeder area. The white paper also charged that some of the chiefs of the Jamote tribe had informed the federal government that because they had opposed the NAP in the 1970 elections, they were apprehensive that the NAP government would try to crush them. This fear was confirmed in December 1972 when nearly 8,000 Jamotes were surrounded and besieged by tribal forces in which the Bizenjo and Mengal tribes to which Governor Bizenjo and Chief Minister Mengal belonged were prominent. In this operation against the Jamotes, the tribal forces were supported by the locally organized Baluchistan Dehi Mohafiz.

The Bhutto regime seemed to be dismayed by the vindictive action of the NAP government against the Jamote tribe in Baluchistan. However, these kinds of political vendettas had been practiced by both central and provincial governments in Pakistan and certainly the Bhutto regime was no exception to this modus operandi. Second, a certain amount of federal forbearance was expected of the Bhutto government because it should have realized that Governor Bizenjo and Chief Minister Mengal were tribal chiefs trying to establish themselves in their new positions by mobilizing political support and by restricting the political activities of their opponents. Having installed a provincial regime led by the sardars, it was not realistic on the part of the Bhutto regime to expect that the sardars would display scrupulous constitutional and political propriety in running their government.

Thus one could see that the conflict between the newly established regional elites and the central elites represented by the federal government had become almost irreconcilable. Given the external pressure from a country like Iran and the fear of the federal government that perhaps another form of Bengali separatism was in the making, it was not surprising that the Bhutto government decided to resort to military action. There is not much evidence that the Bhutto regime explored every possible avenue to reach a compromise with the Baluchi provincial government whereby a central government with its legitimate concerns could coexist with a provincial government committed to increasing provincial autonomy. As in other cases, Bhutto was interested in the aggrandizement of power, not in its sharing.

Military operations in Baluchistan began in May 1973. According to the *White Paper on Baluchistan,* the main centers of insurgency were the Jhalawan subdivision of Kalat district where Mengal tribesmen were active and the Marri area of Sibi district. In the beginning the total strength of the hard-core hostiles was about 400 Mengals and 500 Marris. "This number eventually grew to thousands but most of them were the sympathizers and carriers of supplies to the hardcore hostiles."[7] It has been estimated that during the peak period of insurgency in late 1974 nearly 55,000 Baluch insurgents (some 11,500 of them hard-core units) were engaged in fighting against the Pakistan army. The Pakistan military suffered 3,300 casualties and the Baluch guerrillas 5,300. "A total of 178 major engagements and another 167 lesser incidents during this little known mini-war were officially chronicled by the Islamabad authorities."[8] It was obvious that the Pakistan government had not only failed to crush completely the armed rebellion of the Baluchi guerrillas but also the use of combined superior fire power by the Pakistani and Iranian forces during the 1973-74 conflict had created deep-seated resentment and a desire for revenge among the Baluch guerrillas.

> "If we can get modern weapons," said guerrilla leader Mir Hazar at the Kalat-i-Ghilzai base camp in southern Afghanistan, "it will never again be like the last time. . . . Next time we will choose the time and place, and we will take help where we can get it. In the beginning the Bengalis didn't want independence, but if Pakistan continues to use force to crush us, we'll have no alternative but to go that way."[9]

It would not be fair to suggest that Bhutto was determined to bulldoze Baluchistan into abject submission. As seen, he did use certain political methods before he resorted to military action and, as shall be seen, he abolished the sardari system in order to mobilize political support and establish the political presence of the federal government in Baluchistan. However, even in the pursuit of these political strategies, Bhutto did not want colleagues to work with, but easily dispensable and totally docile instruments who would carry out his orders.

A clear example of his modus operandi was the way he appointed and later dismissed Sardar Akbar Khan Bugti. As pointed out earlier, when Bugti was appointed governor of Baluchistan in February 1973, he had admitted that he had been involved along with the dismissed leaders — Bizenjo and Mengal — in a separatist movement. Thus, of the three leading sardars in Baluchistan, all had been involved in a separatist conspiracy. Did Bhutto expect that Bugti, having undergone a total change in convictions, would now serve Pakistan's national interests? A poacher was now to function as a gamekeeper. Bugti had been convicted of murder and imprisoned in 1960.[10] A diplomat who admired Bhutto commented on his political shrewdness in enlisting the services of the chief of a tribe prone to intertribal violence and killing.[11]

Later, by December 1973, Bugti had outlived his usefulness. Bhutto had started military operations in Baluchistan and also started negotiating with the opposition leaders. Bugti felt that his position both as a governor and as a Baluch was being undermined. Bhutto's comments about Governor Bugti were revealing: "The present Governor is suffering from schizophrenia. He doesn't like having the government negotiate with the opposition. He's frightened now because he betrayed his old friends. Politics is a game of chess and Mr. Bugti played his chess badly."[12]

Certain secret negotiations that Bhutto conducted with the opposition leaders in Baluchistan in 1974 and how he pressured them into reaching a settlement with the government were disclosed by the martial law authorities in January 1979. Bhutto thought that it was proper to let certain members of the provincial assembly in Baluchistan retain their seats in the assembly even though they had been convicted in certain cases and thus were presumably disqualified from holding their seats in the assembly. As regards two NAP members of the provincial assembly, the secretary of the prime minister wrote in his memo: "The two seats in the Provincial Assembly could be used as a lever in obtaining a favourable settlement." The prime minister's comment in his own handwriting was "Exactly."[13]

Former Governor Bizenjo, former Chief Minister Mengal, and Khair Bakhsh Marri, president of the NAP in Baluchistan, were arrested on August 15, 1973. The charges against them had not been verified in the courts. These three political opponents were kept in prison without any trial and Bhutto tried to pressure them into a political settlement while they were in prison. Commenting on their three-year detention and such tactics, the Amnesty International report observed:

> There have been reports in the press that the government has offered the release of the three Baluchistan leaders in exchange for a political settlement. Mr Mengal stated before the Lahore High Court that a government emissary, Mohammed Amin Khoso, frequently visited the detained leaders and asked them to reach a settlement with the government (*Dawn*, 30 November 1974). The London *Times* of 29 August 1974 reported that Mr Bizenjo and Mr Mengal "refused to give up their opposition to Mr Bhutto, the Pakistan Premier, in return for their freedom." And, on 27 July 1974, "the Prime Minister held out an assurance that NAP leader Sardar Khair Baksh Marri would be released if he promised to give up his policy of opposing development work in the Marri areas . . . etc." (*Dawn*, 28 June 1974). Replying to a debate on Baluchistan in the Senate on 16 December, the Prime Minister confirmed that he had tried to bring the Baluchi leaders to the negotiating table.[14]

Did this report indicate the extent to which Bhutto could go in his coercive methods? Even if it were true that Sardar Marri had opposed development work in the Marri areas, how could he as a political leader make a public promise that if released he would not oppose development work?

Perhaps Bhutto would have defended himself by pointing out that all this coercion was for a great cause. He was suppressing the sardars not only for national integration but also for the protection of the small peasants, the tenants, and the serfs who had been oppressed. As seen, under the Sandeman system the sardars had been set up as omnipotent chiefs of their tribal fiefdoms mediating family disputes, handling trade for the whole tribe, and exercising power of life and death over everyone in the tribe. When Bhutto assumed charge of the government of Pakistan, the writ of the federal or the provincial government extended to no more than 134 of the 134,000 square miles that made up Baluchistan. Bhutto claimed that the abolition of the sardari system by his government, which was enacted by the National Assembly in May 1976, eliminated "the worst remnants of the oppressive feudal system."

This measure deprived the sardars and the khans of privy purses, compensations, grants, and so on. Tribal courts, jirgas, and jails were abolished. Tribal courts were replaced by judicial committees to administer justice in accordance with the regular laws of the country. Feudal practices like the tribes offering their lands to their sardar when he was installed as the chief of the tribe were done away with. Lands that were restored to the tribes ranged between 60,000 and 70,000 acres. The sardars had raised their own levies for which they had received allowances from the central government. Under the new act, the government could grant to any person such individual service allowance and thus could establish contact directly with the tribesmen without the sardars serving as intermediaries. Shishak, a tax that varied from one third to one sixth of the produce that the sardar could collect from his tribesmen regardless of the ownership of land, was also abolished.

The sardari system had a long history behind it and had become so firmly rooted in the attitudes and social culture of the tribesmen that it could not be eliminated by government fiat. It must also be borne in mind that Bhutto might have abolished some of the features of the sardari system but had continued to rely on the sardars as his agents in Baluchistan. The greatest of them was the Nawab of Kalat, who was appointed governor in 1974. Similarly, sardars like Raisani, Zehri, and the Jamsahib of Lasbella had served in high government offices during the Bhutto regime. A more important factor was the fact that an institution of ancient lineage like the sardari system could only be progressively eliminated through political means.

Bhutto's Pakistan People's party, to begin with, had no representation and even when members from other parties and independent groups were pressured into joining it, it had never reached the grass-roots level.[15] A more fundamental criticism of Bhutto's reform was that it did not seek to alter the pattern of landholding in Baluchistan. After the abolition of the sardari system, the sardar was expected to return all the lands that had been given to him by the tribe at the time of his installation as a sardar. But as the tribal chief and the feudal landlord, his landholdings were much more extensive than the land that might have been presented to him by the tribe. Under the new system, he might have ceased to be the sardar, but his position as a feudal landlord had a much better legal backing in terms of claims to his land than his original position of merely being a tribal chief. In addition, like his counterparts in Punjab and Sind, he was being brought in closer contact with the capitalists in Karachi. As their junior partner, his income in the trade of gems and marble was likely to increase by leaps and bounds.

However, it must also be noted that Bhutto's abolition of the sardari system and the rhetoric accompanying it did create a sense of liberation among the tenants, the landless laborers, and the workers in mines and oil fields. They had become aware that they had been exploited by the sardars. The abolition of the sardari system could perhaps turn out to be a modest beginning of the end of feudalism in Baluchistan.

PAKHTUN REGIONALISM OR SUBNATIONALISM

In the case of Baluchistan, it was noted how its diversity stood in the way of developing the Baluchi ethnic consciousness and sense of economic grievance into a cohesive regional or national force. In spite of the alleged links of the Baluch movement with the Baluchis in Iran and the military conflict with the Pakistan government, Baluchi regionalism was still in its nascent and amorphous stage. As compared to Baluchi consciousness, the Pakhtuns of the North-West Frontier Province could claim that their ethnicity was backed by greater historic depth as well as a greater sense of cohesion. There were supposed to be 12 million Pakhtuns straddling the northwest sector of the Pakistan-Afghanistan border. According to the 1972 census, the population of the Frontier was 8.38 million, of which approximately 76 percent were Pushtu-speaking Pakhtuns. Twenty-eight percent of the population of Baluchistan were also Pushtu-speaking.

The Pakhtuns held key positions in the civil and military bureaucracies of Pakistan, and in terms of influence and numbers were ahead of the two smaller provinces, Sind and Baluchistan, and were next to Punjab in these two institutions. Even though the Pakhtuns constituted 13.5 percent of Pakistan's population, their share in the armed forces was between 15 to 20 percent. The Pakistan government had emphasized the strategic importance of the province by locating some of the key military establishments in the Frontier. Peshawar was the headquarters of the Pakistan air force and there were air force bases at Peshawar, Kohat, Risalpur, and Chitral. In addition, there was the Pakistan Military Academy at Kakul and the Air Force College at Risalpur, and several other army institutions were located at centers like Risalpur, Nowshera, Kohat, and Abbotabad. A number of Pakhtun generals from time to time had occupied the highest positions in the army and others had been appointed chairmen of important institutions like the Water and Power Development Authority, the National Press Trust, and the Mining Corporation.[16] In addition, several Pakhtuns rising from civil service ranks attained high positions in the government like governor of the State Bank, chairman of the National Bank, secretary-general, secretary of foreign affairs, secretary of the interior, and chairmen of institutions like the Pakistan Industrail Development Corporations, Water and Power Development Authority, and so on.[17]

Unlike Baluchistan, the Pakhtun province had developed its bourgeoisie so that there were three Pakhtun big bourgeois families (the Khataks, the Hotis, and the Khanzadahs) who could be counted among the top 30 capitalist families in Pakistan. The Hotis and the Khanzadahs dominated the sugar mills of the province and the refined sugar that they produced was marketed throughout Pakistan. There were about 31,000 industrial laborers employed in large-scale industry in the province during 1969-70. In addition, there were about 600,000 Pakhtuns in Karachi working in a number of occupations such as factory workers, dock workers, and cab drivers.[18]

There was also the irredentist movement of Pakhtunistan supported by the Afghan government. Ever since the Anglo-Afghan Treaty of 1921, the government of Afghanistan, resting its claim on the clear provision of Article 11 of that treaty, had justified its continuing interest in the well-being of the tribes existing east of the Durand line. The Pakhtunistan movement supported by the Afghan government claimed that the Pakhtuns living in both the North-West Frontier Province and Baluchistan would be included in this state. In 1947, when the British held a referendum in the North-West Frontier Province to decide which state the province would join — Pakistan or India — the Afghan government urged the British to allow the Pakhtuns two additional choices, namely, annexation with Afghanistan or joining an independent state of Pakhtunistan. Reference has already been made to Khan Abdul Ghaffar Khan's Pakhtun movement and his desires to unite the Pakhtuns and change the name of the North-West Frontier Province to Pakhtunistan. Ajmal Khatak, the secretary-general of the National Awami party, who fled to Afghanistan during the Bhutto period, demanded that a separate and independent state of Pakhtunistan on the model of Bangladesh be established.[19]

The Pakhtun sense of ethnic pride and achievement was often accompanied by the bitter complaint that the North-West Frontier Province had been kept in a state of underdevelopment largely because of the dominance of the central government by non-Pakhtuns and particularly by the Punjabis. Wali Khan often pointed out that the federation of Pakistan, particularly in the post-1971 period, was of a unique nature because in no other state, with the possible exception of the Soviet Union, did one province like Punjab have such a numerical majority over all the other provinces. In the National Assembly during 1972-77, Punjab had 82 seats as compared to 60 seats held by Sind (27), North-West

Frontier Province (18), Baluchistan (12), and women (3). Tables 6.1 and 6.2 indicate the relative backwardness of the Frontier in terms of the gross regional product and the regional distribution of large-scale industry.

Table 6.1 indicates that the North-West Frontier Province lagged behind every other province in both gross and per capita regional product. In Table 6.2 one can see that the province again lagged behind Sind and Punjab in the number of large-scale industrial units with its share of such units in Pakistan being as low as 2.7 percent. Similarly, as noted in Chapter 3, Punjab was the main beneficiary of the Green Revolution with 91.2 percent of the tubewells located in that province, whereas in Peshawar division with its fertile agricultural areas there were only 2.7 percent of private tubewells in 1968. In the same year the Frontier had only 5.4 percent of West Pakistan's tractors.

The underdevelopment of the Frontier ever since the establishment of Pakistan was the central theme of the campaigns waged by Khan Abdul Ghaffar Khan and his son, Wali Khan. Both leaders had been jailed by every government in Pakistan. "Out of the eighteen years I spent in Pakistan, fifteen were in jails," said Khan Abdul Ghaffar Khan. During the elections of 1970-71, Wali Khan as the president of the National Awami party tried to mobilize political support from both the landowning classes and the petty bourgeoisie, particularly in areas like Peshawar and Mardan divisions, by stressing the province's underdevelopment at the hands of the Punjabi-dominated center. Other issues raised by the NAP were Pakhtun kwa (pure Pakhtun culture) and revenge against Qaiyum Khan, the non-Pakhtun former chief minister of the North-West Frontier Province who had often functioned as an agent of the center in oppressing and jailing the Khudai Khidmatgars.

The NAP failed to win majority support either in the provincial or National Assembly elections of 1970-71. Table 6.3 indicates that in terms of the total

TABLE 6.1
Gross Regional Product and per Capita Gross Regional Product, by Province, 1968-69 (current factor cost, provisional estimate)

	GRP (in millions of Rs.)	Population (million estimate)	GRP per Capita (Rs.)
Sind	9,805	11.5	854
Punjab	21,356	34.8	614
Baluchistan	769	1.7	455
North-West Frontier	3,714	10.3	360
Total West Pakistan	35,644	58.3	626

Source: Planning Commission, The Fourth Five Year Plan 1970-75 (Islamabad: Government of Pakistan, 1970), p. 547.

TABLE 6.2
Regional Distribution of Large-Scale Industry, 1969-70

	Punjab	Sind	North-West Frontier	Baluchistan	Total
Reporting units					
Numbers	2,052	1,419	98	18	3,587
Percent	57.2	39.6	2.7	0.5	100.0
Value of fixed assets					
Million Rs.	2,180	2,099	554	20	4,853
Percent	44.9	43.3	11.4	0.4	100.0
Average daily employment					
Thousand employees	216.0	169.2	31.0	2.1	418.4
Percent	51.6	40.4	7.4	0.5	100.0
Value of output					
Million Rs.	5,610	5,221	941	28	11,800
Percent	47.5	44.2	8.0	0.3	100.0
Gross value added					
Million Rs.	2,223	2,210	368	10	4,811
Percent	46.2	45.9	7.6	0.2	100.0

Source: Census of Manufacturing Industries, 1970.

TABLE 6.3
**Electoral Strength of Parties in the North-West Frontier
Province, 1970-71**

	National Assembly Elections Votes Obtained	Seats Won
	(percent)	
Qaiyum Muslim League (QML)	325,884 (22.6)	7
National Awami party (NAP)	266,282 (18.4)	3
Jamiatul Ulama-i-Islam (JUI)	366,471 (25.4)	6
Pakistan People's party (PPP)	205,593 (14.2)	1
Jamaat-i-Islami	103,935 (7.2)	1
Independents	86,488 (6.0)	7
Other parties	74,002	
Total	1,428,655	25

Provincial Assembly Elections	Seats Won
Qaiyum Muslim League (QML)	10
National Awami party (NAP)	13
Jamiatul Ulama-i-Islam (JUI)	4
Pakistan People's party (PPP)	3
Independents	6
Other parties	4
Total	40

Source: These figures have been derived from G. W. Choudhury, *The Last Days of United Pakistan* (Bloomington, Ind.: Indiana University Press, 1974), pp. 128-29, and Javed K. Bashir, *N.W.F.P. Elections of 1970. An Analysis* (Lahore: Progressive Publishers, 1973), p. 14.

vote, the Jamiatul Ulama-i-Islam (JUI) obtained the highest vote in the National Assembly elections. It could be argued that the JUI outpolled the NAP because its Islamic appeal won greater support than the ethnic appeal of the NAP in the National Assembly elections. The fact that the NAP was not very successful in mobilizing support on the basis of its ethnic appeal was again borne out by its total vote in the National Assembly election being lower than that attained by the Qaiyum Muslim League. Thus the ethnic factor seemed to have been swamped by the Islamic appeal of the JUI, and the non-Pakhtun Hazara support and the popularity of Qaiyum Khan as reflected in the QML vote. It was true that in the provincial assembly elections the NAP obtained the highest number of seats (13) as compared to 10 for the QML, yet it did not win a majority position in the provincial assembly of 40 members. It was again significant that even though the NAP won the highest number of seats in the provincial assembly, in terms of the total vote it trailed behind the QML.

In their defense the NAP leaders could argue that because of their constant incarceration and the restrictions placed on their political activities, they had not been able to translate the Pakhtun ethnic consciousness into widespread support for their political party throughout the province. The election results indicated that the NAP and the JUI continued to be identified with certain tribes in the areas of their traditional tribal support. In the Peshawar and Mardan divisions, the Yusufzai tribe constituted the majority and the historic hold of Ghaffar Khan over the Yusufzai was inherited by his son, Wali Khan, of the NAP. In Peshawar and Mardan the NAP won only three of the seven seats, but in terms of the total vote outpolled both the QML and JUI in Peshawar division and in Mardan its total vote was more than that won by any other party.[20]

Southwest of Peshawar toward Kohat and Bannu the Yusufzai majority was replaced by the majority of Kirlani tribes like the Waziri, Masud, Afridi, Khatak, Banochi, and Marwat. These tribes were anti-NAP and extremely religious. These factors explain the JUI winning the two National Assembly seats of Kohat and Bannu. In the provincial assembly elections, the JUI won one out of the three seats in Kohat and in Bannu it swept the polls. In the National Assembly elections, the JUI candidate campaigning against the NAP asked the electorate to vote either for the NAP candidate or in favor of the Qur'an. In Dera Ismail Khan, where the majority consisted of Kirlani Pakhtuns, Maulana Mufti Mahmood of the JUI defeated Bhutto of the PPP. The slogan raised was "Socialism Kufar Hai" (Socialism is Ungodly and anti-Islamic). In Hazara the QML emerged as the strongest of all the parties. The popularity of Qaiyum Khan went back to the days when as chief minister he introduced progressive land reforms under which a 20-year tenancy was introduced and it was laid down that no tenant could be evicted without a valid reason. Qaiyum considered himself a Hazarite. Hazara did not have a Pakhtun majority.

Thus the general conclusion that one draws from the elections of 1970-71 is that the NAP, apart from the Peshawar and Mardan divisions, had not been able to establish itself as a clear majority party championing the cause of maximum provincial autonomy for the Pakhtun province.

Does one discern a radical change in the results of the elections of 1977? Serious charges were leveled against the Bhutto government for having rigged the 1977 National Assembly elections. However, these charges were mostly confined to elections for National Assembly seats in areas in Punjab and Sind and the charge of rigging was seldom advanced about the elections in the Frontier. What pattern in terms of support for Pakhtun autonomy emerged from the National Assembly elections of 1977 in the Frontier? Unlike the 1970 elections, when the NAP and the JUI contested the elections separately, in 1977 these two parties along with others were combined into the Pakistan National Alliance (PNA), which won 17 out of 26 seats. Even though the PNA as a combined opposition was fielding candidates in the 1977 elections, one could still see that the PNA candidates in areas like Peshawar and Mardan tended to be from the National Democratic party (NDP), which was the successor of the NAP. Similarly, in the traditional strongholds of the JUI, namely, the southern districts of Kohat, Bannu, and Dera Ismail Khan, the PNA candidates were from the JUI.

Insofar as there took place a virtual elimination of the QML, one could argue that the NDP had been able to mobilize greater support for provincial autonomy and Pakhtun nationalism than it did in the earlier election. However, the JUI, as in 1970 and so in 1977, captured all the National Assembly seats in the southern districts of Kohat, Bannu, and Dera Ismail Khan. This meant that the support for an Islam-oriented party had remained intact. Because the petty bourgeoisie had not developed as much in the southern districts as they had in Mardan and Peshawar, a party like the NDP with its commitment to maximum provincial autonomy based on Pakhtun consciousness did not succeed in mobilizing much political support in these areas. Another noteworthy result of the 1977 election was that the PPP won 8 out of 26 seats, whereas in the 1970 National Assembly elections it had won only one. Did this mean that the PPP's attempt to champion the cause of the lower-income groups and particularly the tenants, landless labor, and small peasants had made a significant dent in the political landscape of the Frontier?

For the first time a government where the Pakhtun leaders could play a commanding role was established in April 1972 when the NAP-JUI government was set up in the Frontier and a similar government was installed in Baluchistan as a part of the constitutional understanding that the central government under Bhutto reached with Wali Khan as the opposition leader. Prior to this, as seen, the Pakhtun movement, drawing its support from Pakhtun nationalism and the demand for maximum provincial autonomy, had been at a distinct disadvantage with all its major leaders being constantly put out of action through their imprisonment. Second, even an active political movement could only mobilize political support, whereas now the NAP-JUI government could think in terms of mobilizing political power.

As pointed out in the case of Baluchistan, an immediate and major source of friction between the central government and the newly established provincial governments was the desire of the latter to make sure that people belonging to the province concerned would occupy key positions in the government, the professions, and the commercial life. As the affidavit of the then chief of staff filed during the Bhutto trial in 1977 stated, in the provinces of Baluchistan and the North-West Frontier a number of police officers, teachers, engineers, and other technical personnel belonging to other provinces and working in these two provinces were pressured into vacating their jobs.[21] Statesmanship and forbearance on the part of the central government demanded that they should have displayed greater sympathy than they actually did toward this understandable grievance, particularly among the Pakhtuns, who even during the British times, had complained bitterly about the domination of the Punjabis in their province.

Even after the formation of the NAP-JUI government in the Frontier, Pakhtun grievances relating to the preempting of all the lucrative forces of revenue by the central government and their alleged unwillingness to make amends for this through generous allocation of central revenues to the province continued. These regional disparities were further heightened by the way the central government had allowed the industrialists to exploit the resources of Baluchistan and the Frontier for the benefit of Punjab and Sind. Voicing his indignation at such injustices, Wali Khan pointed out:

> The natural gas of Baluchistan while providing power to Karachi and the Punjab, has hardly lit any of the dwellings of the common people of that province or brought them other minimum comforts and amenities. The NWFP, which is the biggest producer of raw tobacco, has no cigarette producing plants or factories. The bulk of its hydro-electric power is used for the benefit of others. In keeping with these trends, it is no surprise that the Pathans are used as an easily available pool of cheap migrant labor in Pakistan and elsewhere.[22]

The federal government in reply to such charges pointed out that the distribution of powers of taxation between the center and the provinces had not changed significantly from 1966 to 1972 and that the Bhutto government under the new constitution was making payments to the provincial governments of Baluchistan and the North-West Frontier Province from the revenues that they had realized from natural gas in Baluchistan and the generation of hydroelectric power in the Frontier.[23]

Because Wali Khan had made such statements abroad, he was accused by government spokesmen of being unpatriotic and the usual insinuations of his continuing disloyalty to the very concept of Pakistan were hurled at him. The federal government did not seem to realize that this kind of acrimonious debate did not contribute to national unity and above all it was not coming to grips with the fundamental problem that the smaller provinces had certain legitimate grievances that were likely to be further accentuated by the fact that after February 1973 these provinces were no longer functioning under their own popularly elected governments.

When the NAP-JUI government in Baluchistan was dismissed in February 1973, the NAP-JUI government in the Frontier resigned in protest against the federal action in Baluchistan. In February 1975, when Bhutto's main supporter and the provincial home minister, Sherpao, was killed by a bomb explosion at the University of Peshawar, Bhutto banned the NAP and ordered the arrest of Wali Khan and 60 other top leaders. Later Wali Khan and others were tried by a special court called the Hyderabad Special Tribunal. In the eyes of the Hyderabad Special Tribunal, Wali Khan and the 52 accused had committed acts of high treason. This judgment was based on evidence obtained from questionable sources. The evidence was also not submitted to cross-examination as the defense had staged a walkout.[24] Wali Khan and the other leaders were kept in jail for three years until they were released in early January 1978 by the martial law government following the government's decision to abolish the Hyderabad Special Tribunal.

As in Baluchistan, there were two social contradictions in the North-West Frontier Province. The first was between the emerging regional elites backed by the petty bourgeoisie and the landlords and the national elites represented by the central government. The second contradiction existed mainly between the regional elites dominated by the landowning interests and the great masses of tenants and landless laborers. The regional elites in the Frontier thought that they would be able to take on the central elites better if they were to strengthen their economic and political power structures. Like the central elites, particularly of the 1960s, the regional elites in the Frontier took the view that the only panacea for economic development was to give maximum scope to the private sector. Their hope was that by following such a strategy there would not only be rapid economic development of the Frontier but that the region would have many more of their own capitalists. Through such a capitalist development, the big Pakhtun landowners would have outlets for their surplus capital and be able to join the ranks of capitalists and industrialists.

The NAP-JUI government, which represented the regional elites, soon after its establishment in April 1972 invited capitalists and investors from Karachi and other places to invest in the Frontier, thinking that the capitalists and investors had been so harassed by the industrial turbulence triggered by Bhutto's rhetoric that they would welcome such an opportunity. The finance minister of the new government, Ghulam Faruque, a former chairman of the Pakistan Development Corporation, was obviously in touch with the Pakistani capitalists as he himself was an industrialist. As Wali Khan put it, the government tried to attract capital investment through an assortment of allurements. The capitalists were told that cheap raw material, hydroelectric power, and robust and intelligent labor would be available and that they would be able to enrich themselves and the province in an atmosphere free of labor unrest. "They were told that these backward area [sic] and its inhabitants were also the responsibility of the moneyed class and if they came here, they may probably miss their clubs and other amenities, but they will get understanding, love and protection − No Gherao or Jalao [encirclement or burning] here. . . ."[25]

The response was encouraging, but the capitalists wanted certain guarantees from the central government. According to Wali Khan, the policies pursued by the central government totally frustrated the efforts of the provincial government to embark on this rapid economic development of the region. The central government abolished the tax holiday, which was the primary incentive for the capitalist to invest money in the underdeveloped regions. The Frontier, which had cheap electric power, was to lose this advantage because the hydroelectric power of the province was being made available to other provinces through the newly created transmission system. The last blow was the central government's decision to devalue the currency, which raised the cost of imported machinery.

Thus the NAP was dominated by those landowning interests and the petty bourgeoisie who believed in a strategy of capitalist development and who aspired to become industrial capitalists themselves. As Feroz Ahmed pointed out, the NAP represented "the interests not of those who control the capitalist means of production in the province, but of those who aspire to control them."[26]

One could see that the NAP wanted to resolve the first contradiction between the regional elites and the national elites by launching an accelerated program of capitalist development in the province. Did this mean that eventually the Pakhtun capitalists and the Karachi and Punjabi capitalists would reach an accord and work together? This question of whether the two capitalisms would work separately or together was not clearly answered.

The NAP was most unhappy about the way the second contradiction was developing, namely, the one between the Pakhtun landowners and their tenants and landless labor. As seen in Chapter 1, the NAP's parent movement, the Khudai Khidmatgar, had started originally as a reform movement supported by the small khans and drawing its cadres even from menials and low-income groups in the rural society. However, the movement never became a radical peasant movement with a program to bring about land redistribution. The NAP not only moved away from some of the social service concerns of the Khudai Khidmatgar but also came to be dominated by the medium-sized landlords. When agrarian unrest surfaced during the early 1970s, the NAP viewed it mostly as politically inspired by the center with its origins going back to the expectations that Bhutto's rhetoric had aroused among the lower-income groups. Thus one of the NAP supporters wrote:

> The genesis of the peasant movement can be traced to the pre-election sloganeering days of the PPP when it declared "land for the peasants"

and "mills for the labourers." These catchy phrases found quick adherents among the NWFP farmers, who started illustrating Chairman Bhutto's wishes as far back as 1969. Lands belonging to small land-owners were occupied; the big khans were left untouched as they were equipped with automatics and had fortified themselves.[27]

It would be an exaggeration to suggest that the agrarian unrest owed its origins entirely to Bhutto's rhetoric. The objective conditions that had developed in the Peshawar-Mardan agricultural belt had led to this agrarian unrest. First of all, lands of landlords owning 500 acres or more were surrounded by small land-owners tilling their land with the help of tenants and landless labor drawn from the local areas as well as from areas like Swat and Malakand. According to one observer, in the immediate vicinity of the agricultural areas of Peshawar, there were 17,000 families who owned over 1 acre each and 12,000 who owned 5 to 20 acres.[28] This scarcity of land had also led to many landless laborers and tenants migrating to cities like Karachi in search of employment. An explosive situation emerged when tenant-landlord skirmishes in northern Mardan and the adjoining areas of Malakand Agency took place during 1973-74. As a result of this unrest, the landowners organized a party called the Ittehad party. The cause of the tenants and landless labor was championed by the Mazdoor Kisan party. The NAP viewed these developments with grave apprehension and saw the not very hidden hand of Bhutto in trying to divide and disrupt the Pakhtun movement.

> These happenings in the NWFP are militating against regional unity which is necessary for higher political aims. There are said to be some quarters who precisely favour such a development and the divisiveness gives them satisfaction.[29]

Abdul Ghaffar Khan also, while commenting on the divisive tactics of Bhutto during his term of office, observed:

> Seeds of disunity have been planted among us. Bhutto says I am a socialist who supports the poor and the peasants. But under socialism the state owns the land. Therefore, he should have taken over the land and distributed it among the tenants and landless labor. He did not do this in order to end the conflict because his purpose was to create conflict between the landlord and the tenants.[30]

Afzal Bangash, the leader of the Mazdoor-Kisan party, interpreted the growing conflict between the landlords and the tenants in the Frontier quite differently. His contention was that leaders like Wali Khan would talk in terms of Pakhtun nationalism but the moment they were faced with class conflict in the rural areas they would start emphasizing tribal and clannish divisions and identify themselves with the Muhammadzai tribe. The complaint of some of the landowning khans was that the landlord-tenant conflict had been provoked by the Mohmands and they had started giving a tribal twist to this conflict. According to Afzal Bangash, the landlord-tenant conflict should not be interpreted in terms of tribal conflict but should be viewed as a class conflict. "It is true that Mohmands constitute over 25 percent of the population in Charsadda but in the conflict that is raging tenants belonging to the Muhammadzai tribe are also participating and in fact Muhammadzai tenants have struggled against Muhammadzai landlords."

Giving other instances, Bangash emphasized that in areas like Malakand Agency, Dir, and Hathian both landlords and tenants who were engaged in such conflicts belonged to the Uthmanzai tribe.[31] According to Bangash, in many parts of the Frontier the number of tenants evicted from their lands was growing by leaps and bounds and these evicted tenants, in order to survive, were joining the ranks of agricultural laborers. This factor had contributed significantly to the agrarian conflict.[32]

Both in Chapter 1 and in later discussions reference has been made to the preoccupation of the national leaders with the task of state building rather than nation building. In the early part of this chapter it was pointed out how Bhutto was more adept in thinking about and developing the muscle power of the state than in sensitizing himself to the nerves of Pakistan's diversity. The problem was deeper than the fact that the national leaders, both political and bureaucratic, were Westernized in their living habits and thinking. Pakistani nationalism did not have a long history. Islamic ideology or the concept of an Islamic state was yet to be translated into reality. Many educated Pakistanis had difficulty in reconciling the concepts of modern science or liberalism with some of the traditions, practices, and institutions of Islam. Urdu and its literature came closest to being a national language and literature, but though Urdu in its spoken form was understood by the great majority of the people, only about 7 percent spoke it as their primary language.

In this chapter it has been suggested that Pakhtun regionalism was more cohesive and stronger than Baluch regionalism. It could even be argued that Pakhtun regionalism sometimes displayed the characteristics of a subnationalism. First of all, there was the irredentist demand supported by the Afghan government for the creation of a separate Pakhtun state. It was true that this demand never won the support of a majority of Pakhtuns in Pakistan. However, this feeling of ethnic and linguistic affinity with the Pakhtuns in Afghanistan and above all the intense historic pride that the Pakhtuns had in their culture and identity, along with their sense of alleged economic injustice, gave their movement a character and depth that was probably more vigorous than a more regional movement. Therefore it could be characterized as subnationalism. It is not being suggested that this was necessarily a separatist movement; rather, that within the broader framework of the Islamic nationalism of Pakistan there should be room for subnationalisms to exist. This explains the argument that the national leaders of Pakistan should display sufficient federal flexibility and forbearance to prevent a subnational movement like that of the Pakhtuns from following the same course as the Bengali movement did in 1971.

In order to evaluate and compare the competitive pulls of Pakistan nationalism with those of Pakhtun regionalism or even subnationalism, one should examine the interplay of these two forces and see how the social situation in the Pakhtun region was changing because of this interplay. The first major component of Pakistani nationalism was the appeal of Islamic unity. However, it should be borne in mind that the national leaders, both before partition and after the establishment of Pakistan, had to depend upon certain regional or local religious leaders and influentials to translate the Islamic appeal into political support. In other words, the unifying appeal of Islam rested on a heterogeneous Islamic base. Islam in its rituals and practices was by no means uniform throughout Pakistan. In addition, the religious leaders often pointed out to their followers in the regions and local areas that the Westernized national leaders tended to exploit the emotional appeal of Islam and had not taken any concrete steps to translate the promise of an Islamic state into reality. Though emotionally very potent and sometimes overpowering, the impact of Islam was not uniform throughout the Pakhtun areas. As seen, in the southern districts of Kohat, Bannu, and Dera Ismail Khan and the Tribal Areas, Islam continued to be a potent force in mobilizing political support. As one moved to the Peshawar and Mardan divisions and even in certain adjoining Tribal Areas, the appeal of Pakhtun consciousness or subnationalism was strong with the result that the primary emphasis tended to be on the ethnic and economic factors.

Pakistani nationalism as articulated through language and culture tended to be somewhat tepid in the smaller provinces of Sind, Baluchistan, and the North-West Frontier. It was strong among the Punjabi intelligentsia. First of all, the national official languge, Urdu, was spoken widely only in urban centers like Karachi and Hyderabad in Sind with their large concentrations of Urdu-speaking refugees from India and in urban centers of Punjab like Lahore, Faisalabad, and Multan. Even though it was taught at the primary school level in the rural areas of Punjab, nevertheless it had not yet become the everyday spoken language. In Sind, Baluchistan, and the Frontier, the language of the masses as well as that of the regional elites tended to be the language of their respective province.

In the Frontier one of the major components of Pakhtun consciousness or subnationalism was the intense devotion to the Pushtu language and literature on the part of the intelligentsia and particularly the students. It seemed that the intelligentsia and the students would very much like to have their province named Pakhtunistan to emphasize its linguistic and cultural identity. It was significant that the students had designated the Peshawar University Students Union as the Khyber Students Union. The university in Dera Ismail Khan was named Gomal University and the students union was called Gomal Students

Union. Other student unions that were given such Pakhtun names were Kurram Students Union (Bannu College), Gandhara Students Union (Charsadda College), Zam Students Union (Tonk College), and Kaghan Students Union (Abbottabad College).[33] The Pakhtun Students Federation in May 1979 demanded that the medium of instruction in colleges and universities should be in the language of the region concerned.[34]

The third dimension of Pakistani nationalism was the policy dimension. Here, again, the net impact was varied. It has already been pointed out that the abolition of the sardari system in Baluchistan through a central government fiat was not enough and that in order to produce a more lasting and profound impact the Bhutto government should have used political and ideological means. It was revealing that the *White Paper on Baluchistan* referred to the army's developmental role as if provision of goods and services and road building would convert the so-called Baluchi separatists into fervent supporters of Pakistani nationalism.

Similarly, the *White Paper on Baluchistan* took pride that when the government investment in Baluchistan had never exceeded Rs. 30 million in any year during the entire decade preceding 1970, the Bhutto government in 1974 had allocated as much as Rs. 210 million to Baluchistan. In addition to this allocation for 1974, the central government was spending Rs. 150 million per year through federal agencies. As compared to these federal expenditures, the revenues of the province amounted to only Rs. 88 million, which increased by about another Rs. 138 million in 1974-75 as a result of the central government transferring the sums collected through royalties and excise duties on Sui Gas to the province.[35] Thus the overall picture that emerged in 1974 was that the central government expenditure amounted to Rs. 360 million, whereas the provincial revenue was in the order of Rs. 226 million. In January 1976, when governor's rule was imposed on Baluchistan, the governor's remarks made a strange commentary on the publicity campaign of the central government regarding the large infusion of federal funds in the province. According to the governor, much of this money had been diverted to the chief minister and his colleagues.[36]

It was possible, however, that the federal expenditures in Baluchistan did produce some political support for the Bhutto regime. Some of the oil and gas officials of the central government posted in Baluchistan told the author that even at a time when the military government had publicized unwholesome facts about Bhutto's alleged corruption and high living, they found many Baluchis who, because of the benefits that the Bhutto government had brought to them, were prepared to overlook what they regarded as minor improprieties on the part of Bhutto.

As compared to Baluchistan, the federal infusion of funds into the Tribal Areas of the North-West Frontier Province had dramatic results. Starting with an expenditure of slightly over Rs. 8 million during 1970-71, the expenditure increased more than 30-fold to over Rs. 246 million during 1976-77. The number of primary, middle, and high schools increased by about three times during 1971-76 and the enrollment of students, while nearly doubling in primary and middle schools, went up more than threefold in high schools. Similar increases were reported in areas like health, irrigation, road building, and industrial sectors.

Akbar Ahmed, a civil servant and an anthropologist, while commenting on the impact of these policies and expenditures, pointed out that in the late 1970s a new tribesman with a zest for improving his lot and making a living through business, trade, and other professions rather than through his predatory habits of killing and plunder had emerged. "The battle for the future of the Tribal Areas is neither political nor ethnic but largely economic and it will be decided on this front."[37] It may be noted that in areas like the tribal belt of the Frontier, it was not only a question of channeling Pakhtun consciousness into directions that would run parallel with Pakistani nationalism but also a challenge of using the administrative and political skills of the government in penetrating and transforming a tribal society.

How does one evaluate the conflict between the forces and elites represented by the center and those represented by the province at different levels? At a very broad level it is a competitive struggle between the forces of Pakistani nationalism, which are not fully developed at this stage (and viewed by the regionalists as those dominated by Punjab), and the more entrenched and historic forces of ethnic regionalism reinforced by a sense of economic deprivation or injustice. For purposes of further analysis this basic conflict between the center and the regions should be examined at two levels — the elite level and the mass level.

At the elite level a conflict that was basically between the national and regional elites was personified and symbolized as the tussle for national leadership between Bhutto and Wali Khan. One could see that, during the 1970s, for any political party to capture power at the national level it had to build bases of support in more than one province. Just as Bhutto had built bases of majority support in Sind and Punjab and was planning to develop similar sources of support in the Frontier and Baluchistan, it seemed that the opposition leader, Abdul Wali Khan, had started thinking along similar lines. Starting with his base of support in the Frontier, he wanted to mobilize political support in Punjab. In the beginning of 1974, he toured Punjab and it seemed that his meetings were attracting large crowds. He felt that perhaps in another six months he would be able to take on Bhutto and the PPP in Punjab. According to Wali Khan, Bhutto got so worried by such developments that he had to have him imprisoned under various pretexts.[38] Even if this version is somewhat exaggerated, there is considerable plausibility in it. In any case a government committed to Pakistan's national integration would have allowed Wali Khan to move out of his parochial or ethnic moorings and transform himself into a truly national leader.

Here is one of the most fundamental problems of politics: How is it possible, given the Hobbesian fascination for greater and greater power that most political leaders have, for a national leader like Bhutto to subordinate his appetite for power to considerations of national unity and consensus? Bhutto had more than his share of the primordial lust for power and the result was that he would use every means possible to keep Wali Khan out because he feared the alternative could be his own eventual overthrow. Bhutto not only imprisoned Wali Khan by charging him with high treason but went about publicizing this factor while overlooking the damage that this could cause to Pakistan's national fabric. For central leaders constantly to dub their opponents as traitors undermined the confidence of the average Pakistani in the depth and strength of his country's nationalism. To designate publicly a leader identified with Pakhtun nationalism as a traitor was to inflame further provincial and ethnic animosities between the Punjabis and the Pakhtuns.

At the mass level there exist at least two forces in all the regions — landless labor, tenants, and small peasants and industrial labor — who can serve as unifying links for the country. In Baluchistan and the Frontier there are conflicts between the big landowning groups and the land-hungry tenants and landless labor. Such conflicts exist in Punjab and Sind as well. Therefore it is conceivable that the agrarian proletariat, particularly through the agency of a party like the Mazdoor-Kisan party, may realize that they are engaged in a common struggle. The subnationalisms referred to are by no means cohesive in Pakistan. Just as the borders and adjoining areas of Sind and Baluchistan or Sind and Punjab or the Frontier and Punjab merge into one another, so do linguistic and ethnic groups. If the agrarian struggle in Punjab intensifies, it is bound to have repercussions in the neighboring provinces of Sind and the Frontier.

In the case of industrial labor, the interconnections are even greater. The agrarian proletariat may be mostly Baluchi in Baluchistan, but the labor in the mines of Baluchistan happens to be predominantly non-Baluchi. There are more than 100,000 Baluchi laborers in Karachi. In the case of Pakhtun labor, there are more than a million Pakhtuns in Karachi, making it easily the largest Pakhtun city in Pakistan in terms of Pakhtun population. They have links with their peasant kith and kin in the Frontier. Pakhtun labor, besides being the largest in numbers, is considered to be the most militant in Karachi.

Thus much depends upon the kind of class consciousness that develops among the agrarian and industrial proletariat in Pakistan. If this class consciousness increases under the leadership of a political party, it is bound to undercut regional loyalties.[39] Therefore the problem of Pakistan's national integration is not as intractable as it was prior to 1971 when it was faced with a region like East Pakistan, which was cut off from the West by a physical and cultural distance virtually unbridgeable.

NOTES

1. *Chairman Bhutto's Reply to Gen. Zia's 2nd, Statement in the Supreme Court* (Lahore: Musawaat Press, 1977), p. 42.
2. *White Paper on Baluchistan* (Islamabad: Government of Pakistan, 1974), p. 10.
3. *The Times,* February 13, 1973.
4. It is significant that neither the *White Paper on Baluchistan,* op. cit., nor the affidavit of General Tikka Khan (who was then the chief of staff) filed in support of Bhutto in the supreme court mentioned this seizure of arms incident. See the affidavit of Tikka Khan in *Chairman Bhutto's Reply to Gen. Zia's 2nd, Statement in the Supreme Court,* pp. 94-104.
5. *In the Supreme Court of Pakistan: Written Statement of Khan Abdul Wali Khan* (Peshawar, 1975), p. 48.
6. *Baluchistan Subai Assembly Mubahisat* (Baluchistan Provincial Assembly Debates), vol. 3, no. 7 (January 10, 1973), p. 119. Most of the speeches are in Urdu but the quoted provincial minister's speech is in English.
7. *White Paper on Baluchistan,* p. 25.
8. Selig S. Harrison, "Nightmare in Baluchistan," *Foreign Policy,* no. 32 (Fall 1978): 139.
9. Ibid., p. 140.
10. This was obviously not his first killing. To Sylvia A. Matheson he said, "You must remember that I killed my first man when I was twelve!" Sylvia A. Matheson, *The Tigers of Baluchistan* (Karachi: Oxford, 1975), p. 1.
11. Daniel Sutherland, "Key Men Caught in Baluchistan Storm," *Christian Science Monitor,* December 14, 1973.
12. Ibid.
13. *White Paper on the Performance of the Bhutto Regime,* vol. 3, *Misuse of the Instruments of State Power,* Annex 1 (Islamabad: Government of Pakistan, 1979), pp. A1-A2.
14. *Islamic Republic of Pakistan. An Amnesty International Report Including the Findings of a Mission to Pakistan 23 April-12 May 1976* (London: Amnesty International Publications, 1977), p. 41.
15. One example of how the Pakistan People's party operated in Baluchistan was witnessed by the author when he was present in a public meeting addressed by Bhutto in Chaman in July 1974. Just before the meeting two rival leaders of the PPP were competing against each other as to who should present the welcome address to the prime minister. The deputy commissioner threatened to have them locked up if they continued to wrangle in this way.
16. Even though Ayub Khan tended to identify himself completely with the national elite, he was a Pakhtun who attained the rank of commander-in-chief and later became president of the country. If his two successors, Generals Musa and Yahya, were not fully fledged Pakhtuns, General Gul Hasan, chief of staff in 1972, certainly was. A number of Pakhtun generals rose to positions like governors of provinces and held cabinet posts in the martial law administration of Zia-ul-Haq.
17. Some of these influential and prestigious positions were attained by well-known Pakhtuns like Ghulam Faruque and Ghulam Ishaq Khan. The latter has occupied high positions like the secretary-general of the entire government and in 1979 was minister of finance. Similarly, some of the highest civil service positions in the ministries of foreign affairs and the interior were held by Pakhtuns in 1979.
18. Feroz Ahmed, *Focus on Baluchistan and Pushtoon Question* (Lahore: People's Publishing House, 1975), p. 110. According to Akbar S. Ahmed, Karachi is the biggest Pakhtun city in the world. Akbar S. Ahmed, *Social and Economic Change in the Tribal Areas* (Karachi: Oxford, 1977), p. 70.

19. Feroz Ahmed, op. cit., p. 85.

20. Javed K. Bashir, *N.W.F.P. Elections of 1970: An Analysis* (Lahore: Progressive Publishers, 1973), pp. 1-2.

21. *Chairman Bhutto's Reply to Gen. Zia's 2nd, Statement in the Supreme Court*, pp. 94-95.

22. Letter of Wali Khan, "Pakistan Under Strain: The Politics of Divide and Rule?" *Manchester Guardian*, May 20, 1974.

23. The federal government's rejoinder was to *In the Supreme Court of Pakistan: Written Statement of Khan Abdul Wali Khan*, pp. 39-40. Some of Wali Khan's charges in this written statement were very similar to the charges made in his letter to *Manchester Guardian*, May 20, 1974. For the government's rejoinder, see *Rejoinder in Supreme Court of Pakistan: To Written Statement of Mr. Abdul Wali Khan President of Defunct National Awami Party: In Reference by Islamic Republic of Pakistan on Dissolution of National Awami Party* (Islamabad: Government of Pakistan, 1975), pp. 35-36. See also Hayat Mohammed Khan Sherpao's reply in *Manchester Guardian*, June 11, 1974, to Wali Khan's letter to *Manchester Guardian*, May 20, 1974.

24. *An Amnesty International Report*, pp. 79-85.

25. *In the Supreme Court of Pakistan: Written Statement of Khan Abdul Wali Khan*, p. 42.

26. Feroz Ahmed, op. cit., p. 101.

27. Yusaf Lodi, "The Agrarian Revolt Up North," *Outlook*, 3 (April 20, 1974): 8.

28. *Christian Science Monitor*, October 2, 1974.

29. Yusaf Lodi, op. cit., p. 9.

30. *Naqeeb* (Peshawar), January 1-15, 1978, p. 23. Translated from the Urdu.

31. Pakistan Mazdoor-Kisan Party, *Party Circular*, no. 23, 1973, p. 5. Translated from the Urdu.

32. Ibid.

33. *"Pakhtunistan Kyanv aur Kyanvnahi?"* (Pakhtunistan: Why and Why Not?), *Naqeeb*, December 1-15, 1977, pp. 23-24.

34. *Dawn* (overseas weekly), May 19-25, 1979.

35. *Quarterly Economic Review of Pakistan, Bangladesh and Afghanistan*, no. 4 (1974): 3.

36. Ibid., no. 1 (1976): 3. The author was present in the meeting of Pakistanis in Toronto, March 1976, addressed by Bhutto when the prime minister, turning to the cabinet minister from Baluchistan, playfully chastised him for his corruption and admonished him not to be so corrupt next time.

37. Akbar Ahmed, op. cit., p. 70. For changes in the Frontier, see ibid., pp. 52-71.

38. This is based on Wali Khan's version. See *Naqeeb*, January 16-30, 1978, p. 29.

39. This point has been developed from the insights provided by Feroz Ahmed, op. cit., pp. 42, 110.

7
MASS URBAN PROTESTS AS INDICATORS OF POLITICAL CHANGE IN PAKISTAN

The main thrust of the argument in this chapter is that mass urban protests are more important and suggestive indicators of political change in many developing areas than political innovation and institution building that take place at the top governmental level. Most of the development theorists in the West have concentrated all their concerns and inquiries on the latter almost to the exclusion of the former. Yet, in the first place, the very fact that institution building and certain policy changes are not working is indicated by the kind and intensity of urban protest. Second, urban protests also indicate the nature and direction of some of the major economic and political changes that are taking place in a given society and how some of the existing and new groups are responding to such changes. The ways in which the Ayub regime in 1969 and the Bhutto regime in 1977 were overthrown indicate that the army seizures of power were preceded by certain massive urban protests and demonstrations. It was these urban protests that had so robbed the governments of their legitimacy and rendered them so ineffective that the military intervened in the name of law and order and stability.

What factors trigger such violent ebullitions of social and urban discontent? What groups play a predominant part in such demonstrations? How are such groups led and organized? What political issues and interests lie behind such

First published in *Journal of Commonwealth & Comparative Politics* 17, no. 2 (July 1979): 111-35, and reprinted by permission of Frank Cass & Co., Ltd., London.

group demonstrations? Are such demonstrations outcomes of certain policies or are they organized and launched to extract new policies from the government? Answers to such questions will also reveal the kind of political development and the nature of developmental change that took place in Pakistan during 1958-78.

In 1961, out of a total population of 46.8 million in what was then West Pakistan, 22.5 percent were urban and 77.5 percent rural. In 1977, out of a total population of 73.4 million in Pakistan, the urban component was 26.5 percent and the rural 73.5 percent. During both 1968-69 and March-July 1977, most eruptions took place in urban centers. During the 1968-69 period, the demonstrations against Ayub were organized both in West and East Pakistan. In West Pakistan the centers of protest were almost entirely in urban areas, such as Karachi, Lahore, Lyallpur, Rawalpindi, and Peshawar, whereas the protests in East Pakistan were not confined to urban centers but spread to the rural hinterlands of such urban centers as Dacca, Mymensingh, and Khulna. During the Bhutto era, Karachi and Lahore continued to be the dominant centers of massive urban upheavals. However, other cities like Hyderabad in Sind, Faisalabad (formerly Lyallpur), Multan, and Sialkot in Punjab, and Peshawar in the Frontier also became important centers of massive and violent protest. In addition, there were large numbers of mundi (market towns) that also participated in the protests against the Bhutto regime.

In terms of population, the urban areas were dominated by metropolitan centers like Karachi, which had a population of 4.2 million in 1975. In addition to a city like Lahore with 2.1 million in 1972, other cities like Lyallpur, Hyderabad, Rawalpindi, and Multan emerged as urban centers with populations of over half a million by 1972. Table 7.1 lists the ten cities with populations in excess of 200,000. There were at least 20 cities in Pakistan with populations exceeding 100,000.

Tables 7.2 to 7.5 indicate, respectively, the urban distribution of the population, the labor force by major occupation groups, the number of registered trade unions and their membership, and the enrollment of students during 1971-76. From these tables one can see that the principal groups in urban areas in terms of numbers were industrial and construction labor, those engaged in commerce, and college and university students. In addition, there were professional groups like lawyers and religious groups who often played an influential role in urban demonstrations. Groups like refugees or those living in self-made huts and slums called kutchi abadis also showed various degrees of cohesiveness and organization for purposes of urban unrest. Refugees in Karachi, Lahore, and Multan played an important role in the demonstrations against the Bhutto regime, but the dwellers of the unplanned kutchi abadis, were more or less quiescent spectators during the urban protests against the Bhutto regime. It was only at a later stage when Bhutto granted them proprietary rights to their miserable dwellings that a large procession of them came out in Lahore in April 1977 in support of the Bhutto regime.

TABLE 7.1
Population of Cities, 1961 and 1972

City	Population (in thousands) 1961	Population (in thousands) 1972	Percentage of Change, 1961-72
Karachi	1,913	3,469	81.3
Lahore	1,296	2,148	65.7
Lyallpur	425	820	92.7
Hyderabad	435	624	43.4
Rawalpindi	340	615	80.9
Multan	358	544	52.0
Gujranwala	196	366	86.7
Peshawar	219	273	24.7
Sialkot	164	212	26.9
Sargodha	129	203	57.4

Source: Census of Pakistan, 1972.

TABLE 7.2
Urban Distribution, West Pakistan, 1961, and Pakistan, 1972

Urban Category	1961 Population (in thousands)	1961 Percentage of Total Urban Population	1972 Population (in thousands)	1972 Percentage of Total Urban Population
Metropolitan areas	3,549	36.8	6,309	37.9
Secondary cities (over 100,000)	2,640	27.3	4,086	24.5
Large towns (50,000 to 100,000)	888	9.2	1,367	8.2
Small towns (less than 50,000)	2,577	26.7	4.902	29.4
Total	9,654	100.0	16,664	100.0

Source: Richard F. Nyrop, Beryl L. Benderly, Cary C. Conn, William W. Cover, Melissa J. Cutter, Newton B. Parker, *Area Handbook for Pakistan,* 4th ed. (Washington, D.C.: U.S. Government Printing Office, 1975), p. 85.

TABLE 7.3
Labor Force by Major Occupation Groups, 1974-75
(percentage of total)

	Pakistan	Rural	Urban
Agriculture, forestry, and fishing	54.8	72.1	6.2
Mining and quarrying	0.2	0.1	0.2
Manufacturing	13.6	9.3	25.7
Electricity, gas, and water	0.5	0.2	1.2
Construction	4.2	3.4	6.4
Commercial trade	11.1	5.8	25.9
Transport and communications	4.9	2.9	10.3
Financial services	0.7	0.1	2.3
Community, social, and personal services	9.8	5.7	21.3
Other	0.2	0.4	0.5

Source: The Economist Intelligence Unit, *Quarterly Economics Review of Pakistan, Bangladesh, Afghanistan.* Annual Supplement 1977, p. 7.

TABLE 7.4
Number of Registered Trade Unions and Their Membership in Pakistan

Year	Trade Unions	Membership
1971	1,997	581,219
1972	4,452	525,062
1973	5,345	570,202
1974	7,172	741,174
1975	8,196	695,667
1976	8,611	718,331
1977 estimated*	9,110	760,300

*Labor Division's estimates.

Source: Pakistan Labour Gazette (Islamabad: Labour & Manpower Division), January-March 1977.

TABLE 7.5
Enrollment of Students, 1971-76

Stage	Position in 1971-72	Likely Achievement, 1975-76	Percentage Increase
Primary	4.21 million	5.37 million	+ 27.55
Secondary	1.32 million	1.68 million	+ 26.64
College	186,000	211,000	+ 13.44
University	17,000	23,000	+ 35.29
Polytechnic/technical college	2,766	3,300	+ 19.31
Graduate engineering	1,648	2,172	+ 31.80

Source: Ministry of Education.

During 1968-69, when there were few well-organized trade unions of industrial labor, there was considerable labor militancy, whereas in 1977, when there were as many as 9,110 trade unions with a total membership of 760,300, apart from the "wheel jam" strike (total transport strike) in April, industrial labor did not play as important a role as the shopkeepers, small traders, and merchants during the demonstrations against the Bhutto regime. The importance of the latter group can be seen in Table 7.3, which shows that commercial trade constituted 25.9 percent of the labor force in the urban areas as compared to manufacturing, which made up 25.7 percent of the urban labor force.

URBAN PROTESTS AGAINST THE AYUB REGIME

How does one explain the demonstrations that took place against the Ayub regime? The Ayub regime had been hailed, particularly in the West, as a showpiece of what foreign aid combined with sound government and local capitalism could achieve. Economist Gustav Papanek justified income inequalities in Pakistan by arguing that income inequality, by creating economic incentives for the "robber barons" of Pakistan, would eventually lead to a real improvement for the lower-income groups.[1] Similarly, Samuel Huntington had hailed Ayub as a "Solon or Lycurgus or 'Great Legislator' on the Platonic or Rousseauian model" of the third world.[2] What had gone awry with the economic development and political institution building that had taken place under the Ayub regime? What groups or classes of people came out in the streets to challenge the Ayub regime?

Several commentators have catalogued such grievances as rising prices, corruption in high places, and gross inequality between rich and poor, all accompanied by a highly autocratic government and police repression, as causes that triggered the series of almost uninterrupted demonstrations that lasted for 132 days from November 1968 to March 1969.[3] Thus Mushtaq Ahmad argued: "The problems of poverty, disease and ignorance were at the root of political unrest and disaffection."[4] But the same writer, after pointing out how Ayub's land reforms and economic development had not benefited the poorer sections, admitted: "Numerically the largest and politically the least conscious, these classes constituted no threat to any government and were not a source of trouble to the Ayub regime."[5] Similarly, *The Economist* observed:

> Pakistanis have plenty of grievances against their government, but there are no burning issues on which the opposition can focus. The pleas for a return to parliamentary democracy which Ayub abolished when he took over ten years ago, appeals to the urban intelligentsia, but little to the masses. Economic injustices abound, but resentment does not run deep: spectacular growth during the 1960s has brought some benefit to everyone.[6]

If it were not the very poor who were rebelling and if there were no explosive issues of popular desire for democratic rule, then who were the disaffected groups and why were they rebelling?

First of all, corruption at the government level and excessive concentration of industrial and economic power in the 22 big industrial families had robbed Ayub's government of a sense of legitimacy. Ayub's son, who had retired from the army as a captain, by promoting and aligning himself with a number of business enterprises, had managed to amass a fortune of $3.3 million.[7] Another estimate indicated that the total wealth of Ayub Khan and his family at the time of his relinquishing the presidency on March 25, 1969 was in the order of $10 to $20 million.[8]

Bhutto, who had been Ayub's foreign minister, and other political leaders had created the impression, which was gaining increasing currency, that Ayub under international pressure had made concessions to Indians in the matter of Kashmir in the Tashkent agreement of January 1966 and thus lost at the negotiating table what the army had tried to win at the battlefront. In East Pakistan it was almost universally believed that the central government under the domination of West Pakistani interests had initiated the war of 1965 purely for pursuing its interests in Kashmir and had thus exposed East Pakistan to invasion by India. Bhutto's assertion that the Chinese would not have tolerated such an outcome confirmed all the apprehensions of East Pakistanis.

Some political scientists have extolled Ayub for his political planning and incomparable institution building.[9] However, the centralization of the constitution rendered the National Assembly effete and made the provincial governments mere fiefdoms of the president. The institution of Basic Democracies, for which Huntington gave high marks to Ayub, had neither provided any forum of expression to the opposition politicians nor afforded means of redress to the disaffected professional groups and industrial labor.

The political air was thus thick with discontent, and Ayub's increasing unpopularity and declining effectiveness had increased the possibilities for the privileged and aroused expectations among those who were knocking at the citadels of power. Power in the last resort was that of the army. And Bhutto knew that in the face of massive political demonstrations in the cities of West Pakistan, a predominantly West Pakistani army would not use its firepower merely to keep an unpopular president in power.

There was thus no widespread misery or suffering among the urban masses but there was definitely a growing awareness that the benefits of economic growth and prosperity had been appropriated by the industrialists and some of the members of the government. There was growing resentment and even anger against inequity and repression. Thus the rebelling groups took to the streets because they considered that the political and economic system had become both inequitable and vulnerable. It is in this context that one has to view the uprisings, some of which were spontaneous and some planned.

An example of the sporadic outbursts was the student-police confrontation in early November 1968 that initiated a series of uprisings against Ayub. Students of a college in Rawalpindi came out in a procession to protest against the seizure by the police of the purchases they had made at Landikotal, a border point to the north of Peshawar. In politics, as in other areas, small and strange beginnings sometimes lead to awesome consequences. Thus a small student demonstration for the purpose of recovering their purchases of contraband goods started a series of violent student-police confrontations. It may be noted that the students already had a grievance against the university ordinance issued by the Ayub regime that had prescribed penalties like the confiscation of university degrees from students who had indulged in political and nonacademic activities. Thus discontent was there, but student protests had not been systematically organized on a large scale against the university ordinance. However, in a student-police confrontation in Rawalpindi during November a student was killed. This resulted in more violence and even the army had to be called in to aid the civil power.

Later, on November 11, Ayub Khan was fired upon when he was addressing a meeting in Peshawar. It was suspected that the assailant might have been a Pakhtunistan activist. It was significant that in the eyes of the government all these incidents had clear political overtones and on November 13, Zulfikar Ali Bhutto, Wali Khan, and ten other leaders were arrested under the Defense of Pakistan Rules. The charge against Wali Khan was that he had advocated the breakup of the integrated West Pakistan province and the creation of a North-West Frontier province of Pakhtunistan. The arrests of Bhutto and other members of the Pakistan People's party were made because the government feared that they would seize the opportunity of incipient student protest to launch a political campaign against the Ayub regime. The arrests resulted in demonstrations in some of the Punjabi and Frontier districts like Multan, Mianwali, Jhelum, Mardan, Charsadda, and Abbottabad.

In the escalation of demonstrations a more or less clear pattern could be discerned. During the early student demonstrations, student demands very largely centered around the university ordinance and certain proposed changes in the administration of higher education. In addition to their sense of outrage that their degrees could be confiscated for taking part in politics, they were concerned about matters like examination pass levels and various administrative regulations. When Bhutto supported the student demands, student leaders organized demonstrations in support of political issues like the restoration of civil rights and parliamentary institutions, the release of political leaders, and so on.[10] The killing of a student by the police in one town would trigger a series of demonstrations of students in other towns leading to further confrontations with the police and more killings.[11] By mid-February 1969, in cities like Lahore and Karachi literally thousands of students, supported by other groups like women, some workers' unions, and the bar associations, had become capable of organizing such massive demonstrations and rallies that the police were heavily outnumbered. The Ayub regime saw the writing on the wall, repealed the university ordinance, and released Bhutto.

Student power skillfully supported and used by a politician like Bhutto and professional groups like the lawyers had exposed the obvious weakness of the Ayub regime, its alienation of the urban intellectuals and professional groups. But the power of industrial labor demonstrated that even a relatively new, weak, and unorganized group like labor unions could attack the regime in an area where it claimed to be at its strongest, economic development.

The Ayub regime in its eagerness to accelerate the industrial growth of the country had followed the doctrine of functional inequality under which the private entrepreneurs would receive maximum incentives. Groups like industrial labor were being exhorted to count their blessings in the form of job opportunities and wait for the full fruits of economic growth like higher wages to come their way, perhaps in the long run. Ayub had argued that "present labour policies represent a very carefully worked out balance between the interests of the employers on the one hand and the interests of labour on the other."[12] The policy as it stood represented income transfers from consumers, industrial workers, and farmers to the industrialists and trading groups. To make matters worse, the war of 1965, followed by a decline in foreign aid and mounting military expenditures, increased inflationary pressures in such a way that the real wages of industrial labor suffered a sharp decline. Even government spokesmen were admitting that the major beneficiaries of the "development decade" (1958-68) were the 22 privileged families who under government patronage and protection controlled most of the industrial and bank assets.

Perhaps no one was as aware of the system of inequality and the conspicuous consumption of the entrepreneurial families as the industrial laborer, who was facing a steady decline in his real wages. He probably felt that the regime in its eagerness to promote this kind of rapid economic growth had made sure that he would be deprived of his right to strike through the collective efforts of his trade union. As an editorial in *Dawn* observed: "The virtual banning of the right to strike accompanied by the practice of promoting unions controlled by hirelings has dealt a serious blow to responsible trade unionism."[13]

In addition to the decline in real wages, another factor that explains the intensity of labor militancy against the Ayub regime was the growing hostility between trade union leaders and the Basic Democrats elected in urban areas. Under Ayub's political system, the Basic Democrat in the urban areas tended to be the influential community patron or ward leader who as an elected member of the local council acted as a broker between the urban dwellers and the city administration. His contacts with the city administration enabled him to seek redress for the grievances of his constituents. He also helped his constituents if they were involved in criminal proceedings or if they were being harassed by the police. For such services he charged fairly high fees.

The Basic Democrats also became fairly affluent overnight by obtaining transport licenses and permits for government ration shops. They had obtained such favors from the government for mobilizing votes and political support in their respective areas. The rapid and enormous increase in the wealth of the Basic Democrats was so conspicuous that it was bound to lead to their widespread unpopularity. Some writers have commented upon the unpopularity of Basic Democrats among urban dwellers but have not taken into account the role of labor leaders and workers in the overthrow of the Ayub regime.[14]

It was significant that, by early March, labor power had replaced student power in the urban confrontation with the Ayub regime.[15] How does one explain the massive upsurge of labor militancy when all genuine trade union activity had virtually been disallowed by the Ayub regime? Labor not only displayed the capacity to take on the police apparatus of the regime but also developed an organizational capacity to wage strikes, to combine with unions belonging to other trades and professions, and to formulate certain concrete demands relating to wages, living conditions, and certain desired changes in the economic and political system.

The appearance of the East Pakistani populist and peasant leader, Maulana Bhashani, in West Pakistan explained some of this militancy. He put forward the technique of gherao (forcible confinement of owners and management in the factory by workers until they agreed to their demands) as developed in West Bengal. In his fiery speeches throughout West Pakistan he justified virtual confiscation of private industrial wealth through wholesale nationalization of all industries on the plea that this kind of socialism was sanctioned and blessed by Islam: "Islam says whatever is beneath the sky or over the surface of the earth belongs to Allah. I want to put that concept in practice. I want everything nationalized in the name of Allah and distributed equally to the people."[16]

It may be noted that Bhashani during these speeches stated the basic demands of the workers as food, clothing, and shelter (roti, kapra aur makan).[17] This slogan was later picked up by Bhutto in his 1970 election campaign where he used it to his full advantage. No other East Pakistani leader had ever stirred the poorer sections and particularly the industrial labor of West Pakistan as much as Bhashani did in early 1969.[18] He even put forward the concept of national unity through class consciousness. "In our struggle we are neither Bengalis nor Punjabis, Sindhis, Balochis or Pathans, but common victims of oppression and exploitation."[19]

This upsurge of labor militancy in West Pakistan created greater problems for the Ayub regime than did the counterpart agitation in East Pakistan, as West Pakistan was industrially much more developed than East Pakistan. This development ran counter to the widely held belief in East Pakistan that political consciousness in West Pakistan always tended to be at a more tepid level than in East Pakistan because of the dominance of feudal landlords in West Pakistan. The events of 1969 demonstrated that in terms of sustained and more widespread labor militancy, West Pakistan was getting ahead of East Pakistan. However, the upsurge in rural areas in East Pakistan was in contrast to the relative quiescence of the West Pakistan countryside.

One could say that the militancy that one finds in Bhashani's rhetoric was actually reflected in the pronouncements and activities of certain trade union leaders and their followers. During early March both the Karachi Port and its industrial area were affected by labor unrest and violence resulting in the death of two laborers. Kaniz Fatima, president of the Karachi Shipyard Workers Union with a membership of about 10,000 workers, warned the industrialists to see the writing on the wall and demanded that at least 25 percent of profits should be given to the workers as an annual bonus.[20] Similarly, Ahmad Bakhtiar, president of the West Pakistan Federation of Trade Unions, addressing a rally of 30,000 workers in Lahore, referred to the negotiations that were going on between the political leaders and President Ayub and warned that a mere change in the top leadership would not satisfy the workers, who were demanding basic changes in the economic system. He declared that the political leaders should understand that it was because of the agitation of workers and students that the president had been forced to withdraw his name from the forthcoming presidential election.[21]

What organizational strength lay behind this rhetoric? In order to answer this question, one has to explain the way the trade union organization was built up despite the formidable and repressive obstacles introduced by the Ayub regime. The secret of this organizational strength was the links that developed between the militant federation leaders at the top and the workplace leaders below, particularly in the industrial area of Karachi. Workplace leaders lived in the workers colonies, which were situated around the mills and factories. Below the workplace leaders there were militant shop floor activists. Thus, whenever strikes occurred as, for example, the March 1963 strike in Karachi when militant federation leaders were arrested, the leadership of the strike would pass into the hands of workplace leaders and those student and other underground activists with whom the police and the administration were not familiar.

In this manner coordinating links and organizational interaction developed between militant federation labor leaders, the workplace leaders, student leaders active in the labor field, and shop floor activists. This coordination emerged in the form of labor action committees during the 1968-69 labor movement. These new labor action committees were linked further to new labor federations that tended to articulate their goals in more politically ambitious terms than those of mere wage settlements. As regards the success and strength of the labor organization in Karachi, Zafar Shaheed has written:

> Although the movement against Ayub Khan was a nation-wide effort, and involved strata of society in addition to the working class — notably professionals such as lawyers, teachers, doctors, etc. — the factory workers of Karachi showed a militancy which was not paralleled anywhere else in the country. . . . By 24 March, virtually all the factories of Karachi, comprising some 40% of Pakistan's industrial capacity, were on strike.[22]

During March 1969, when labor militancy in Karachi and Lahore was at its peak, one also notices trade unions trying to combine with other unions in the same field in order to make their strikes and demonstrations more effective. Thus the Transport Workers Action Committee consisted of the Bus Workers Union, Auto Rickshaw Drivers Union, Karachi Omnibus Service Workers Union, and Karachi Drivers Union. It must be noted that development theorists often refer to institution buiding in terms of political and legal innovations of government leaders at the top. They seem to ignore completely the institution building that is undertaken under grave disabilities by trade union leaders, workplace leaders, and shop floor activists.

Thus it was because the Pakistan trade union movement was able to develop this kind of organizational depth and power, particularly in areas like Karachi and Lahore, that it could hurl defiance at the Ayub regime throughout the month of March. On March 4, 1969, 5,000 workers of the Valika textile and woolen mills threatened strike action if their demands relating to the payment of certain basic wages for skilled and unskilled workers, bonuses, dearness allowances, and the immediate reinstatement of 224 workers were not complied with.[23] Later it was reported that the workers of the Valika textile and woolen mills had set fire to the offices of the Valika textile mills in Karachi.

In Lahore the millworkers attempted to burn the Kohinoor textile mills belonging to the Saigol family. The workers by such action created fears among the industrialists that industries belonging to the 22 big industrial families had become the targets of labor violence.[24] In Karachi workers took over two of the largest mills. This led not only to stoppage of all industrial activity in the area but also to flight of capital abroad with a sharp decline in the foreign exchange value of the rupee and a 40 percent rise in the price of gold. All this created so much panic among the factory owners that weeks before martial law was declared on March 25 they were appealing to the government to send troops to the industrial areas, as the police were totally unable to cope with trade union violence.[25]

During the first week of March the workers throughout West Pakistan celebrated "Labor Demands Week." During this week the Workers Action Committees put forward their eight-point demands, which included the unconditional right to form unions and the right to strike, repeal of black laws, fixation of Rs. 150 as minimum wage, free accommodation, educational and medical facilities, bonus, security of employment, distribution of government land among farmers, and land measuring less than 16 acres to be exempted from tax.[26] Later other demands were added that included immediate nationalization of all heavy industries and banks and insurance companies and the appointment of a tripartite labor commission to frame labor laws.[27] On March 17 a general strike was observed throughout West Pakistan in answer to the call of the West Pakistan Labor Council. It was reported that as many as 2.5 million workers took part in this strike in West Pakistan.[28] There was no public transport available and all factories and most of the shops and offices were closed.

An equally significant phenomenon of this period was that for the first time white-collar workers like the clerical staff of banks and particularly those of the National Bank of Pakistan, doctors, engineers, and central government employees staged strikes. On March 6, the clerical staff of the National Bank of Pakistan in Karachi resorted to gherao with the result that the president and the mananging director were confined to their offices until midnight when they accepted the demands of the striking staff. Similarly, demands for better pay scales, better opportunities for promotion from a lower class to a higher class, and better working conditions were put forward by the Income Tax Inspectors Association, All-Pakistan Attached Departments Superintendents Association, the Central Government Servants Association, and the West Pakistan Railway Workers Union. Some of these associations issued threats that if the government did not comply with their demands, they would resort to direct action. Threats to strike by government employees must have come as a shattering experience to the government, for government servants in Pakistan were always known for their docility and willingness to obey government orders and accept their working conditions.

Another noteworthy feature of this unrest among government employees was the demand put forward by engineers urging the government to give them an improved status and publish and implement the Cornelius report. One of the central thrusts of the report by Chief Justice Cornelius was that the privileged and monopolistic position that the Civil Service of Pakistan (CSP) enjoyed in the matter of top policy and administrative jobs in the government should be abolished and specialists like engineers and doctors should be given top policy positions in ministries relating to such technical functions of the government. The CSP constituted the steel framework of the government of Pakistan and any challenge to its privileged position meant that the authoritarian structure had become quite shaky and that the rebellious forces were defiant enough to suggest ways and means to reconstitute the government structure on a different basis.

Ayub tried to defuse the alarming situation by appointing new governors in East and West Pakistan. The governor in West Pakistan tried to win the confidence of industrial labor by assuring them that he would try to meet their eight basic demands relating to wages, medical care, housing, profit sharing, and so on. But it looked as if the situation had slipped beyond Ayub's control. Ayub in his broadcast on March 25 said: "The mobs are resorting to gherao at will and get their demands accepted under duress." Because no one could control this situation and the economy was being crippled, the president declared that he was handing over the government to the defense forces.

In what significant ways had this urban upsurge transformed the politics of Pakistan? It was true both during the pre-Pakistan and pre-Ayub periods that some of the political energy and dynamism originating from a few urban centers tended to spread into the countryside. However, particularly in areas of West Pakistan, the feudal landlords with their secure power bases could dilute and change this political dynamism in such a way that the political programs of the Muslim League party never assumed any radical character. In any case, prior to the Ayub period Pakistan's industrialization had not sufficiently changed the social character of the urban areas. But during the Ayub period the industrialization of cities like Karachi, Lahore, and Lyallpur had generated new urban forces. Cities were attracting peasants, landless laborers, and tenants from the surrounding countryside and the new industrial and urban climate had created new issues and aroused new expectations. Thus the relatively quiescent countryside, particularly around the urban areas, was becoming aware of the growing restlessness in areas to which they wanted to migrate in search of jobs. Also, in the urban centers politics was becoming so radicalized that for the first time conflicts between the supporters of right and left had emerged and some of them erupted in street battles.

In March 1969, when negotiations were going on between the Ayub regime and the political leaders, it was expected that under Sheikh Mujibur Rahman's leadership a new political alliance, including the Awami League, the Muslim League, the Jamaat-i-Islami, the National Awami party led by Wali Khan, and other religious and political groups, might emerge as "a workable parliamentary alternative to the Ayub regime."[29] But the leftist groups led by Bhutto and Bhashani made it clear that the mere restoration of parliamentary government under the old politicians without a settlement of the economic issues would be challenged by the new militant forces.

One could see how serious this challenge was when a leader like Mujibur Rahman became apprehensive about the inroads that the militant forces might make into his province. It was reported that Mujib demanded "that the East Pakistan administration reassert itself against the violence of antisocial elements in the province."[30] Thus the politicians could no longer be confident about their former secure political bases. During the labor strikes and demonstrations in Karachi in March, the All-Pakistan Trade Union Council in a telegram to the political leaders who were negotiating with Ayub made it clear that a settlement that merely restored parliamentary democracy "without economic democracy would not be acceptable to the workers and peasants."[31]

TABLE 7.6
Percentage of Votes Won by Parties in Punjab and Sind
in the 1970 Elections

Party	Punjab	Sind
Pakistan People's party	41.6	44.9
Muslim League (combined vote of three separate factions)[a]	23.1	20.2
Islamic parties (combined vote of three parties)[b]	19.7	22.0
Pakistan Democratic party	2.2	0.4

[a]The three factions were Pakistan Muslim League Council, Pakistan Muslim League Convention, and Pakistan Muslim League Qayyum.
[b]The three parties were Jamaat-i-Islami, Jamiatul Ulama-i-Pakistan, and Jamiatul Ulama-i-Islam (Hazarvi).

Source: These percentages derived from Mushtag Ahmad, Politics Without Change (Karachi: Space Publishers, 1971), p. 169.

URBAN UNREST OF THE EARLY 1970s

It is in terms of the growing militancy of the urban areas of West Pakistan and their spreading effects on the surrounding countryside that one can explain the surprising victory that Bhutto won in the 1970 election. This development seemed to refute the continuing myth that West Pakistan was so completely dominated by feudal landlords that the polity of West Pakistan was totally different from that of East Pakistan.[32] Table 7.6 indicates how the Pakistan

People's party gained ascendancy at the expense of conservative Muslim League groups and religious parties.

In terms of broad regions, the Indus River was the great divide in the 1970 elections. To the east was the semiprosperous Punjab, where the PPP with its espousal of Islamic socialism won the majority. To the west lay the poorer Frontier, which returned more conservative, tribal, and ethnic-oriented parties.

The main areas of the PPP strength in Punjab were the relatively prosperous areas of Lahore Division, eastern Multan Division, and all along the Grand Trunk Road where lay areas of industrial development and agricultural prosperity. The PPP also obtained much higher electoral support in districts that were relatively more urbanized and more literate and had more roads. It has been estimated that in nine districts with 586 persons to a square mile, a road mileage of 13.5 per 100 square miles of area, a literacy percentage of 15.1, and an urban population of 25.9 percent, the PPP won 52 percent of the votes. As compared to this, in ten other districts with 185 persons to a square mile, a road mileage of 7.9 per 100 square miles, 7.9 percent literacy, with an urban population of 14.1 percent, the share of the PPP vote turned out to be only 25 percent.[33]

However, if one looks at the political topography that had emerged after the elections, there were areas, particularly in Sind, where the PPP was able to defeat the old feudal landlords by mobilizing support from their rivals and in some cases the lesser known landlords. Therefore what is being suggested here is not that the political structure of West Pakistan had been totally transformed but that the PPP, capitalizing on the militancy in the urban areas, had made a major dent in the semifeudal and traditional political structure of West Pakistan.

Bhutto had the double advantage of witnessing from both inside and outside the government how the developmental process initiated by Ayub had generated certain forces of discontent. He has often been credited with considerable political acumen. Therefore he must have discerned that the political forces generated by economic development in the urban areas would help him to win a decisive victory in the elections in provinces like Sind and Punjab. However, after the elections it must have also been apparent to him that even though he had obtained convincing majority support in the two largest provinces, yet if the conservative opposition parties had combined against him in Punjab and Sind, their combined vote would have been higher than that of the PPP in Punjab and only slightly lower in Sind.

From Table 7.6 it may be seen that the PPP polled 41.6 percent of the vote in Punjab, while the combined opposition vote came up to 45 percent. In Sind the PPP vote was 44.9 percent and the combined opposition vote was 42.6 percent. This suggested the kind of danger that Bhutto and the PPP faced if the conservative forces were provoked and antagonized into combining against the government. In Karachi, where most of the antigovernment rallies and revolts started, the PPP managed to win only two out of seven National Assembly seats with its arch enemy, the Jamaat-i-Islami, also winning two seats.

One of the seats in the city of Multan was won by Bhutto (56,297 votes), but if the votes of the two opposing candidates belonging to religious parties had been combined, they would have totaled 71,033. The conservative forces had been trounced, but by no means eliminated.

In urban areas, as shown in Table 7.3, those occupied in manufacturing industry in 1974-75 constituted 25.7 percent of the people in the urban areas, but those engaged in commercial trade constituted 25.9 percent. Thus the conservative parties in a deteriorating economic situation could mobilize support from the relatively more prosperous groups like white-collar workers, traders, merchants, and civil servants. In addition, there were other issues like language and religion that could be used by the opposition to organize demonstrations and protests against the government.

The language riots that at first simmered during March and April 1972 and then exploded during June and July 1972 were caused by both the pent-up grievances of the Sindhis against the refugee settlers in Sind and the determination of the refugee settlers to hold on to the vested interests they had acquired in dominating the economic and commercial life of urban areas like Karachi and Hyderabad. Sindhis, and particularly the educated middle class, had acquired new confidence because they felt that the newly established provincial government and Bhutto, the Sindhi prime minister, would offer them better job opportunities and also create new conditions for the development of their culture and language. On July 7, the Sind assembly passed a language bill declaring Sindhi to be the sole official language of the province. Opposition demands to make Urdu an additional official language were rejected. This was in contrast to the other three provinces of Pakistan, which had adopted the national language of Urdu as their provincial official language. Another development that added fuel to the fire was a nonofficial resolution moved in the Sind assembly that made the learning of Sindhi in three months by government employees compulsory, failing which the employees would be dismissed.

All this presented a grave threat to the entrenched position of the refugee settlers who constituted nearly 40 percent of the population of Sind. Maulana Maudoodi, leader of the Jamaat-i-Islami party, which had considerable influence in areas like Karachi and Hyderabad, probably expressed the feelings of the settlers when he suggested that the exclusive promotion of Sindhi and prejudice against Urdu would encourage Sindhi provincialism based on unity between the Sindhi Hindus and Sindhi Muslims.[34] Obviously, in the views of the settlers, such an outcome would deal a deadly blow to the very foundation of Pakistan.

Bhutto was in a difficult situation. While reprimanding his Sindhi followers for burning Urdu papers, he could not afford to alienate them because the PPP, which had obtained a bare majority in a house of 60 in the 1970 elections, had drawn nearly all its support from the Sindhis. However, he aroused the intense animosity of the refugees by reminding them that in certain areas they had converted the local population of Sind into a minority. "Remember in America, the Red Indians were converted into a minority and history has not forgiven America until today."[35]

Demonstrations and riots erupted predominantly in Sind's urban centers, Karachi and Hyderabad. Press notes issued by government authorities reported that supporters of the Sindhi and Urdu languages attacked each other with offensive weapons and that mobs of thousands of agitators were involved in setting fire to colleges and printing presses, attacking police stations, and raising road barricades.[36] The district magistrate of Karachi in a press note admitted that the civil administration had collapsed in certain areas of Karachi and only with the assistance of the military could law and order be restored. The refugees demanded that Karachi should secede from Sind to become a separate province.[37] It was apparent that the right-wing parties, the Jamaat-i-Islami and the Jamiatul Ulama-i-Pakistan, were leading the pro-Urdu demonstrators. According to one source, some of the radical groups in Karachi felt that "Urdu extremism is being stoked up by Karachi industrialists in a bid to divide the working class and the poor."[38] Probably what the industrialists were aiming at was the disaffection of industrial labor, over 90 percent of whom were Urdu-speaking, from the PPP and Bhutto. Bhutto, appreciating how explosive the situation was, brought about a quick settlement between the two sides. A new ordinance was issued providing that, notwithstanding the provisions of the Sindhi Language Act, for a period of 12 years from the commencement of the ordinance on July 16, 1972 no person otherwise eligible for appointment or promotion to any civil service in Sind would be discriminated against only because of his inability to communicate in Sindhi or in Urdu.

In March 1969, some of the Jamaat leaders were reported to have threatened "to crush the Socialists."[39] With mounting dismay, the Jamaat-i-Islami must have witnessed Bhutto's ascent to power and the subtle way in which he was trying to usher in what it regarded as socialism and secularism. It has already been noted how Bhutto was viewed with grave apprehension by other conservative political parties and perhaps notably by the industrialists in Karachi and Lahore. Therefore his policies and pronouncements were kept under very close surveillance by the conservative forces.

Bhutto's strategy was both to placate and outwit the religious and conservative opposition. He had in his cabinet a conservative political leader, Kausar Niazi, a former member of the Jamaat-i-Islami. When the anti-Ahmadi demonstrations broke out in Lahore and Lyallpur in June 1974, resulting in widespread rioting, destruction of property, and army units being called, Bhutto more or less surrendered to the demands of the religious groups. In September 1974, through legislation, the government declared the Ahmadi community to be a minority and a non-Muslim community because they did not believe in the finality of the Prophet Muhammad. Even though the Ahmadi community had supported him in the 1970 elections and even though the prime minister was averse to religious orthodoxy of this kind, the Ahmadis became non-Muslims in the eyes of the law under his government. Apparently he was compelled to make this major concession because he feared "that opposition politicians and extremist Muslim religious leaders would use the issue against him."[40]

In the author's interviews with religious and conservative groups in Pakistan, it was constantly emphasized that behind the political facade of Bhutto there lurked deep designs to introduce socialism and secularism that would strike at the very roots of Pakistan. When asked for evidence, the complainants would refer to the insidious propaganda that was being spread through the radio and television networks. Executives of the Pakistan Chamber of Commerce complained that the message that was being purveyed through plays and short stories was that the capitalist or the trader was always the villain. Some of the antireligious, socialist, and secular messages were detected when the well-known Urdu novel, *Khuda ki Basti* (God's Populace), was serialized on television.

To the religious factor were added other factors that may have been even more important in turning some of the urban classes against the Bhutto regime. The most important factor that turned all this pent-up resentment against Bhutto into hatred was the periodic terror that the opponents of the regime were being subjected to through threatened kidnapping of family members and destruction of property. The Federal Security Force was the most visible instrument of this terror and oppression. Its victims were both individuals and political parties. The government argued that certain processions and public meetings were being organized to overthrow the regime. During a National Assembly session in November 1975, when a constitutional amendment limiting dissent was being pushed through, the Federal Security Force was brought in. Several protesting opposition members of the house were beaten up and physically thrown out of the assembly.[41] The expenditure on the Federal Security Force went up from Rs. 36.4 million in 1973-74 to Rs. 107.7 million in 1976-77. This expenditure did not include the Intelligence Bureau, which was under the prime minister's cabinet division and for which Rs. 25.8 million was spent in 1976-77.[42]

From interviews with businessmen and industrialists, it appeared that one of the most worrying problems that the Bhutto regime had created for them was the way labor groups had been encouraged to keep escalating their demands for wages and bonuses in spite of there being a decline in labor productivity and their unwillingness to work hard to match the wages and benefits they had been accorded. The government had devised a system of wage-price packages in an attempt to link wages with prices in such a way that periodic adjustments were made in taxes, in wage rates for different classes of workers, and price increases on essential products like kerosene, vegetable ghee, electricity, sugar, and so on. In addition, prices of commodities like wheat were subsidized and 60 percent of the government's subsidies consisted of those relating to wage goods. This explains why industrial labor and other poorer sections in the urban areas, with the exception of those employed in service and food industries in Karachi (where the Jamaat had been successful in gaining support), more or less abstained from any active participation in the demonstrations against the Bhutto regime during March-July 1977.

1977 URBAN CONFLICT AGAINST BHUTTO

In the 1970 election, religious and conservative parties like the Jamaat-i-Islami, the Jamiatul Ulama-i-Islam, and the Muslim League were divided and ran their own candidates. In the 1977 March elections, Bhutto's repression and his alleged socialist and secular policies had united these parties into the Pakistan National Alliance (PNA). The bonds of unity were both economic and religious. The class interests that each of the components of the PNA represented were given from a Marxist standpoint and in somewhat exaggerated form in a paper prepared by the Pakistan Study Group in Lahore. Some of the major interests with their party spokesmen were listed as follows: Muslim League (kulaks, small and middle-sized capitalists), Jamaat-i-Islami (middle-sized traders and businessmen), Jamiatul Ulama-i-Pakistan and Tehrik-i-Istaqlal (trading capitalists and monopoly capitalists; Tehrik-i-Istaqlal was also aligned with the military and civilian bureaucracy), and National Democratic party with its main area of support in the Frontier and Baluchistan (landlords and kulaks, petty bourgeoisie, and the middle class who were opposed to Sindhi and Punjabi feudals and landowners).[43]

Why did the PNA resort to massive urban demonstrations and seek violent confrontation with the government? An obvious explanation was that the rigging of elections had triggered all this. But the resulting explosion was much too big and involved too many risks and loss of human life on the part of the demonstrators to be explained by this alone. It was apparent that big business had suffered because of nationalization. Private investment had declined. The refugee middle class had suffered because of shrinking job opportunities caused by decline in private investment and by the quota system of the new government. The lower middle class, who were under the influence of the Jamaat and the Jamiatul Ulama-i-Pakistan, really felt that Bhutto would cause incalculable harm to the Islamic ideology. These misgivings were further reinforced by his repression. The mounting expenditure on the Federal Security Force was a clear example of how the Bhutto regime had tried to stamp out all forms of opposition. In addition, the PPP strongmen and the Mohalla chairmen (locality chairmen) derived benefits from the government like a ration depot or a route permit and used their position to extract fines, bribes, and payments from the merchant class.[44] These sorts of grievances came through when the author interviewed the leaders of merchant groups in the walled cities of Lahore and Multan.[45] They felt that it was divine help and the Islamic fervor of the masses for Nizam-i-Mustafa (state based on the teachings of the Prophet) that had enabled them to overcome Bhutto.

Table 7.7 indicates how the PNA movement during March-July was a middle-class phenomenon with women's processions being next in importance to students in numbers. Labor demonstrations, probably the most important in the anti-Ayub campaign of 1968-69, are noticeably absent as a category, suggesting that labor did not play a significant role in the Anti-Bhutto campaign.

As observed in the anti-Ayub campaign, the politics of Pakistan had changed so much that urban movements seemed to be based on some organizational depth and therefore could sustain themselves even after the arrests of the top national leaders. In contrast to the anti-Ayub movement, the anti-Bhutto movement drew most of its inspiration and sustenance from middle and lower-middle classes consisting of small merchants, traders, and professional groups like lawyers reinforced now and again in the case of Karachi by some trade unions. The movement against Bhutto was more widely based in the sense that the centers of protests were not only Karachi, Lahore, Faisalabad, Peshawar, and Rawalpindi but also Hyderabad, Multan, and Sialkot and mundi (market) towns as well. The hard-core organization of the movement came from religious parties like the Jamaat-i-Islami in Karachi and the Jamiatul Ulama-i-Pakistan in Multan. For cohesion and strength one should look at organizational units and cells like the madrasahs (religious schools) and mosques, commercial associations or federations, and some trade unions, notably in Karachi.

Mosques and walled cities provided certain advantages. For example, during the agitations, when Section 144 of the Criminal Procedure Act banning the assembly of more than five persons was imposed, mosques where more than five persons assembled for prayers and other activities did not normally come under the purview of Section 144. When mosques became the nerve centers of the demonstrations where Bhutto and his socialism were denouced as anti-Islamic

TABLE 7.7
PNA Processions, March-July 1977

Province	Public	Women	Lawyers	Ulama	Students	Boys/Children
Punjab	2,537	105	71	12	92	17
Frontier	870	14	20	3	70	2
Sind	338	140	3	4	93	38
Baluchistan	575	3	1	–	28	11
Total	4,290	262	95	19	283	68

Source: Mr. A. K. Brohi, Counsel for Federation. Statement in the Supreme Court of Pakistan (Islamabad: Government of Pakistan, 1977), p. 65.

forces, members of the police and Federal Security Force did enter the mosques either to arrest or beat the demonstrators. Such action was regarded as sacrilegious and tended to provoke more violence and demonstrations. Furthermore, it was not easy for the police to chase or arrest demonstrators in the walled cities where the narrow lanes and streets restricted movements of personnel and vehicles.

An important cementing and sustaining force was the commercial and monetary interests of the shopkeepers and merchants who were against the government because of its nationalization of big industries, declining private investment, and above all, nationalization of cotton ginning and rice husking mills in July 1976, which meant that the small merchants and traders could not become investors and small industrialists by investing in such mills. It was the nationalization of these rice and cotton mills that attracted the artis (middlemen) of the mundi (towns) in their thousands to the PNA movement. The merchant class, particularly those trading in cloth, had a vast network that linked cities like Karachi, Lahore, Faisalabad, and Multan. The Lahore merchants would get their textiles, silk, and tetron from Karachi. Other supply centers were Multan with its bedsheets and Faisalabad with its shirting cloth. It was significant that with these interlinked interests and contacts the merchant class in all these cities supported the demonstrations. This explains how quickly the movement spread throughout Punjab and Sind. Another cementing force in the movement was the fact that traders, merchants, lawyers, and civil servants in cities like Karachi, Hyderabad, Multan, Lahore, and Faisalabad were refugees who had come mostly from eastern Punjab and western Uttar Pradesh in India. Within certain cities like Multan, the refugees also belonged to certain baradaris (kinship groups), which accentuated or reinforced their sense of solidarity.

If the movement was by and large organized and sustained by the petty bourgeoisie, then one has to explain how this class was able to confront and withstand the police, the Federal Security Force, and after April 21, the military. It is the religious link that provides the explanation. Bhutto's government had not only created the impression of being determined to secularize Islamic Pakistan but Bhutto had openly admitted in Lahore that he drank liquor. This enabled the maulvis to harangue in the mosques that it was the religious duty of the Muslims to wage war against such a regime, as the idea of the leader of an Islamic state drinking liquor was intolerable. Thus for both religious and practical reasons, processions would start from the mosques in Karachi, Hyderabad, Lahore, Faisalabad, and Multan.

The slogan that inspired the processionists to face the police lathis or even bullets was the establishment of Nizam-i-Mustafa. This was a powerful symbol because it combined the religion of Islam and the personality of the Prophet Muhammad. Devotion to Islam was there, but the love that the Prophet's personality inspired for the common man was perhaps even more electrifying. This explains why the name of Haji Aftab, a cloth merchant of Lahore, became a legend for he led the procession against police fire. Some eyewitness accounts have suggested to the author that this encounter was perhaps one of the deadliest blows struck at the Bhutto regime. When the author in February 1978 toured parts of the walled city of Lahore that had been the battleground of the movement, he was repeatedly told that the movement was not created by any political party or an organization. It was a "miracle" that could not be explained by reason or logic. People who did not strictly follow Islam advanced to face bullets in the name of Nizam-i-Mustafa.

Within the same movement and within the same class of petty bourgeoisie, one detects fairly significant differences depending upon whether the class was concentrated in a metropolitan city like Karachi with a much larger industrial and commercial base or a smaller city like Multan with a smaller industrial and commercial base. In Karachi, the Jamaat-i-Islami with a more complex and tightly knit organization and with its links with some trade unions was the principal organizer of the movement. The result was that the leadership was much less charismatic and much more organization and party oriented. The Jamaat's links with the trade union movement were almost entirely through the Pakistan National Federation of Trade Unions. It was this union that organized the Paiya Jam (wheel jam) strike on April 20, 1977 in Karachi. They were supported by their counterparts in Hyderabad and Lahore. It was reported to be so successful that, as the name implies, not a vehicle of any kind moved in the streets. In interviews with the officers of the Pakistan National Federation of Trade Unions, the author found that out of the 264 constituent trade unions, over 150 unions were clearly unions not of industrial labor but of employees of banks, commerce, service, food, and transport industries. From a Marxist point of view the wage earners belonging to such unions could be regarded as members of the petty bourgeoisie.

As compared to Karachi, the movement in Multan was largely led by Maulana Hamid Ali Khan, a charismatic leader belonging to the Jamiatul Ulama-i-Pakistan. In terms of ideology, the Jamiatul Ulama-i-Pakistan offered a much more simple and popular view of Islam than the Jamaat-i-Islami. The religious ideology of Nizam-i-Mustafa that the JUP put forward had been influenced by its concern about rituals and ceremonies associated with saints, pirs, and their mausoleums. This kind of Islam had a greater appeal for the common man than the Jamaat-i-Islami's more fundamentalist views concerning Islamic state and Islamic law. It was also significant that it was largely under the influence of an organization like the Jamiatul Ulama-i-Pakistan that the concept of Nizam-i-Mustafa was put forward by the Pakistan National Alliance. Above all, the JUP claimed that Nizam-i-Mustafa could be implemented within six months if the PNA came to power. Thus the movement in Multan centered around the personality of Maulana Hamid Ali Khan, who derived most of his support from two sources: the Rohtak baradari members, most of whom lived within the walled city and were engaged in trade, and students of three religious schools supported by the traders and merchants and that produced scholars skilled both in theology and rhetoric. "If the Traders Associations can have the shops closed within a few hours, the supporters of Maulana Hamid Ali Khan and the students of religious schools can unleash a political movement in the interior of the city.'[46]

The interests and political action of the small and medium-sized merchants, traders, professionals, white-collar workers, and labor belonging to service and food industries have been identified as those of the petty bourgeoisie. It is this class that had organized and sustained the PNA movement. However, their religious and political attitudes and interests should be viewed in a broader economic setting. Their interests in present-day Pakistan were closely identified with those of the big industrial and commercial groups. In a city like Faisalabad in the suth mundi (yarn market), the yarn traders, consisting of eight or ten main groups, bought yarn from the textile mills as their agents and sold it to the local loom operators. Mill owners supplied yarn to the traders at a certain rate and the trader made a 1 percent commission. The traders speculated by withholding the yarn from the power loom operators, hoping that the price would shoot up. The mill owner was aware of this and took his share of the profit that the trader made from speculation. The income tax department had been trying to break this arrangement for the past 30 years. However, the political interests of the Bhutto government were such that the income tax officers were told to "pinch the tax evaders but not bite them too hard."

Those who took a cynical view of both the commercial operations and the religious attitudes of the petty bourgeoisie would probably agree with a former PPP cabinet minister who said: "They live in a dream world of corrupt money and easy heaven. Bhutto had facilitated their entry to heaven by providing unlimited opportunities for their pilgrimages to Mecca." Although the yarn traders were probably not hit "too hard" by the income tax officials, yet they were nevertheless liable to be anxious on account of tax inquiries. They were also fearful that the nationalization of rice husking and cotton ginning might be followed by similar action in respect to gasoline pumps, cinema houses, and other ventures in which many had been investing. These considerations were sufficient to outweigh the facilitated journeys to Mecca.

Thus what is being suggested here is that, as part of the general crystallization of class interests in Pakistan, the petty bourgeoisie were also becoming increasingly aware of their common interests as a class regardless of social origins and of region. The PNA movement was an instrument for concerted action on the part of those interests and in that respect it was also an aspect of national integration across regional divisions.

Perhaps no other party was more aware of who exercised how much political power and influence in Pakistan than the Jamaat-i-Islami. Several years before General Zia was appointed chief of staff in March 1976, it was known to the Jamaat that he was a devout Muslim. Soon after he was appointed chief of staff it was disclosed in several newspapers that he regularly read some of the journals and publications of the Jamaat. Another announcement that impressed the Jamaat and other religious parties was that one of the first actions General Zia took as chief of staff of the Pakistan army was to declare that the three mottoes of the Pakistan army would be iman (faith), taqwaa (piety), and jihad (struggle in the name of God). The *Urdu Digest,* one of the journals that supported the Jamaat point of view, in an editorial in its March 1976 issue, welcomed his appointment as chief of staff and in a later editorial of August 1976 commended General Zia for his laudable action in formulating the mottoes of the army in Islamic terms. It may also be noted that General Zia was a refugee from east Punjab. The head of the Jamaat-i-Islami party was one of the prominent political leaders who applauded the imposition of martial law on July 5, 1977. Bhutto, while making his statement in the Supreme Court, observed: "I appointed a Chief of Army Staff belonging to Jamaat-i-Islami and the result is before all of us."[47]

It may be noted that while referring to the characteristics and attitudes of the petty bourgeoisie, Marxist writer Nicos Poulantzas pointed out:

> Both small holders and those wage earners who live out their exploitation in the form of "wages" and "competition" far removed from production present the same political and ideological characteristics for different economic reasons: petty bourgeois individualism; attraction to the *status quo* and fear of revolution; the myth of "social advancement" and aspirations to bourgeois status; belief in the "neutral State" above classes; political instability and a tendency to support "strong States" and bonapartist regimes; revolts taking the form of "petty bourgeois" jacqueries.[48]

Obviously with some modifications, this holds true of the petty bourgeoisie class of Pakistan. However, one of the major shortcomings of the Marxist theory regarding the way the petty bourgeoisie functions in a country like Pakistan is that it has not explained how a religiously inspired or influenced petty bourgeoisie class behaves. How long will this link with religion continue or under what conditions will it snap?

The tendency on the part of certain political scientists to characterize institution building at the central or top government level as developmental and ignore or exclude protests and demonstrations at the lower societal levels from this developmental process has been criticized. This is precisely the kind of view of the developmental process that has gained currency in a number of U.S. and other Western universities. Thus Peter H. Merkl points out:

> According to Huntington, new states require above all strong, centralized authority in order to deal with the enormous problems of development. Failing this and generally lacking a well-institutionalized order, they are forever endangered by the waves of (democratic) participation

and frequent violence produced by the maladjustments and unsatisfied aspirations of transitional societies.[49]

Similarly, Bhutto's political strategy to establish his control over the civil and military bureaucracies has been characterized as "patrimonialism" by Gerald A. Heeger and his inability or unwillingness to develop the PPP as a participatory and mobilizing instrument as "demobilization." Heeger regards Bhutto's patrimonialism and demobilization as "de-developmental processes."[50]

All along it has been emphasized that under both Ayub and Bhutto there have developed organized forms of urban mass protests and that these should also be regarded as essentially developmental tendencies. Both Huntington and Heeger, in their inability to view the total developmental process as something beyond institution building at the top, have failed to take into account these forms of political activity. This shortsightedness leads to consequences that are more than academic or theoretical. Huntington, carried away by Ayub's institution building, failed to see what was simmering on the ground, and within a few months of the publication of his book his hero was overthrown by the very urban forces that he had supposedly outflanked. Heeger also failed to discern that in spite of Bhutto's alleged patrimonial and demobilizing strategies, he had aroused so much political consciousness and support through his land and labor reforms in the rural and urban areas that the military regime did not hold elections even after more than two years of Bhutto's overthrow.

Some development theorists, while conceding that the urban protest movements in Pakistan have demonstrated certain organizational skills and viability, may point out that for such movements to become an integral part of the broader developmental process, political parties should have stepped in to aggregate or accommodate such protest movements. If they had done this, the bargaining process in a recognized forum like the legislature would have resulted in certain policies that could have avoided mass violence and the overthrow of governments.

Such arguments do not take into account two factors in Pakistan's politics. The dominant role of the military and their alignment with conservative forces have not allowed the politics of accommodation to function. Second, the increasing class polarization created a climate of confrontation in which the contestants were not prepared to play or abide by the rules of the so-called democratic game. The military regime dominated by the rightist forces believes in the elimination of the left. The Jamaat-i-Islami, who were a part of the PNA movement organized ostensibly against the rigging of elections by the Bhutto regime and for the holding of new elections, joined the government in August 1978. Of these rightist groups the Jamaat-i-Islami was most committed to the view that the process of accountability and the punishment of the Bhutto group should take precedence over the holding of elections. Bhutto was executed on April 4, 1979 following his conviction by the Supreme Court for having ordered the murder of a political opponent. Bhutto has become a martyr to vast sections of lower-income groups — industrial labor and small peasants, tenants, and landless laborers.

NOTES

1. Gustav F. Papanek, *Pakistan's Development: Social Goals and Private Incentives* (Cambridge, Mass.: Harvard University Press, 1967), p. 242.
2. Samuel P. Huntington, *Political Order in Changing Societies* (New Haven, Conn.: Yale University Press, 1968), p. 251.
3. Herbert Feldman, *From Crisis to Crisis: Pakistan 1962-1969* (London: Oxford University Press, 1972); and Mushtaq Ahmad, *Government and Politics in Pakistan* (Karachi: Space Publishers, 1970).
4. Ahmad, op. cit., p. 315.
5. Ibid., p. 306.
6. *The Economist,* November 16, 1968.
7. Feldman, op. cit., p. 305-06.
8. Ibid., pp. 287, 306. As a result of the acquisition of so much wealth, Ayub was rated as one of the wealthiest presidents in the world. In Pakistan his family was one of the 22 families controlling the bulk of industrial and banking assets.
9. Karl von Vorys, *Political Development in Pakistan* (Princeton, N.J.: Princeton University Press, 1965), p. xiii; and Huntington, op. cit., pp. 251, 253.
10. *Quarterly Economic Review of Pakistan and Afghanistan,* 1st quarter 1969 (London: The Economist Intelligence Unit), p. 2.
11. *New York Times,* January 31, 1969.
12. Cited in Feldman, op. cit., p. 259.
13. *Dawn,* March 12, 1969.
14. Lawrence Ziring, *The Ayub Khan Era: Politics in Pakistan 1958-69* (Syracuse, N.Y.: Syracuse University Press, 1971).
15. *Le Monde,* March 8, 1969; *Manchester Guardian,* March 11, 1969.
16. *New York Times,* March 30, 1969.
17. *Dawn,* March 23, 1969.
18. Even as late as 1977 and 1978 some of the trade union leaders in Lahore recalled to the author the great role that Bhashani had played in the struggle against the Ayub regime.
19. *Dawn,* March 23, 1969.
20. *Dawn,* March 19, 1969.
21. *Dawn,* March 8, 1969.
22. Zafar Shaheed, "Union Leaders and Strikes: The Case of Karachi 1969-72." Discussion paper presented to Seminar on Third World Strikes, Institute of Social Studies, The Hague, September, 1977, pp. 12-13. See also Zafar Shaheed, "The Organisation and Leadership of Industrial Labour in Karachi" (Ph.D. diss., University of Leeds, 1977).
23. *Dawn,* March 5, 1969.
24. *New York Times,* March 7, 1979.
25. Feldman, op. cit., p. 258.
26. *Dawn,* March 7, 1979.
27. *Dawn,* March 9, 1969.
28. *New York Times,* March 18, 1969.
29. *The Economist,* March 22, 1969.
30. Ibid.

31. *Dawn,* March 7, 1969.

32. Even after the overthrow of the Ayub regime in which industrial labor in West Pakistan played an important role, Rehman Sobhan continued to cling to the view that West Pakistan was dominated by feudal interests. Rehman Sobhan, "East Pakistan's Revolt Against Ayub," *The Round Table* 59 (1969): 305-07.

33. Herbert Feldman, *The End and the Beginning: Pakistan 1969-1972* (London: Oxford University Press, 1975), p. 94.

34. *Dawn,* June 18, 1972.

35. *Dawn,* April 1, 1972.

36. For press note of the district administration, Hyderabad, see *Dawn,* July 10, 1972.

37. *Dawn,* July 10, 1972.

38. Dilip Mukerjee, "Pakistan's Growing Pains: Language Riots in Sind," *Times of India,* July 17, 1972.

39. *The Economist,* March 22, 1969.

40. *New York Times,* July 9, 1974.

41. *The Guardian,* February 6, 1976.

42. For the 1973-74 figures, see Finance Division, *The Budget 1975-76: Demands for Grants and Appropriations* (Islamabad: Government of Pakistan, 1975), p. 218. For 1976-77 figures, see *The Budget 1976-77: Demands for Grants and Appropriations* (Islamabad: Government of Pakistan, 1976), pp. 5, 215.

43. Pakistan Study Group, *Analysis of PNA Class Character and Movement* (photocopy).

44. The unpopularity of the PPP because of these factors was admitted by the prime minister's special secretary. See *White Paper on the Conduct of the General Elections in March, 1977* (Rawalpindi: Government of Pakistan, July, 1978), Annexure 63, pp. A203-04.

45. Lahore, Multan, and Delhi are walled cities built originally by the Mughals and other Muslim rulers. Their narrow lanes and closely packed houses are all enclosed within gates or doors like the Lohari Gate and Mochi Gate in Lahore and the Lohari Gate, Haram Gate, and Daulat Gate in Multan.

46. "Interior of the city" refers to the walled city of Multan. *Maiyar,* April 23-30, 1977, pp. 15-17.

47. *Chairman Bhutto's Reply to Gen. Zia's 2nd Statement in the Supreme Court,* October 31, 1977 (Lahore), p. 88.

48. Nicos Poulantzas, "Marxism and Social Classes," *New Left Review* 78 (March-April 1973): 37-38.

49. Peter H. Merkl, *Modern Comparative Politics,* 2nd ed. (Hinsdale, Ill.: Dryden Press, 1977), p. 24.

50. Gerald A. Heeger, "Politics in the Post-Military State: Some Reflections on the Pakistani Experience," *World Politics* 29 (January 1977): 254-61.

8
THE NATURE AND DIRECTION OF
POLITICAL CHANGE IN PAKISTAN

One can say that a country may experience political change at several levels. There may be a change in its ideology or belief system. Ideology provides the link between action and fundamental belief. Individuals are expected to mold their political behavior in conformity with or in relation to a principle or set of principles. One can also say that the country is experiencing political change when the character of its government changes. This may involve a change in the class composition of the government, or the change could be less fundamental than that in the sense that other institutional groups may enter the oligarchy that is dominating the government. Instead of the government being dominated by civil servants, the government may come under the dual domination of both the military and the civil servants.

A third way of looking at political change is to examine and assess the strength of major social classes like industrial labor in the cities or landless labor, tenants, and poor peasants in the rural areas. These classes come into being and become increasingly militant as a result of economic changes like urbanization and industrialization in the urban areas and the emergence of nascent forms of capitalist agriculture in the rural areas. Urbanization and industrialization brought about by capitalist development in the urban areas of Pakistan has created income inequality, unemployment, and growing class consciousness. This chapter examines the kinds of explosive forces that are emerging in the rural and urban areas and how the military regime in Pakistan is responding, through certain policies and ideological means, to such explosive forces.

What sort of changes does one detect in the belief system that is Islam and that provides an important ideological underpinning for the state in Pakistan? In Chapter 1 it was indicated that the leaders of the Pakistan movement, by putting forward the goal of Pakistan as the establishment of an Islamic state, were able to mobilize considerable political support during 1945-47. Later, in August 1947, the founder, Jinnah, by drawing a line of demarcation between matters pertaining to religion and those pertaining to the state, was perhaps returning to his earlier secularist and liberal leanings. In his other addresses he ruled out the possibility of Pakistan becoming a theocracy. He also recommended the principles of social justice and Islamic socialism as foundations for the new state.[1] However, even Jinnah, and certainly his successors like Liaquat Ali Khan, when faced with the problems of regional discontent and divisiveness, would declaim about the mission of Pakistan to set up an Islamic polity.

For the masses, thanks to the preachings of the ulama and the religious leaders, the gap between the promises that had been made and the state performance continued to widen. Perhaps more important than the fact that the political leaders were not seen to be very Islamic in their deportment was the realization that Pakistan was emerging as a neocolonial state with practically no efforts being made to follow the principles of social justice. Some even felt that the plight of the common man in terms of rising food prices, corruption, and maladministration had become even worse under the brown Englishmen. The religious disturbances in the early part of 1953 that were analyzed in Chapter 2 erupted in support of the demand that the Ahmadis, who did not believe in the cardinal Islamic doctrine of the finality of Muhammad's Prophethood, be removed from government positions and declared a minority community. Again, the fact that the government of Pakistan, still committed to the objective that Pakistan should be an Islamic state, had given high positions in the government and the army to Ahmadis indicated the extent of the credibiility gap that had arisen in the eyes of the common man between government promise and government performance.

The common man had been told that perhaps the greatest factor responsible for the establishment of Pakistan against overwhelming odds was the Islamic bond, which could overcome any divisions. After the establishment of Pakistan, the wranglings of politicians, the dismissal of governments — all accompanied by intense internecine regional conflicts between Bengalis and West Pakistanis and between Punjabis and Sindhis, and Punjabis and Pakhtuns — confirmed the common skepticism and disillusionment about Islamic unity and the Islamic state. The trauma of more than 50 percent of the Pakistan population breaking away from their West Pakistani brethren and establishing themselves as the state of Bangladesh in December 1971 was perhaps the most shattering blow to the belief that Pakistan could perhaps eventually become an Islamic state based on social justice. The ruling elites could produce explanations like the villainous role of India in the dismemberment of the country, but the gnawing and growing doubts were too strong to be overcome by such explanations.

During the national and provincial elections of 1969-70 a radical change had taken place in the religious and political attitudes of the electorate in Punjab and Sind. They returned the PPP with over 60 percent majority in these two provinces, if one takes into account both the National and provincial assembly elections. In winning this impressive victory, Bhutto not only had trounced some of the Islam-oriented parties like the Jamaat-i-Islami and the Muslim League but also had overcome the propaganda that the Islamic socialism that he was advocating ran totally counter to the principles of Islam.

During 1972-73, Bhutto provided dynamic leadership to the country and created the impression that he had extracted victory from the jaws of defeat so far as Pakistan's relations with India were concerned. India released 90,000 prisoners of war and returned 5,000 square miles of Pakistani territory that it had captured during the 1971 war. Bhutto was also successful in having the constitution of 1973 adopted by reaching a settlement with the opposition on the question of provincial autonomy. However, as seen in Chapter 6, by the early part of 1973, serious rifts had emerged between the Bhutto government and the Pakhtun and Baluchi leaders. During July-August 1974, when the author visited Pakistan, one could see that pessimism was once again emerging as a result of the growing corruption, mounting inflation, and regional differences. One heard repeatedly remarks or statements being made of the following nature: "This nation has become so depraved that even if Prophet Muhammad were to appear now, I doubt whether it could be put on the right course."

During November-December 1977, the author discussed with some of the social scientists at Quaid-i-Azam University in Islamabad the findings of the village surveys that they had carried out in some of the districts of Punjab like Rawalpindi, Campbellpur, and Faisalabad. According to these findings, it seemed that there was a distinct decline in the observance of religious rituals and prayers among the villagers. In order to do a sample test of some of these findings, the author questioned a gathering of 50 villagers in the immediate vicinity of Pakpattan in Punjab where a famous shrine is located. The villagers were asked how many of them prayed five times a day. Only three in the audience said they did — two of them elderly and one a young man. How many of them prayed on Fridays? Only ten replied in the affirmative. To the question, how many fasted throughout the month of Ramadan, only five replied in the affirmative.

It would not be fair to suggest that all this meant that the people in general were moving away from Islam. Their devotion to its basic principles remained undiminished. But even the poorer sections of the rural and urban masses had become aware that it was no longer possible for them to follow blindly the dictates of the ulama and the village mullah in political and social matters: They had become vitally interested in their economic well-being, in the education of their children, and in job opportunities, and they were not prepared to dub a political party that offered social justice as anti-Islamic at the behest of the mullah.

The astute Bhutto had detected these changes in the attitudes of the masses. In an address to the PPP, he is reported to have said:

> The anti-Pakistan mullahs and monopolists of Islam correctly foresee that in the new Pakistan when the exploited and the oppressed classes shall become the ruling classes they will be ruined. Since they will be ruined they are crying hoarse that that will be the end of Islam. . . .
>
> The level of consciousness of the poor and oppressed Pakistani people has become so high that they are paying no heed to the reactionaries and a handful of anti-Pakistan elements.[2]

Although Bhutto constantly referred to Islamic socialism, neither he nor the party spelled out clearly how Islam and socialism were to be combined or were to influence each other. In the election manifesto of the PPP of 1970, the four mottoes of the party were stated as: "Islam is our faith, Democracy is our polity. Socialism is our economy. All power to the people." It was significant that in such a formulation, Islam was described only as a faith and was neither linked clearly with democracy nor with the socialist economy. When one reads the manifesto in its details, one again finds that there is no mention of how Islam justifies or supports nationalization of certain industries or measures and objectives like land reforms and the elimination of feudalism.

Were Bhutto and the PPP being deliberate in putting forward the concept of Islamic socialism but not explaining how Islam would inspire or justify certain radical measures that the party was advocating? Did they perhaps feel that Islam as a religion or as an ideology could not be readily used for purposes of creating class consciousness and launching a class struggle? A well-known scholar like Maxime Rodinson has pointed out:

> How can one proclaim: "in the name of Islam, such and such property must be socialized," when the owners of this property are paragons of devotion, when the majority of the religious are ready to proclaim (and rightly) that Islam sanctifies private property, when Islam is bound up historically in everyone's mind with that traditional society of which the practically untouchable status of private property is, after all, one of the fundamentals? How can one denounce as adversaries of Islam all these personalities whose attachment to Muslim practices and beliefs is obvious, demonstrative, even ostentatious, and when none of these their beliefs or practices is being attacked?[3]

Bhutto was able to defeat the Islam-oriented and conservative parties in the 1970 elections with the help of a radical program and a political slogan like Islamic socialism. During 1972-77, his regime and his policies created sufficient class tension that, in turn, alarmed the conservative forces to such an extent that he was eventually overthrown through urban demonstrations in 1977. It is conceivable that had his party produced an intellectual and political synthesis between socialism and Islam he might not have been as vulnerable. This is a question that has never been systematically explored. The fact remains that in the eyes of the conservative groups who had coalesced in the PNA movement against Bhutto and the military regime that finally toppled him Bhutto's policies had heightened class conflict to alarming proportions.

PROBABILITIES OF URBAN AND RURAL UNREST

In the previous chapter it was shown how demonstrations against the Ayub regime organized during 1968-69 and the protest movement against the Bhutto regime staged during the spring of 1977 were mostly confined to the two large metropolitan centers and certain large cities. One could see that during the Ayub period the demonstrations were confined to metropolitan cities like Karachi and Lahore and urban areas like Rawalpindi and Peshawar. It was true that the Ayub regime faced similar demonstrations in East Pakistan as well. By 1977, when the demonstrations against the Bhutto regime took place, the urban population of Pakistan not only had spread from Karachi and Lahore and a few urban centers to many other cities but the old metropolitan cities and urban centers had swollen in population. According to the 1972 census, in addition to Karachi and Lahore, there were four cities with populations exceeding well over 500,000. There were four other cities with populations in excess of 200,000 and ten cities with populations well in excess of 100,000. Thus one could say that by 1972 there were 20 urban centers with populations in excess of 100,000.

In this chapter the potential for civil unrest that exists in the expanding urban centers in Pakistan will be discussed. If one looks at the overall increase in urbanization that took place during 1960-75, the increase is by no means great. In 1960, the urban population constituted 22 percent of the total population, whereas in 1975 it was 26 percent with the average annual growth during 1960-75 hovering around 4 percent. However, the average annual growth of the urban population was 4 percent, whereas the average annual growth of the population as a whole during the period 1960-70 was only 2.8 percent and during 1970-77 was 3.1 percent. Moreover, one finds that the urban bulge is increasing at a very fast rate in cities of over 500,000. In 1960, there were only two cities with populations in excess of 500,000, whereas in 1975 there were six such cities. In 1960, only 33 percent of the urban population lived in cities of over 500,000, whereas in 1975 50 percent of the urban population was concentrated in cities of over 500,000.[4]

Thus, although the proportion of urban to rural population is not increasing dramatically, the population of some of the large urban centers is increasing at a very rapid pace, and it is in the latter areas that the potential for civil unrest exists. The capability of a government in coping with problems arising from the concentrations of the urban population in certain large cities depends upon factors like the industrial growth rate, employment opportunities, rate of inflation, and on certain safety valves like emigration.

Table 8.1 shows that the annual average percentage rate of increase in industry during 1971-72 to 1976-77 was only 2.9. Table 8.2 indicates that employment in the manufacturing sector in 1967 was 16.2 percent of total employment and in 1975 it came down to 13.6 percent. The military regime claims that the gross domestic product at market prices is likely to increase to 6.4 percent during 1979-80, whereas when it assumed charge it was 2.2 percent during 1976-77 (see Table 8.1). As Table 8.1 indicates, the growth rate in both industry and gross national product had slowed down considerably during the 1970s. Even under the military regime, in spite of assurances given to the private

TABLE 8.1
Real Growth, by Sector, 1971-72 to 1976-77
(annual average percentage rate)

Sector	1971/72- 1973/74	1974/75- 1976/77	1971/72- 1976/77
Agriculture	3.0	1.9	2.3
Industry	8.1	− 0.4	2.9
Services	10.0	3.3	5.9
Gross domestic product	6.9	2.2	4.1

Source: Ministry of Finance, Planning, Development and Provincial Coordination. Data obtained from Ministry of Finance.

TABLE 8.2
Employment, FY 1967 and FY 1975
(percent of total)

	Employment	
	FY 1967	FY 1975
Agriculture	53.4	54.8
Manufacturing	16.2	13.6
Other	30.4	31.6
Total	100.0	100.0

Source: Data obtained from Statistics Division, Ministry of Finance.

sector, there are as yet no signs of buoyancy in private sector investment or the industrial growth rate.

When one looks at the figures relating to employment/unemployment and the projections for future years, one can see that there are many more people entering the labor force each year than can be absorbed through gainful employment in the economy. According to government estimates made by the Manpower Division, the labor force is increasing at a rate of 3.2 percent per year with the net addition each year to the labor force being in the order of 770,000 persons. By the end of the five year plan of 1978-83, as many as 3.8 million additional persons will enter the labor force.[5] According to government figures, out of an estimated population of 77.86 million in 1978-79, 22.97 million were in the labor force with 5.60 in the urban areas and 17.37 million in the rural areas. As regards unemployment, the government's estimate is that 380,000 persons were unemployed during 1977-78 and 390,000 in 1978-79.[6] Given the stagnant nature of the economy during recent years and its slow growth during the immediate future, this means that the economy is not likely to provide adequate employment opportunities for absorbing these increasing numbers of people entering the labor market.

One could see that, starting from the Ayub period onward, the government was trying at least partially to tackle the unemployment problem by encouraging rapid emigration, first to Britain and later during the Bhutto period to the Middle East. Table 8.3 indicates that in 1971 the number of workers who emigrated was only 3,734, but in 1977 it had reached the peak figure of 140,445.

Strange as it may sound, the government has been opening training centers so that the country may be able to meet the rising external demand for skilled

TABLE 8.3
Labor Force Emigration from Pakistan

Year	Number of Workers
1971	3,734
1972	4,530
1973	12,300
1974	16,328
1975	23,077
1976	41,690
1977	140,445
1978 (provisional)	128,041

Source: Finance Division, Government of Pakistan, Pakistan Economic Survey 1978-79 (Islamabad: Government of Pakistan, 1979), p. 6. These are official figures. The real net migration can sometimes be twice as high.

manpower and thus drastically reduce the supply of badly needed skilled manpower for its own economy. Emigration may partially alleviate the unemployment problem but it can also retard economic growth and lower industrial
productivity. It has been estimated that at least 60 percent of legal migration
to the Middle East consists of skilled craftsmen and construction workers
like welders, electricians, plumbers, carpenters, masons, steel erectors, fitters,
and joiners.

An equally serious factor that promotes social unrest is the runaway inflation that Pakistan has been experiencing during the 1970s. According to the
World Bank's World Development Report 1979, the average annual rate of
inflation during 1960-70 was 3.3 percent, which increased to 15.2 percent
during 1970-77. The inflation rate in 1979 has been unofficially estimated at
30 percent with monetary expansion exceeding 20 percent annually during the
last three years. In the 1979 budget the government at first announced increased
duties on kerosene oil and powdered milk and higher rates on gas for domestic
consumers but these measures were immediately withdrawn when the government was faced with bitter opposition from both the lower- and middle-income
groups. As measures of pacification for the lower-middle and even some middle
classes, the wealth tax on self-occupied houses was modified and relief was
offered in the form of dearness allowances to government servants in the low
and middle brackets.

As seen, some of the factors that triggered the demonstrations against the
Ayub regime were the increased inflationary pressures following the 1965 war
and the sharp decline in real wages of industrial labor. Nothing arouses the ire
of the petty bourgeoisie as galloping inflation, which destroys all their hopes of
either maintaining themselves at their present living standards or joining the
ranks of the upper-income groups. Inflation is likely to radicalize the petty
bourgeoisie and induce them to join hands with labor, as they did during the
Ayub regime in organizing protests against the government. It has been seen that
during the demonstrations against Bhutto, industrial labor did not join hands
with the petty bourgeoisie, but galloping inflation can be a great unifier of these
two classes. The Jamaat-i-Islami, which represents the petty bourgeoisie, has
recorded its indignant opposition to the 1979 budgetary measures and described
the budget as a "deep conspiracy." A publication of the Jamaat, *Zindagi,* has
warned the government that the public despair and hostility that the budget has
provoked may take a highly dangerous turn: "It should be known to President
Zia-ul-Haq that those groups or classes who have been waiting for opportunities
to arouse unrest will not let this golden opportunity go by."[7]

Far more wretched than the condition of industrial labor or other low-
income groups is that of refugees and other transients who live in self-made huts
in slums called kutchi abadis. These settlements (kutchi abadis), numbering 500
of les miserables of Pakistan, may be found in all major cities and towns of
Punjab. In Lahore alone there are as many as 90 such settlements where 700,000

people out of Lahore's population of 2.5 million (1975), or 28 percent, live in unsanitary conditions. Bhutto's socialism had promised the inhabitants of kutchi abadis proprietary rights in the election campaign of 1969-70, but it was only when the Bhutto regime was faced with massive demonstrations in the spring of 1977 that the then prime minister gave them proprietary rights. One of the very few big processions that were organized in support of Bhutto was by the dwellers of these kutchi abadis in and around Lahore. Thus they represent one of the most politically explosive elements in the cities, and if organized and aroused, would contribute to urban unrest.

Agrarian relations and the modes of production in the Pakistan of the late 1960s and 1970s are a far cry from the kind of predominantly feudal and semifeudal relations that existed in agriculture during the period 1920-1940 that was discussed and analyzed in Chapter 1. It is true that in the canal colonies like Lyallpur the middle-sized farmer had emerged, but this was a relatively small tract in terms of political and economic power as compared to the predominantly feudal and semifeudal districts of west Punjab and Sind. During the 1960s, as a result of the modest land reforms, but largely because of the Green Revolution, the agrarian situation underwent a substantial change. In 1960, according to the Pakistan Census of Agriculture, the 1,000 big landowning families that owned more than 2 million acres in 1949 were in possession of only 1.1 million acres.

More significant than the shrinkage of land owned by large landholders was the increase in both numbers and size of holdings of the middle-sized farmers. In 1960, the middle-sized farmers of Punjab owned 19.4 million acres as compared to the 12.9 million acres that they owned a decade earlier. This increase of nearly 50 percent of land in their possession came about as a result of their acquiring lands from both the large landowners and the small farmers.

A lively controversy has taken place in the *Economic and Political Weekly* as to what extent Indian agriculture, particularly in Punjab, has been penetrated by the capitalist mode of production.[8] A similar but by no means as fierce a controversy has surfaced among Pakistani academics.[9] It is not quite relevant to the analysis here to get involved in this controversy. What should be emphasized here is that in Pakistan, though the capitalist mode of production has not emerged as the dominant mode, nevertheless it coexists with other modes and relations of production. In spite of land reforms and other measures, semifeudal relations continue to exist in all four provinces in varying degrees.

According to the Pakistan Census of Agriculture of 1972, 58 percent of the farmers in Pakistan in 1972 rented all or part of the lands they cultivated.[10] According to the same 1972 census, 34 percent of the farmers were tenants who did not own any land. If one were to add to this number the thousands of landless laborers, one can see the extent of land deprivation that exists in Pakistan's agrarian economy. As a result of land reforms and the Green Revolution, under which subsidized inputs have become available to large and middle-sized farmers, capitalist agriculture or agricultural production for the market has emerged. The capitalist farmer possessing and making use of the new means of production like tractors, tubewells, fertilizers, and employing wage labor has emerged.

Also, there is the self-employed peasant possessing some of the means of production and hiring others, but producing mostly with family labor and hiring additional labor to a small degree. In addition, there are the tenants working and renting land on the farms of the large and middle-sized landowners. The so-called capitalist farmer is using both wage labor and tenants in the cultivation of his land and this explains why some observers have taken the view that fully fledged capitalist farming has not yet emerged. Finally, there is the landless peasant possessing no means of production and offering his labor for wages. According to some, he is emerging as a part of the rural proletariat. Thus, even if the farming operations of the middle-sized farmers (50 to 100 acres) are regarded as a constricted form of capitalism, the fact remains that this constricted form is penetrating and transforming the relations of production and also creating the necessary conditions for class conflict in Pakistani agriculture. Increasing numbers of small peasants, tenants, and landless labor are being squeezed out of agriculture and are moving to towns and cities in search of employment.

If one looks at how there has been a marked increase in the number of tractors, tubewells, and quantity of fertilizer used in Pakistani agriculture, one can see how agriculture has become increasingly profitable over the years. According to the 1972 Census of Agriculture, the total number of privately owned tractors in 1972 was only 2,427. According to government sources, during 1976-79, as many as 40,635 tractors had been imported and used in farming operations.[11] During 1965-70, 10,000 private tubewells were installed each year, but the number came down to 3,000 per year during 1970-75. During 1977-79, the number of tubewells installed each year was close to 9,000 and the total number by the end of 1978-79 was expected to be 170,530.[12] The consumption of fertilizer has increased from 553,830 nutrient tonnes in 1975-76 to 720,203 nutrient tonnes in 1977-78.[13] An equally important feature of capitalist farming is the use of permanent hired agricultural labor. According to the Census of Agriculture in 1972, the number of permanent hired workers was 512,207. The census also reported that the employment of casual labor was 418,057 in terms of the number of man-days.

Even though semimodern mechanized farming has emerged under which commodities like rice, wheat, sugarcane, and cotton are being produced as profitable operations for the market, many observers are not prepared to rush to the conclusion that this kind of farming in which wage labor is being employed will automatically create class conflict in Pakistan's agrarian economy. Peasants do not develop class consciousness as easily as the industrial proletariat. To paraphrase Marx, under these early forms of capitalist farming insofar as landless laborers as wage earners become increasingly conscious of their unequal status and conflict of interests with the capitalist farmers, they form a class or are on their way to becoming a class. In the same manner, Marx would argue that insofar as this new "identity of their interests begets no community, no national bond and no political organisation among them, they do not form a class."[14] Marx was obviously suggesting that it was difficult to create class consciousness among peasants who lived in relative isolation from each other and under semifeudal conditions.

In India and Pakistan, even after capitalist farming has emerged, it has not been easy for agricultural laborers to unite and organize against their employers. They sometimes continue to look upon their employers as their protectors against the police or against the big landowners on whose farms they might have worked as tenants or casual laborers. One observer writes that although organizations of agricultural laborers have existed for quite some time in Punjab, nevertheless agricultural laborers have not yet developed much class consciousness for purposes of peasant struggle. He ascribes this inability to the inferior status that the lower classes among the Punjab peasants and farmers occupy in the caste or baradari structure of the villages. In contrast to this, the small peasant and agricultural laborers in the North-West Province, even though they belong to different tribes, regard themselves as equals of the big landowners or the more prosperous farmers. Thus the peasants and agricultural laborers, according to this observer, were able to wage fairly sustained and successful peasant struggles against the big landlords in areas like Hashtnagar, Malakand Agency, Swat, and Dir during the 1960s and 1970s.[15]

As seen in Chapter 1, during the 1930s and 1940s the Pakhtun also displayed greater political consciousness as compared to his counterpart, the Punjabi. Throughout this period, he tended to support anti-British governments, whereas Punjab, even though economically more prosperous, was under the domination of pro-British Unionist government.

It is in Punjab, because of the infusion of much larger numbers of tractors, tubewells, and fertilizers into agriculture, that capitalist farming has made significant strides. It has been suggested that the thousands of workers who are working in units ranging from a few to as many as 50 power looms in cities like Faisalabad, Gujranwala, and Kasur are those tenants and agricultural laborers who have been squeezed out of agriculture as a result of farm mechanization in Punjab.[16] According to one estimate, there are as many as 150,000 power looms producing cloth out of the yarn supplied by textile mills in Punjab.

If capitalist farming has not as yet created social unrest in the rural areas of Punjab, is it more likely that mechanized or capitalist farming through its eviction of agricultural laborers and tenants will create urban unrest? It was expected that industrial development in the cities and particularly the textile industry would be able to absorb the surplus of manpower from the rural areas. If one goes by recent trends, this has not worked out quite as well as expected because of the fact that there have been a series of serious shortfalls in the cotton crop accompanied by sustained stagnation in the textile industry. It was also noted earlier that the prospect in terms of overall industrial development leading to job opportunities is somewhat pessimistic because of the slow growth of the economy and manufacturing industry throughout the 1970s.

Both this chapter and the preceding chapter have tried to analyze the social and economic contradictions that have surfaced in modern Pakistan since the first military government under Ayub introduced a rapid industrialization program under the doctrine of functional inequality. These contradictions and the continuing regional conflicts that plague Pakistan's politics make one wonder whether Pakistan is politically governable. It has been seen how some of the fundamental values, attitudes, beliefs, and expectations relating to Islam and relevant to politics have been changing. In the strategies of rapid industrialization and higher growth rates in agriculture under the Green Revolution pursued by regimes dominated by classes like the big bourgeoisie and landowners and institutions like the civil service and the military, not even scant attention has been paid to considerations of equity and social justice. The heightened class consciousness and class conflict that have been produced by such policies have been further aggravated by the slow economic growth and a limited resource base.

The net impact of these problems and policies is such that governments in Pakistan are facing a host of new challenges. There is the challenge of redefining Pakistan's political values that is so formidable that the intellectual and political leaders have to put forward a new ideology that will carry conviction and create commitment among the various classes and groups. This could be either Islamic socialism or some other progressive version, but it needs to be defined and stated in clear, concrete, and convincing terms. There is the political challenge posed by the emergence of new groups and classes as represented by industrial labor and the petty bourgeoisie in the urban sector and the peasants, tenants, and landless labor in the rural sector. So far Pakistan's government and the policymaking structures have been dominated by the civil-military oligarchy, the big landowners, big business, and some of the professional elites. Can the ruling elites accommodate or co-opt these new classes and groups? Can they formulate a more acceptable and concrete ideology than just vague and emotional references to Islam? Will they be able to pursue policies more efficient in economic terms and more equitable in social terms?

When the government at a given time cannot fulfill the demands and expectations through economic policies and the mobilization of internal and external resources, the unfulfilled demands will have to be absorbed and cushioned through ideological and political means. In the final analysis, politics has to take command and new political structures have to be created before new policies can be pursued. This may mean a revolution, or, if Pakistan is lucky (and no third world country has been so lucky so far), it may be able to bring about these changes through a series of elections. However, a more pressing question is what is being done about the challenges that Pakistan faces by the military regime, which is answered in the following section.

CONSERVATIVE RESPONSE OF THE MILITARY REGIME

The way the military regime under Zia-ul-Haq has responded to the social challenges and contradictions that Pakistan faces is indicated by the manner in which the regime has diagnosed the social situation in the country. Military leaders have often been taught to reduce some of the most complex problems to their simple dimensions. According to Zia-ul-Haq, some of the malaise of Pakistan that could have been tackled through a united and strong central government inspired by an Islamic ideology have been magnified into almost insoluble problems, sometimes by the bungling of politicians and sometimes by certain deliberate objectives and policies that the Bhutto regime pursued. The general seems to be in agreement with what was said earlier, that there is considerable class consciousness that may lead to a social upheaval, except that he blames this all on the Bhutto regime. Zia in an interview pointed out:

> If you stay here for a few more days you will find out the environment. It is now getting better but there is a tremendous polarisation — polarisation between the right and the left, the poor and the rich, among the students and the labour, and between the haves and the have nots. This was all an intentional doing of the former Government that you have various elements whom you could manipulate. We are a developing country and it is more important for us that we have no polarisation. The objective must be one, the ideology of Pakistan should be in the forefront, and then people should have clean politics devoid of agitation.[17]

As shall be seen, this statement explains many of Zia's conservative policies as well as his attempts to Islamicize Pakistani society. The candor with which Zia has expressed his views regarding politics and society is quite engaging, but the social implications of his views are frightening. To cite a few examples:

> The Musalmans have one God, one Prophet, one Book; how can you have two hundred leaders ruling you? You have got to have an Amir.[18]

> Gen. Zia-ul-Huq said the second aspect in his opinion was that the Pakistani society was basically a tribal society whether people belonged to the Punjab, Sind, Frontier or Baluchistan. In cities there still existed "bradari" system. Fifty years ago a numberdar was elected who was supposed to be a better man financially or emotionally [Using this as an argument, the general recommended elections based on local bodies — presumably a system similar to Ayub's Basic Democracies.][19]

He said that Martial Law administration was determined to award severest punishment to law-breakers. A few more hangings would help maintain peaceful conditions in the country.[20]

Q. There are rumours in and outside Pakistan that yours is a rightist regime and you intend to suppress the leftists before holding elections. Would you comment on this?
    A. I have no dispute on this. I am a rightist. . . .
    Q. There are different types of leftists: extremists, moderates, etc.
    A. There is nothing much to choose between the leftists. I can tell you this.[21]

These statements, and some of the policies that the military regime has pursued, have created an unmistakable impression that the regime is determined to follow a rigidly rightist course of action. Denationalization of the flour mills and rice husking mills was announced soon after the imposition of martial law. As regards the cotton ginning factories, of the 579 such factories that had been taken over in 1976 by the Bhutto government, 297 were returned to their owners. Interviews with several managers of both public and private companies revealed that the managers after the imposition of martial law had acquired a new air of confidence bordering on arrogance and felt that it would no longer be possible for industrial labor to demand bonuses and higher wages despite declining productivity.

In these interviews, two themes that were emphasized were how the Bhutto regime had brought the country's economy to the brink of disaster and that the only hope for future growth and stability was a regime similar to that of martial law. Industrialists were assured by the martial law regime that any kind of industrial unrest resulting from strikes or any other trade union activity would be prohibited. Maximum punishment to the offenders was three years' rigorous imprisonment and/or whipping.[22] Rumors soon were circulating that a number of trade unionists and industrial laborers had been whipped.

A clear indication of how the climate had changed against trade union activity and strikes came on January 2, 1978 when 19 workers were shot dead by the police in Multan. The management of the Colony Textile Mill in Multan had sought assistance from the police in its dispute against the striking workers. Even though an enquiry commission was set up and cases registered against the policemen who were charged with ruthless killing and wounding of workers, industrial labor could see the writing on the wall and conclude that the martial law regime was in no mood to tolerate any form of labor militancy.

Notwithstanding the martial law regulation prohibiting strikes, there have been occasional strikes and labor protests. One of the frequent charges of the striking workers and trade union leaders has been that the right-wing and seemingly pro-government organization, Jamaat-i-Islami, has been trying to infiltrate the trade union movement. According to the striking workers of the Karachi Shipyard and Engineering Works, a strike organized by their union was sabotaged by the leaders of the Pakistan Trade Unions Federation with which the Shipyard Workers Union was affiliated. While the union leaders were in jail, the leaders of the Pakistan Trade Unions Federation started negotiating with management without consulting the Shipyard Workers Union. In addition, some of the leaders associated with a minority union led by the Jamaat were working closely with management in trying to have the members of the striking union dismissed.[23]

After the imposition of martial law, many landlords were reported to have told their tenants to seek the protection of their benefactor, namely, Bhutto. One source estimates that after martial law thousands of tenants had been forcibly evicted from the various districts. In the district of Mianwali 1,100 cases of eviction were registered. The author's figures from the district of Sahiwal obtained from the Official Fortnightly Statement showing the disposal of complaints filed by the forcibly ejected tenants up to November 30, 1977 were as high as 1,958.[24]

It was noted earlier that in an area like Hashtnagar in the Frontier there have been a series of armed clashes between landlords and tenants. The matter of eviction of tenants in this area had come before the High Court in 1973 when the High Court ruled that the landowners were legally entitled to evict the tenants. The Bhutto government, which was in political conflict with the big landowners, including Wali Khan, would not enforce the court order. The imposition of martial law gave an excellent opportunity to the landowners to ensure the enforcement of the High Court order. This was also facilitated by two factors. First, the lands from which the tenants were to be evicted belonged to the big landowners influential with the government, with one of them being a highly placed general in charge of the martial law administration. Second, under the martial law regime the landowning influentials brought about the eviction of tenants from their lands with the help of the police and the Frontier Constabulary.[25]

While the government pursued these policies in the matter of industrial disputes and eviction of tenants, labor groups and a leftist political party, the Pakistan Mazdoor-Kisan (workers and peasants) party, voiced its strong opposition. The All-Pakistan Labor Conference, announcing labor's seven-point charter, declared that it was totally opposed to denationalization of public sector industries and their return to private owners. The Conference also condemned the eviction of tenants and demanded that the evicted tenants should be allowed to reoccupy their lands.[26] The Unity Congress organized to unite all leftist groups and parties by the Pakistan Mazdoor-Kisan party also denounced what it alleged as the antilabor policy pursued both by the government and management and supported the strikes organized by workers in various industries. The resolutions of the Congress demanded that the policy of evicting tenants should be ended forthwith.[27]

As has been suggested all along, the raison d'etre for the military to seize power in July 1977 was to move Pakistan along a conservative course of action and thus reverse or abandon some of the policies that the Bhutto government was pursuing. The two major planks in the program of action were, one, to reassure the main propertied classes (the industrialists, the petty bourgeoisie, and the landowning groups) that the new government would abandon all the so-called radical policies of the Bhutto regime, and, two, to make it crystal clear to industrial labor and the poorer sections in the rural sector that any signs of militancy on their part would be suppressed.

General Zia and his supporters both in the military regime and outside have devised a two-pronged strategy to deal with the class antagonisms that have emerged in Pakistani society. The first, which has already been discussed, relates to the kind of firm measures that have been taken against industrial labor and agricultural classes like the tenants and landless labor. The second component of this strategy is to use certain Islamic reforms as instruments to defuse class antagonisms and support the status quo. One of the persistent themes in General Zia's pronouncements has been that all Pakistani governments since the establishment of the country have waxed eloquent about how Pakistan as an Islamic state would enable its citizens to mold their lives in accordance with the teachings and requirements of Islam, but none of them took any concrete steps to translate this objective into legislative and administrative realities.

After dealing with this problem in a piecemeal fashion through a number of martial law orders and regulations, General Zia finally put forward a coherent and broad-based plan on February 10, 1979. The measures that he announced were designed to set up a new Islamic system of socioeconomic welfare. These measures consisted of zakat (state-administered assistance to the poor through collection of taxes and contributions), ushr (tax on agricultural produce), and certain punitive measures to deal with offenses like drinking, adultery, theft, and false allegation. If one analyzes some of the principal measures like those relating to zakat, others pertaining to guarantees for payment of compensation to owners of industrial concerns in the event of their nationalization, and certain other punitive measures dealing with theft, one can see that the central purpose behind all these measures is to use Islam in support of the conservative philosophy and policies of the regime.

While announcing his measures relating to zakat and ushr, Zia declared: "To narrow the gap between the rich and the poor and to look after the indigent and the destitute are important principles of an Islamic society and these are also the cornerstone of the policy of the present Government."[28] The principle of zakat, as outlined with such modest objectives, calls to mind the Elizabethan poor laws. It is stated clearly that the state collection of zakat would be at the rate of 2.5 percent on all visible assets like bank accounts or savings made by individuals from their rents of buildings and so on. This means that the goal of both zakat and ushr (which will be collected at the rate of 5 percent of agricultural produce) is extremely modest and that it is alleviation of poverty and not its elimination.

The problem of poverty in Pakistan, as Table 8.4 indicates, is simply massive. Households with a monthly income of less than Rs. 200 constitute 52.4 percent of the rural population and 28.4 percent of the urban population. As for households with incomes ranging between Rs. 200 to Rs. 399, they comprise 38.6 percent of the rural households and 46.8 percent of the urban households. These figures vividly describe the depth of abject poverty that exists in Pakistan, and it is astonishing that the military regime is putting forward such modest proposals to tackle such a massive problem.

According to the penal measures relating to theft, the punishment for theft of property of about Rs. 840 or more is amputation of the right hand.[29] The law also states that a person who commits theft in a situation when he is in "apprehension of death due to extreme hunger or thirst" will be exempt from the prescribed punishment. First of all, it is difficult to imagine how a person who is so hungry that he is on the point of dying will commit theft. This means that a person who is half-starved and therefore has sufficient energy left may commit theft but in the eyes of the law may face the prescribed punishment. Second, the prescribed punishment is for offenders who commit thefts of a value of Rs. 840 or more, which suggests that the law is designed to protect the property of the well-to-do or propertied classes. It may be pointed out that the laws and regulations relating to theft and punishment of theft are all listed under the ordinance entitled "Offenses Against Property (Enforcement of Hudood Ordinance).".

TABLE 8.4
Income Distribution in Rural and Urban Areas, 1971-72

	Percent of All Households	
Monthly Income per Household	Rural	Urban
Less than Rs. 200	52.4	28.4
Rs. 200 to Rs. 399	38.6	46.8
Rs. 400 to Rs. 499	4.3	8.9
Rs. 500 to Rs. 749	3.1	8.9
Over Rs. 750	1.6	7.0

Source: Finance Division, Government of Pakistan, Pakistan Economic Survey, 1974-75 (Islamabad: Government of Pakistan, 1975), p. 28.

It is significant that the law that states that no industrial property shall be compulsorily acquired by the state without adequate compensation being given to the person or corporation concerned was announced by General Zia-ul-Haq as an integral part of the Islamic laws. While referring to the new measure regarding adequate compensation for acquired industrial properties in his speech on the Islamic laws, General Zia pointed out

> There were many factors responsible for the wrecking of national economy. The policy of nationalisation which was applied indiscriminately also played a major role in it. Islam confers the right to possess property both on the citizen and the state. The public and private sectors are wheels of the same cart.[30]

The liberals in reacting to these Islamic laws would assert that the enormous dynamic potential that Islam has for reformation and modernization is being ignored. Asghar Khan, the president of the Tehrik-i-Istaqlal (movement for solidarity) party and a former commander-in-chief of the Pakistan air force, has criticized General Zia's Islamic laws. Asghar Khan, as a former head of the air force, probably represents liberal sections of the military establishment because the air force, as compared to the army, has been preponderantly drawn from urban areas and the minimum qualifications even for its lowest ranks is high school graduation. Asghar Khan has observed:

> The face of Islam which Pakistan is presenting to the world and to our own people is of a religion concerned only with harsh punishments. To convert a great religion, vitally concerned with the welfare of the human individual, into a mere penal code of crime and punishment is to do it a great disservice.[31]

Zia and the military regime have prescribed certain sovereign remedies for all the major maladies that Pakistani society is afflicted with. Zia proposes to reform what he calls Pakistan's "degenerate society" through the Islamic reforms that he has proposed. As for the integrity of the country, "it will not be safeguarded by politicians, I am sorry to say this, but you can take it from me, that the country's integrity will be safeguarded by the Armed Forces alone."[32] What General Zia and the military generals have in mind is that the army "should have certain constitutional powers to act in an emergency." In practice this would mean that Pakistan's military leaders would have the power and the right "to ask a government to resign in the event of what they considered to be a crisis." General Zia has referred to this approach as "the Turkish solution" and such constitutional changes would provide for "the doctrine of necessity."[33]

What wide support this kind of thinking has in the army may be seen in the views expressed by Asaf Hussain. Asaf Hussain was invited in 1975 by General Tikka Khan, then chief of staff of the Pakistan army, to carry out a study on the political role of the Pakistan army. Asaf Hussain wrote:

> Given the military-state relationship, the ME [military elite], it can be predicted, will always take over the political arena whenever such crises threaten the state. The military thus serves to act as a check on the system whenever some elite group (like Bhutto's) becomes dictatorial and does not share power with others. . . . It would therefore be in order to give the military a constitutional role, that is, to take over the political arena under certain conditions. . . . Suffice it to say that the interests of the masses must be the main guiding factor in political coup d'etats. The military must be the saviours and not the oppressors of the Pakistani masses.[34]

What dangers, risks, or threats lurk in General Zia's mind? The military regime knows that even after three years of its rule the great majority of Pakistanis may still vote its arch enemy, the PPP, into office. The results of the elections for local bodies held in September 1979 indicated that the candidates identified in the public mind as candidates backed by the PPP had done exceedingly well in Punjab, Sind, and the Frontier. This was conceded not only by neutral observers but also by sources hostile to the PPP.[35]

If the PPP were to be successful in the national elections, the military regime would be faced with grave risks threatening its very existence. This explains why General Zia announced a series of measures to ensure the elimination of the PPP as a likely threat when he was contemplating the holding of national elections scheduled for November 17, 1979. According to the Political Parties (Amendment) Ordinance of 1979, it was made clear that any party that propagated any views designed to defame or bring into ridicule the judiciary or the armed forces of Pakistan would not be registered by the Election Commission as a political party eligible to contest the election. In this connection it may be added that some of the PPP leaders from time to time had threatened to try the generals associated with the military regime on charges of high treason according to Article 6 of the 1973 constitution. According to this article, parliament would provide for the punishment of persons found guilty of high treason, which was defined as any action or attempt designed to abrogate or subvert the constitution by use of force.

Even before the decision to postpone the elections indefinitely was announced on October 16, 1979, the PPP had been rendered ineligible for contesting the elections because it had not met certain requirements laid down by the Election Commission. First of all, the PPP had rejected the requirement that a political party could not criticize certain actions of the armed forces and the judiciary during the election campaign. Second, it did not submit its accounts and details regarding party membership to the Election Commission.

Another step that General Zia took to forestall the possibility of the PPP winning majority support in the general elections was to introduce a system of proportional representation, which would have meant that the electoral support of each party would be translated into its relative position in the assembly more or less in strict accordance with the percentage of votes obtained in the national elections.

Even though political parties and particularly the PPP had been hamstrung with so many disabilities, General Zia decided not to take any risks when he announced the cancellation of elections scheduled for November 17. In the same announcement all political activities were banned and stricter press censorship imposed. It was also made clear that no industrial strikes would be tolerated under any circumstances. General Zia, while announcing these decisions, emphasized that in spite of martial law considerable uncertainty and lack of confidence in the business community, other upper-income groups, and civil servants had existed and that his new measures would usher in an era of renewed confidence and discipline in the industrial, educational, and governmental sectors. "No longer industrialists will have fears about their investments nor farmers face uncertainty about the continuance of the present agricultural policies."[36]

As for the future, General Zia has clearly indicated the kind of political blueprint that is emerging in his mind and how he hopes to create an assembly packed with safe, conservative, and docile members reminiscent of the Ayub regime. This would be ensured through the abolition of universal adult franchise, an attempt to reduce the number of parties to the bare minimum, and above all through the requirement that candidates be practicing Muslims. All this goes to suggest that industrial growth pursued largely through private enterprise in Pakistan can best be ensured under a military Leviathan that combines the sticks of supression of civil liberties with the carrots of economic growth.

Reference has already been made to the plans of the military regime to assign to the military a pivotal position in the constitution as the final custodian of the country's integrity. In addition to these long-term plans, the regime has made sure that military officers are planted in key positions in a number of ministries both to implement the regime's policies and also to gain access to all the major decision-making layers of the government for a long time to come. In addition to appointing military officers to such top positions as secretaries in ministries like defense, information, interior, communications, and housing and labor, a number of military officers have also been appointed at the level of joint and deputy secretaries. Another major change of this nature that the military regime has introduced is to make sure that a certain quota of jobs in ministries and departments are reserved for ex-servicemen. General Zia has pointed out that as many as 25,000 men leave the army every year. Because he would not like them to leave as "disgruntled soldiers," he would like to place them in suitable positions in the government.[37] With infusion of such large numbers of army personnel into the departments and ministries of the government, and given the strong esprit de corps of the army, the army would soon occupy a dominant and entrenched position in the administration.

The above analysis suggests that Pakistan for quite some time is likely to be saddled with a military regime or a series of military regimes, all lacking political support and constantly racked by regional strife. As indicated, the military regime is unwilling to hold elections and thus allow a civilian regime to mobilize political support. Given its military character, it is also incapable of mobilizing political support for itself through a mass or totalitarian party. It has turned to Islam not for the purposes of deriving from it a social or political program of a progressive nature but for evolving a penal code that makes the regime and Pakistan look like a retrograde society. Given its class and ideological predisposition, Pakistan's military regime has turned increasingly toward the Saudis. The Saudis have provided investment funds and loans to finance some of Pakistan's power and electric plants and also its arms' purchases. In return Pakistan has provided its well trained military and technical manpower to the Saudis who, like Pakistanis, also feel threatened by a Soviet-supported state — South Yemen. The threat to Pakistan largely comes from the Soviet-backed regime in Afghanistan.

The use of the Soviet military power in Afghanistan in support of a pro-Soviet regime that is facing armed insurrection by Afghan rebels has provoked profound apprehension and intense hostility on the part of the United States, Western Europe, Pakistan, and a great majority of Muslim countries led by Saudi Arabia. As General Zia has ponted out: "The threat that has been created is not only a threat to American interests, it is a threat to sea lines, to oil, to Western European economic requirements."[38] The question that arises is that even if Pakistan were to receive massive economic and military aid from the United States and Western sources, would it be able to cope with the political and military challenges that Soviet incursion into Afghanistan poses for Pakistan. Pakistan was a recipient of massive military and economic aid during the Ayub era but since the military regime during that period failed to correct or arrest the growing economic disparity between East and West Pakistan, the country suffered dismemberment in 1971. Throughout the 1970s, both during the Bhutto and Zia regimes, Pakistan has been faced with continuing regional discontent bordering on threats of secession in the Pakhtun and Baluchi areas. These threats would become even more menacing if the Communist regime in Afghanistan backed by Soviet military and economic resources starts capitalizing on regional discontent, particularly in the Baluch areas. General Zia has admitted that in Baluchistan "the ground is ripe for seeds of subversion, because of deprivation and lack of resources."[39]

The response of the Zia regime to these challenges has been two-fold. First, Pakistan is hoping to strengthen its military defenses by seeking military aid from the United States. Second, Pakistan has mobilized political support from Islamic countries and the West against Soviet incursion in Afghanistan. However, it is significant that even though the Islamic Conference held in Pakistan in January 1980 demanded the withdrawal of all Soviet troops from Afghanistan, this conference of Muslim countries did not address itself to the ideological and political threat that Soviet Communism posed to an Islamic country like Afghanistan, and other Muslims like the Pakhtuns and the Baluchis living in the border areas of Afghanistan and Pakistan. The Islamic Conference organized by Pakistan and Saudia Arabia did not offer any program of social and economic justice for the Afghans, the Pakhtuns, and the Baluchis, the great majority of whom have lived under semifeudal conditions of poverty and despair.

The long-term threat of Soviet Communism to Pakistan and other Islamic countries is not only from outright Soviet military incursion but also from the way the Soviet-backed regime in Afghanistan is planning to transform the Afghan society. It is reported that the Communist regime has already introduced radical land reforms and abolished rural debt and usury.[40] It may also be noted that some of the mullahs who are spearheading the revolt against the regime were former landowners. Once the Soviet-backed regime in Afghanistan consolidates its hold over the country and starts probing the Baluchi and Pakhtun areas, it will not only try to capitalize on the regional discontent that exists in these areas but also impress upon the peasants and the intelligentsia that their regime has much more to offer in terms of a social program than the Zia regime can with its primary emphasis upon the Islamic penal code.

The military regime in Pakistan also faces certain challenges from within. The U.S. and Western military assistance that Pakistan is likely to attract in order to cope with the Soviet threat to its borders may set in motion an internal shift within the power structure of the Pakistan army. The bulk of the improvements in the military defenses of Pakistan may be concentrated in the border areas of Baluchistan and the North-West Frontier Province which may mean that not only the Pakhtun and Baluchi areas may benefit but also that the Pakhtun officers and generals may emerge increasingly powerful in the command structure of the army. However, the army is so predominantly Punjabi that it is not likely that the Pakhtun officers by themselves can dominate the command structure and decision making. They would have to work in partnership with the Punjabi generals. It may also be noted that some of the influential members of the Zia regime holding key positions as ministers of Finance and Defense Production in the cabinet and as top civil servants in the ministries of Interior and Foreign Affairs are all Pakhtuns.

The more serious threat that Zia's military regime faces is from the social and political forces that have been referred to earlier, namely, the more awakened peasant class consisting of the small landowners, the tenants, the landless laborers and, above all, the industrial proletariat and the petty bourgeois groups like students, lawyers, and civil servants. There may be urban protests and rebellions but there is not much likelihood of a social revolution in the near future. It will take quite some time before classes cutting across regional lines will crystallize and for classes like the industrial labor and the peasants combining with other groups to seize power through a social revolution. In any case revolutions cannot spring entirely from below. Given the power and institutional structure in Pakistan, classes like the industrial labor and the peasants would have to seek alliances with institutional groups like the military in order to overthrow the existing conservative power structure.

A political leader like Bhutto had not only won an election but also enjoyed the support of some of the powerful generals in the army. There does not seem to be a leader of Bhutto's stature on the scene and the army is not likely to leave the political arena. Therefore in any new power alignment the army officers are likely to play key roles. The more ambitious and politically skillful military officers holding the ranks of majors-general, brigadiers, or even colonels when faced with political crises or the likelihood of massive urban protests may combine with the dissastisfied and militant classes to provide Pakistan with a regime that enjoys the support of both the urban masses and the army. Presumably such a political coalition would follow a radical and even a socialist program.

NOTES

1. *Quaid-i-Azam Mohammad Ali Jinnah: Speeches as Governor-General of Pakistan 1947-1948* (Islamabad: Government of Pakistan, n.d.), p. 103. According to Bhutto, under the directions of the information minister, General Sher Ali, attempts were made to have this speech burnt or removed from the records. *In the Supreme Court: Rejoinder by Chairman Bhutto* (Lahore: Musawaat Press, 1977), p. 78.

2. Mubashir Hasan, "On Bhutto's Revolutionary Outlook," *Pakistan Times*, May 14, 1976.

3. Maxime Rodinson, *Islam and Capitalism* (New York: Pantheon, 1973), p. 230.

4. This information has been mostly derived from World Bank, *World Development Report 1979* (Washington, D.C., 1979), pp. 158, 164.

5. Finance Division, Government of Pakistan, *Pakistan Economic Survey 1978-79* (Islamabad, 1979), p. 3.

6. Ibid., pp. 3-4.

7. *Zindagi* (Lahore), July 6-12, 1978, p. 5. Translated from Urdu.

8. See particularly Utsa Patnaik's Rejoinders to A. Rudra: "Capitalist Development in Agriculture: A Note," *Economic and Political Weekly*, September 1971, and "Capitalist Development in Agriculture: A Further Comment," *Economic and Political Weekly*, December 1971.

9. For Pakistani points of view, see S. J. Burki, "Agriculture's New Entrepreneurs," *Pakistan Times*, June 24, 1972; and Feroz Ahmed, "Is Capitalism Emerging in Agriculture?" *Pakistan Forum*, December 1977. Feroz Ahmed concedes that certain features of capitalism have emerged but the agricultural laborers have not become laborers in the Marxist sense and tenancy farming continues to be an important feature.

10. Agricultural Census Organization, Government of Pakistan, *Pakistan Census of Agriculture 1972: All-Pakistan Report* (Lahore: Government of Pakistan, 1975), p. 1, Table 3.

11. *Pakistan Times*, August 6, 1979.

12. *Pakistan Economic Survey, 1978-79*, p. 29.

13. Ibid., p. 30.

14. K. Marx, *The Eighteenth Brumaire of Louis Bonaparte* (Moscow: Progress Publishers, 1972), p. 106.

15. Tala Muhammad, "Zarii Sarmayadari aur Kisan Tehrik" (Capitalist Farming and Peasant Struggle), *Pakistan Forum*, February 1978, pp. 27-30.

16. Punjab Mazdoor-Kisan Party, *Party Circular*, no. 22, 1973, p. 11.

17. *Pakistan Times*, April 10, 1978.

18. *General Zia-ul-Haq Meets the Press* (Rawalpindi: Government of Pakistan, 1977), p. 54.

19. *Pakistan Times*, March 28, 1978.

20. Ibid.

21. Ibid., April 10, 1978.

22. Martial law regulation no. 12. See *Martial Law Regulations July 1977* (Islamabad: Government of Pakistan, 1977), p. 16.

23. *Viewpoint*, August 26, 1979, p. 14. For similar charges against the Jamaat by the leaders of the Pakistan Railway Workers Union, see ibid.

24. "Fortnightly Statement Showing the Disposal of Complaints Filed by the Forcibly Ejected Tenants in Sahiwal Districts up to 30.11.77." Obtained from the Office of the Land Commissioner, Sahiwal.

25. For a detailed account, see *Pakistan Forum*, February 1978, p. 30.

26. *Viewpoint*, May 13, 1979, p. 14.

27. *Pakistan Forum*, August 1979, p. 21.

28. *Introduction of Islamic Laws. Address to the Nation. President General Zia-ul-Haq* (Islamabad: Government of Pakistan, 1979), p. 12.

29. The law as announced in ordinance no. 6 of 1979 states that the punishment for theft, which is amputation of the right hand, is applicable to persons who have committed thefts of a value equal to 4.457 grams of gold or more. Ibid., pp. A24-A27.

30. Ibid., p. 16.

31. *Dawn* (overseas), September 15, 1979.

32. *General Zia-ul-Haq Meets the Press*, p. 55.

33. For General Zia's views, see his interview with Michael Charleton of the BBC, *The Listener*, June 28, 1979, p. 871; and *New York Times*, August 17, 1979.

34. Asaf Hussain, *Elite Politics in an Ideological State* (Folkestone: Dawson, 1979), p. 145.

35. *The Economist*, October 27, 1979. Even the *Urdu Digest*, October 1979, p. 12, which is pro-Jamaat-i-Islami, conceded that the PPP supporters were successful in the elections because of their alleged electoral malpractices.

36. *President Ends Political Uncertainty. Address to the Nation. President General Mohammad Zia-ul-Haq* (Rawalpindi, October 1979), p. 16.

37. *General Zia-ul-Haq Meets the Press*, p. 31.

38. *The Economist*, January 26, 1980, p. 45.

39. Ibid., p. 46.

40. *The Economist*, September 1, 1979, p. 44.

INDEX

Afghanistan, 122, 132, 186-87
agrarian conditions: under Ayub Khan, 55-57, 62-63; under Bhutto, 89, 91-94, 109; capitalist farming, 174-77; unrest, 130-32, 136, 174-77; (*see also* land reforms, landless laborers, landlords, tenants, and peasants)
Ahmad, Mirza Ghulam, 38
Ahmad, Mushtaq, 144
Ahmadis: 1953 agitation against, 11, 16, 34-35, 36, 37-38; 1974 agitation against, 155-56
Ahrars, 9
Alavi, Hamza, 89, 108
Ali Bogra, Muhammad, 34-35, 39, 41, 43
Ali, Chaudhri Muhammad, 43
All-Pakistan Labor Conference, 180
Apter, David, 86
Asiatic mode of production, 2-3
astanadars (*pirs* and custodians of shrines in the North-West Frontier Province), 23
Awami League party, 36, 40, 45-46, 66, 69

Baluchistan: area and population, 114; central allocations, 134-35; imprisonment of Baluch leaders, 119-20; irredentist movement, military action by Bhutto, 115-16; natural gas in, 128; revenues, 134; Sandeman system under British, 3-4; sardari system and abolition by Bhutto, 114, 118, 120-21, 134; social and economic conditions, 114-15; social and political contradictions, 116-17; Soviet incursion in Afghanistan, 187; (*see also* Sandeman system, sardari system)
Bangash, Afzal, 132
Bangladesh, 113, 167
Barth, Fredrik, 23
Basic Democracy, 55, 144-45

Basic Democrats, 55, 147
Basic Principles Committee Report, 34
Bhashani, Maulana, 147-48, 151-52
Bizenjo, Mir Ghaus Bakhsh, 115-20
Bhutto, Zulfikar Ali: and Baluchistan, 114-21, 168; Bonapartist state; 89-91; use of civil armed forces, 106-08; and class conflict, 169; constitution of 1973, 105-06, 168; demonstrations against, 139-43, 157-62; 1970 election, 87-88, 152-54, 168, 169; and Islam, 169; Islamic Socialism, 169-70; and Jamaat-i-Islami, 155-56; labor policies, 99-102; land reforms, 91-94; language riots, 154-55; nationalization of industries, 95-99; and N.W.F.P., 121-36; PPP as populist movement, 86-87; desire for power, 103-04, 105-07; pricing policy, 102-03; relative autonomy, 109; state capitalism, 97-99; (*see also* Pakistan People's party)
Bonapartist state, 96, 108-09
bourgeoisie, petty: against Bhutto, 110, 143, 158-61, 173; characteristics of, 162; Marx's view of, 2; in N.W.F.P., 123, 127
Britain, British: as representative of bourgeoisie, 2; in Baluchistan, 3-4; in N.W.F.P., 3-4, 17-24; in Punjab, 4-6, 7-16; in Sind, 6-7
Bruce, Richard, 3
Bugti, Sardar Akbar Khan, 115-20

canal colonies, 6, 15-16, 174
capitalist development: in agriculture, 174-77; in Baluchistan, 116; under military protection, 46-51, 89; in N.W.F.P., 129-31
CIA, 46
civil bureaucracy: civil-military oligarchy 1947-58, 28, 33-51; coercive powers, 55;

190

demonstrations against Ayub Khan, 150-51; East Pakistanis in, 33, 39-40; as ruling elite under Ayub Khan, 70-82; West Pakistan dominance in, 26, 33-34, 68
Civil Service of Pakistan: under Ayub Khan, 70-82, 151; Bengalis in, 33, 39-40; under Bhutto, 89, 109, 150-51; under Jinnah, 26-27
class conflict, 63, 136, 163, 169-70, 175-77, 178, 181
Congress party, 19-24, 25
Connor, Walker, 68
constituent assembly, 33, 43
constitution of 1973, 104-06, 168
Cunningham, Sir George, 20-21, 26, 28

Darling, Malcolm Lyall, 5-6, 7
Daultana, Mian Mumtaz, 36-37, 38, 42
Deutsch, Karl, 68, 84-85, 113

East Bengal: central rule imposed, 41-42; in civil service, 39-40; conflict with Punjabis, 33, 34, 43-44; economic grievances, 33-34; industrial riots, 40-41; Muslim League defeat 1954, 40; population, 33; social structure, 33, 66; West Pakistan view of, 67 (see also East Pakistan)
East Pakistan: Awami League's Six Points, 69, 113; in civil service, 77, 81; dismemberment, 63, 65, 82, 136, 186; disparity between East and West Pakistan, 57-58, 63, 76-81; opposition to strong center, 68-69; and West Pakistan power elites, 65-82 (see also East Bengal)
Easton, David, 65, 68
economic development: in agriculture, 174-77; in industry, 171-72; 1947-58 period, 46-49, 50-51; 1958-68 period, 55-62, 76-81
elections: 1937 provincial elections, 10-11, 25; 1946 provincial elections, 13-16, 21-22; national and provincial elections 1969-70, 63, 81, 152-54, 157, 168, 169; 1970-71 provincial assembly elections, 115, 123-27; 1977 elections, 127, 157; September 1979 local elections, 184
elites: civil service elites, 70-76, 81-82; military elites, 70, 71-76; national

versus Baluchi elites, 116-17; national elites versus Pakhtun 129-30, 135; power or ruling elites, 1, 28, 65-66, 68, 69-74, 75-76, 80-81; vernacular elites, 39, 41
emigration, 172, 173
employment, 171-72

Fallaci, Oriana, 103
Federal Security Force, 88, 91, 103, 106-08, 109, 110, 156, 157
feudal, semi-feudal conditions, 62, 84, 87; in Baluchistan, 114, 120-21; under British, 2-4, 5-9, 13, 14, 15, 36, 174-75; in Punjab, 36-37, 44, 151, 152

Green Revolution, 56-57

haris (tenants at will), 6-7
Heeger, Gerald, 163
Huntington, Samuel, 55, 85, 143, 144, 162, 163
Huq, Fazlul, 41
Hussain, Asaf, 183-84

ideological change, 62, 167-70, 177
India, 32, 41, 67, 82, 85, 168
industrialists: under Ayub Khan, 57-60, 62, 76, 144; in Baluchistan, 116; under Bhutto, 88-89, 155, 157; drawn from trading communities, 46-48; and East Pakistan, 40-41; and labor, 156-57; in N.W.F.P., 122, 128-30; under Zia-ul-Haq, 179-81, 185
industrialization: under Ayub Khan, 55-60, 76, 151; in N.W.F.P., 128-30; rate of, 171, 172; in urban areas, 166; West Pakistan favored region, 33, 84, 177
inflation, 61-62, 85-86, 102, 146-47, 173
Iqbal, Sir Muhammad, 9, 10
Iran, 115, 121
Islam: and Bhutto's secularism, 155-56, 157-61; used by British, 8, 17, 20-21; and ideological change, 167-70, 177; in N.W.F.P., 20, 23, 133; in Punjab, 8-12, 14-16, 35; raison d'etre of Pakistan, 1; redefinition needed, 177; Zia-ul-Haq's Islamic views and measures, 178-79, 181-83, 185-86
Islamic socialism, 63, 87, 169-70

Jamaat-i-Islami Party: and Bengalis, 67; and

Bhutto, 155, 157, 160-61; and labor, 101, 160; and Zia-ul-Haq, 162, 173, 179-80

Jamiatul Ulama-i-Islam Party (JUI), 115, 123-27

Jamiatul Ulama-i-Pakistan Party (JUP), 157, 160

Jinnah, Muhammad Ali: administration, 26; and East Bengal, 26-27, 66; economic views and policies, 25-26, 27; Islamic appeal, 10-11, 25, 167; and Khizr Hyat Khan, 12-13; 1937 provincial elections, 10-11, 25; political timing, 23; secularism, 27, 167; and Sikander Hyat, 10, 12; strategy in Punjab before partition, 10-16

jirga (council of tribal leaders), 21, 28, 120

Kalat, Khan of, 3, 114

Kay, Geoffrey, 2

Khan, Sir Abdul Qaiyum, 18, 23

Khan, Asghar, 183

Khan, Khan Abdul Ghaffar, 18-19, 21, 22, 23-24, 123, 131

Khan, Muhammad Ayub: demonstrations against, 139-53; developmental policies, 55-62; economic development, 46-49; Green Revolution, 56-57; and industrialists, 46-49, 50-51; industrialization, 57-60; land reforms, 56; and Mirza, 44-45; poverty under, 60-62; strong presidential system, 54-55, 62, 68; and Suhrawardy, 46; and United States, 46, 49-51; view of East Pakistanis, 75

Khan Sahib, Dr., 18, 19, 20, 22

Khan, Sir Sikander Hyat, 10, 11-12

Khan Tiwana, Khizr Hyat, 12-13

Khan, Wali, 115-16, 122, 123, 128, 135-36

khans (landlords), 17, 21

Khilafat movement, 8, 18

Khizr Hyat, (see Khan Tiwana and Khizr Hyat)

Khudai Khidmatgar (servants of God), 17, 18-19, 20-21, 24, 123, 130

Khuhro, Muhammad Ayub, 42-43

Krishak Sramik (Peasants and Workers) Party, 36

kutchi abadis (self-made huts in slums), 140, 173-74

labor: agitation against Ayub Khan, 146-50; Baluch, 136; and Bhutto, 91, 99-102,

156-57, 163-64; Pakhtun, 122, 136; and Zia-ul-Haq, 166, 172, 179-81

Laclau, Ernesto, 87

Lahore resolution, 11

land reforms: under Ayub Khan, 56; under Bhutto, 89, 91-94, 109; Jinnah fails to introduce land reforms, 27

landless labor, 5-7, 27, 35, 136, 164, 174-75, 187-88

landlords: and Ayub Khan, 56; and Bhutto, 88-90, 91, 92, 109; declining power, 174; eviction of tenants, 180-81; feuds, 36; landlord-tenant conflict, 130-32, 136, 175-76; power of, 5-7, 9-10, 35-37, 54; protected by British, 4-5, 17-18

Maddison, Angus, 59

Marshall, Charles Burton, 46

Marx, Karl, 2, 62, 94, 108, 175-76

maulanas (learned men in Islam), 37

maulvis (some formal schooling in Islamic theology and therefore qualified to lead prayers), 14-15, 159

Mengal, Sardar Ataullah Khan, 115-19

Merkl, Peter H., 162-63

military: under Ayub, 41-42, 44-45, 46, 49-51; topples Bhutto, 110, 170; and capitalist development, 46-51; civil-military oligarchy, 28, 33-51; future role, 187-88; Punjabi domination, 33, 34; U.S. support, 46, 49-51; under Zia-ul-Haq, 183-86

Mills, C. Wright, 70

Mirza, Iskander, 41, 43-46

Mudie, Sir Francis, 36

Muhammad, Ghulam, 34-35, 43, 50

mullahs (preachers), 17, 20, 37, 168-69, 187

Munir report, 74

Muslim League: anti-Ahmadi movement, 37-39; in first constituent assembly, 33; in second constituent assembly, 43; defeat in East Bengal, 40; in 1937 provincial elections, 10-11, 19, 21-23, 25; in 1946 provincial elections, 13-16, 21; lack of organization, 28, 32; landlords in, 36-37; in pre-partition N.W.F.P., 19-24; in pre-partition Punjab, 10-16; relations with Unionist party, 10, 12-13; religious appeal, 11-12, 14-16, 25, 36

National Awami party: in Baluchistan, 115-19; in N.W.F.P., 123-32; and One Unit, 44

nationalism, 132-36

Nazimuddin, Khwaja, 34-35, 39, 66, 67

Nizam-i-Mustafa (state based on the teachings of the Prophet), 158, 159-60

North-West Frontier Province: agrarian unrest, 130-32; bourgeoisie, 122; British support of tribal chiefs, 3-4; Congress ministry and Muslim League, 19-21; 1937 provincial elections, 19; 1946 provincial elections, 21-22; 1970-71 elections, 123-27; federal expenditure in Tribal Areas, 134-35; grievances, 122-23; irredentist movement, 122; role of Khan Abdul Ghaffar Khan, 18-19, 21, 22, 23-24; NAP-JUI government 1971-73, 127-29; Pakhtun consciousness, 17; referendum, 22-24; regionalism vs. nationalism, 132-36; social contradictions, 129-32; Soviet incursion in Afghanistan, 186-87

O'Dwyer, Sir Michael, 5, 7

One Unit, 42-45, 113

Pakhtuns: and Khan Abdul Ghaffar Khan, 18-19, 21, 22, 23-24; Pakhtun consciousness, 17; Pakhtun regionalism vs. Pakistani nationalism, 121-36 (see also North-West Frontier Province)

Pakhtunwali (Pakhtun code of honor), 17

Pakistan: under Ayub Khan, 54-63; under Bhutto, 84-136; under Jinnah, 25-28; under parliamentary system 1947-58, 32-51; under Zia-ul-Haq, 166-88

Pakistan Mazdoor-Kisan (workers and peasants) party, 131, 136, 180

Pakistan National Alliance (PNA), 127, 157-61, 170

Pakistan People's party (PPP): and Ahmadis, 155-56; in Baluchistan, 120; Bhutto fails to use support of PPP, 110; 1970 election, 63, 87-88, 152-54; September 1979 local elections, 184; as populist movement, 86-87

Papanek, Gustav, 57, 80, 143

peasants: in Punjab, 5-7, 8, 15-16; under Bhutto, 91, 92-94, 127; under Jinnah, 27; unrest, 130-32, 174-77, 187

Pentagon, 50

pirs (spiritual guides), 5, 6-14, 15, 16, 23, 35, 36, 54

political change: and agrarian change, 174-77; in the future, 186-88; and ideological change, 167-70, 177; and industrial growth, 171-72; and inflation, 173-74; and unemployment, 172-73; and urbanization, 170-71; urban protests as indicators of political change, 139-64

political institutionalization, 85, 162-63

political parties: Awami League, 36, 40, 45-46, 66, 69; Congress, 19-24, 25; Jamaat-i-Islami, 67, 101, 155, 157, 160, 161-62, 173; Jamiatul Ulama-i-Islam, 115, 126-27; Jamiatul Ulama-i-Pakistan, 157, 160; Krishak Sramik, 36; Muslim League, 10-17, 19-25, 28, 32, 33, 36-39, 40-41, 43, 66; National Awami, 44, 115-21, 123-32; Pakistan Mazdoor Kisan, 131, 136, 180; Pakistan National Alliance, 127, 157-61, 170; Pakistan People's, 63, 86-88, 110, 120, 152-54, 155-56, 184; Qaiyum Muslim League, 125-27; Republican, 44-45; United Front, 36, 40-41; Unionist, 7, 10-16 (see also subject headings throughout the index)

Political Parties (Amendment) Ordinance 1979, 184

political system, 65-66

populism, 86-87

Poulantzas, Nicos, 162

poverty, 60-62, 181-82

Punjab: British and landowning interests, 4-7; British and religious interests, 8-10; economic and social changes, 11-12; 1946 provincial election, 13-16; Unionist Party vs. Muslim League, 10-13 (see also West Punjab)

Punjab Alienation of Land Act 1900, 4, 6, 7, 9, 11-12

Qaiyum, Sir Abdul (see Khan, Sir Abdul Qaiyum)

Qaiyum Muslim League, 125-27

Quaid-i-Azam (see Jinnah, Muhammad Ali)

Rahman, Sheikh Mujibur, 152

referendum, 24, 122

Republican Party, 44-45

Rodinson, Maxime, 169

sajjada nashins (hereditary custodians of shrines or tombs), 8-9, 14-16, 35, 36
Sandeman, Sir Robert, 3-4
Sandeman system, 3-4, 120
sardari system, 114; Bhutto abolishes sardari system, 118, 120-21, 134
sardars, 114, 115, 116, 117, 118, 119-20, 121
Sattar, Pirzada Abdus, 42
Saudi Arabia, 186
Seal, Anil, 4
Shaheed, Zafar, 149
Shariat (Islamic law), 16
Sikander Hyat Khan (see Khan, Sir Sikander Hyat)
Sind: feudalism in, 6; and landlords, 92; language riots, 154-55; and One Unit, 42-44, 113
social mobilization, 84-85
Soviet Union, 186-87
state capitalism, 97-99
students: in Bengal, 40; in N.W.F.P., 133-34; protests against Ayub Khan, 62, 145-46
Suhrawardy, H. S., 39, 45-46, 66, 67

tenants: under Bhutto, 91, 92, 94, 180; eviction of, 180-81; under Jinnah, 27; landlord-tenant conflict, 130-32, 136, 175-76; in Punjab, 5-7, 8, 35, 37
Thorburn, S. S., 4
Thornton, Thomas Henry, 3
Tikka Khan, General, 117
trade unions: and Bhutto, 99-102, 110, 143; conflict between trade union leaders and Basic Democrats, 147; demonstrations against Ayub Khan, 143, 147-50, 152; membership, 99-100, 140; and Zia-ul-Haq, 179-80
Tribal Areas, 3-4, 133, 134-35
tumandar (chief), 3

ulama (learned authorities on Islam), 9, 14, 15, 23, 28, 37, 167, 168

unemployment, 172
Unionist party, 7, 10-16
United Front party, 36, 40-41
United States, 186; CIA, 46; economic assistance, 50; military aid, 50; Pentagon, 50; support of Ayub, 46, 49-51; support of Zia, 186
urban protest demonstrations: against Ayub Khan, 139-53; against Bhutto, 103, 139, 157-64
urbanization, 140, 151, 166-67, 170-71
Urdu language, 40, 67, 132, 133, 134
ushr (tax on agriculture produce), 181-82

von Vorys, Karl, 54

Wavell, Lord, 13, 22
West Pakistan: disparity between East and West Pakistan, 57-58, 75-81; dominated by landlords, 33; East-West conflict, 33-34, 43-44, 65-66, 68-69; economic development, 33-34; infeuding, 44; integration of, 42-45; One Unit plan, 42-44; population, 33; regional conflicts in, 63
West Punjab (province of Pakistan): anti-Ahmadi movement, 37-39; capitalist farming, 175-76; conflict with East Bengal, 34; Green Revolution, 56-57; landlords in, 36-37; language in, 133; martial law imposed, 38-39; peasants in, 93 (see also Punjab)
White Paper on Baluchistan, 117, 134
Wilson, W. R., 7

zakat (state administered assistance to the poor through collection of taxes and contributions), 181-82
zaildars (village headmen), 5, 9, 17, 20
Zia-ul-Haq, Muhammad: conservative policies, 179-81; and Jamaat-i-Islam, 161-62, 173, 180; and role of military, 183-84, 185-86, 187-88; foreign relations, 186-87; Islamic views and policies, 161-62, 178-79, 181-83, 186; views on class conflict, 178

ABOUT THE AUTHOR

Dr. Khalid B. Sayeed was born in India. He was educated at Madras University, the London School of Economics and Political Science, and at McGill University. He has taught not only in Indian and Pakistani universities, but also at University of New Brunswick, Duke University (as a visiting associate professor), McGill University (as a visiting professor), and is now professor of political studies at Queen's University, Kingston, Ontario. He has also served as United Nations adviser in development administration to the Plan Organization, Government of Iran. Dr. Sayeed is the author of *Pakistan the Formative Phase* and *The Political System of Pakistan,* of numerous articles published in learned journals and encyclopedias, and of chapters in edited works.